A Glassware and Pottery Collection

Original Catalog Reprints from the

"Baltimore Price Reducer"

A Merchandise Catalog of

The American Wholesale Corporation

An Old Line Publishing Reference Book

Hampstead, Maryland

Printed in The United States of America

Compiled and designed by Craig S. Schenning

ISBN-13: 978-0-9786948-9-0

ISBN-10: 0-9786948-9-9

Looking for a publisher?

At Old Line Publishing we are always looking for authors and original manuscripts. We hope that you will contact us and share your thoughts, ideas, stories, and/or already written material with us so that we can help you turn your idea into a timeless treasure and share it with the world.

Old Line Publishing, LLC

P.O. Box 624

Hampstead, MD 21074

Toll-Free Phone: 877-866-8820

Email: oldlinepublishing@comcast.net

Website: www.oldlinepublishingllc.com

Table of Contents - Index

Table of Contents - Index

Baltimore Price Reducer

MORE GOODS FOR SAME MONEY

MARCH, 1919

SAME GOODS FOR LESS MONEY

Protect Your Profits

YOUR profits for the year will depend to a large degree on the prices you pay now for your Spring and Summer goods; so you ought to consider the price carefully on every item you buy and place all your orders where you can get the biggest values. The best protection against paying too much for your goods is to READ OUR CATALOG and make it a rule not to buy any item anywhere until you have first looked up our price for same goods. You will find that we can supply the most of your goods at prices below the market on an average—also HUNDREDS OF SPECIAL BARGAINS which will be a big help to you in besting your competitors and increasing your sales. IT PAYS TO READ OUR CATALOG.

Prices herein guaranteed against any advances to March 25, 1919, inclusive. You will get the benefit of any reductions in effect at the time your order is received, without asking for same

As this Catalog goes to press there is a bill pending which imposes War Taxes on some few items of merchandise; and if this bill should become a law before our next Catalog is issued (March 25), we will on such few items add the amount of the taxes to the prices quoted herein, beginning the day the law goes into effect.

Baltimore Bargain House

WHOLESALERS OF GENERAL MERCHANDISE

TRADE MARK REG. U.S. PAT. OFF.
Baltimore, Md.
ESTABLISHED.1881

MFRS.OF CLOTHING,SHIRTS, OVERALLS,CLOAKS & SUITS.

Our Prices Guaranteed

against any advances to March 25, 1919, inclusive.

You will get the benefit of any reductions in effect at the time your order is received, without asking for same.

As this Catalog goes to press there is a bill pending which imposes War Taxes on some few items of merchandise; and, if this bill should become a law before our next Catalog is issued (March 25) we will on such items add the amount of taxes to the prices quoted herein, beginning the day the law goes into effect.

Our Liberal Terms
See Below

All Bills of Goods bought from the Baltimore Bargain House and shipped between Dec. 26 and April 1, which together aggregate $500.00 or more, ARE PAYABLE JUNE 1st.

All other bills are payable in 60 days, NET
No discounts, no interest allowed for anticipation

This Is The Guarantee That Makes Your Buying SAFE!

1—WE GUARANTEE that all goods listed in our Catalogs are the same quality as sold by other first-class Wholesale Houses; and—

2—Exactly as described and represented by us.

3—All articles listed in our Catalogs are strictly FIRST QUALITY (with only two exceptions, which are: a few items in Enameled Ware sold as "Run-of-Kiln", and Rubber Boots and Shoes which we handle in three grades, First, Second and Third, which are fully described as such and are handled by all other first-class wholesalers).

4—We further guarantee our prices to be 5% to 15% lower, on an average, than other wholesalers charge for the same goods, except on such few items as the manufacturer through his brands and trade marks establishes the wholesale selling price.

5—You are privileged to return to us, WITHIN 5 DAYS after arrival at your store, any goods purchased from any Baltimore Bargain House Catalog if they do not come up to your expectations.

Signed — *Baltimore Bargain House*

TABLE GLASSWARE

ASSORTED GLASS TABLEWARE
Large pieces to sell at popular prices

AO2032—Crystal glass, smooth finish, Colonial and Imitation Cut Glass pattern. Asst. comprises ½ doz. each of 20 styles as illustrated. 10 doz. in bbl. wt. 108 lbs ......Doz. **72c**

DECORATED BLUE BIRD AND STRAWBERRY DINING SETS—
FIRED DECORATION—WILL NOT WASH OFF

AO2132—Raised Blue Bird and Strawberry design, fire polished crystal glass, decorated in bright colors. Asstd. as follows
2 only 4-pc. Table Sets (sugar, covered butter, cream and spoon holder to set.
2 only 7-pc. Berry Sets (large bowl and 6 nappies to set).
2 only 7-pc. Lemonade Sets (large jug and 6 tumblers to set)
6 sets in bbl. Wt. 80 lbs .... Set, **90c**

CRYSTAL GLASS TABLEWARE
Attractive pattern, well selected and evenly balanced assortment of staple items

AO2036—Fire polished, crystal glass. Asst. comprises the following:

1 3 doz. Cov. Butters.	1 6 doz. 10-in. Berries	2 Extra Large
1 3 doz. Sugars.	1 doz. 5-in. Berries.	Berry Sets.
1 3 doz. Cream Pitchers.	4 Tea Sets.	
1 3 doz. Spoon Holders.	1 doz. 10½-in. Celery Trays.	
¾ doz. Large Pitchers.	1 3 doz. 8½-in. Pickle Dishes	3 Water Sets.
1½ doz. Tumblers.	1 3 doz. Ftd. Jelly Bowls	
¾ doz. 8½-in. Berries.	1 3 doz. 6½-in. Bell. Preserves.	
1½ doz. 4½-in. Berries.	1 3 doz. 6½-in. Vases.	3 Berry Sets.
1 6 doz. 7½-in. Salads.	1 doz. Fancy Goblets.	
1 doz. 4½-in. Salads.	¾ doz. Tall Celery Holders.	2 Salad Sets.

10 doz. in bbl. Wt. 140 lbs. .... Doz. **$1.05**

FLORAL PATTERN TABLE CLASSWARE

A very attractive pattern of well-selected staple items

AO2035—Crystal glass, smooth edges, fire polished. Asstd. as follows

½ doz. Covered Butters		¼ doz. 8-in. Footed Salads	
½ doz. Covered Sugars		1½ doz. Footed Salad Napples	3 Salad Sets
½ doz. Spoon Holders	4 Tea Sets	½ doz. Footed Jelly Comports	
½ doz. Creams		½ doz. Pickles	
½ doz. ½ gal. Pitchers		½ doz. 9-in. Berry Bowls	
2 doz. Water Glasses,	4 Water Sets	1½ doz. Goblets	
¼ doz. 8-in. Berry Bowls		¼ doz. Roll Trays	
1½ doz. Berry Napples	3 Berry Sets	¼ doz. Celery Holders	

10 doz. to bbl. Wt. 150 lbs. .... Doz. **$1.10**

PLAIN TABLE CLASSWARE
Large pieces that can be retailed at 10c, 15c and 25c each

AO2037—Heavy crystal fire polished glass, star bottom. Asstd. as follows:

½ doz. Covered Sugars.	½ doz. Footed Jellies.
½ doz. Cream Pitchers.	½ doz. 7½-in. Deep Berry Bowls.
½ doz. Spoon Holders.	½ doz. Covered Bowls.
½ doz. Covered Butters.	½ doz. 10½-in. Celery Trays.
½ doz. ½-pt. Jugs.	½ doz. 7½-in. Pickles.

Total 5 doz. in bbl. (wt. 135 lbs)...................... Doz. **$1.55**

NOVELTY IRIDESCENT GLASSWARE

AO2258—Floral and Fancy raised design, Royal Blue and Golden glass, blended with oriental colors. ½ doz. each of 12 styles (as per illustration). 6 doz. in bbl. Wt. 90 lbs. .... Doz. **98c**

BRIGHT STAR CRYSTAL GLASS TABLEWARE

AO2033—Heavy crystal, fire polished, imitation cut Sun Burst Star. Asst. comprises the following pcs.:

- ⅓ doz. Butter and Cover, ⅓ doz. Sugar and Cover, ⅓ doz. Cream, ⅓ doz. Spoon } 4 Tea Sets
- ¼ doz. ½ Gallon Pitcher, 1½ doz. Tumblers } 3 Water Sets
- ¼ doz. 8½ in. Berry, 1½ doz. 4¾ in. Berry } 3 Berry Sets
- ¼ doz. 7½ in Berry, 1½ doz. 4¾ in. Berry } 3 Berry Sets
- 1½ doz. Goblets
- ¼ doz. 6½ inch Bowl and Cover
- ¼ doz. 5½ inch Bowl and Cover
- ¼ doz. Tall Celery
- ¼ doz. Celery Tray
- ½ doz. 8½ inch Pickle
- ¼ doz. Vinegar Cruet
- ¼ doz. Footed Jelly

10 doz. in bbl.; wt. 150 lbs. .... Doz. **$1.15**

"CLEAN EASY" PLAIN GLASS TABLEWARE

AO2034—Crystal, fire polished, star bottom. Asst. comprises the following:

- ¼ doz. Covered Butters, ⅓ doz. Covered Sugars, ⅓ doz. Cream Pitchers, ⅓ doz. Spoon Holders } 4 Tea Sets
- ¼ doz. Large Water Pitchers, 1½ doz. Table Tumblers } 3 Water Sets
- ¼ doz. Medium Pitchers, 1½ doz. Goblets } 3 Lemonade Sets
- ¼ doz. 7½-in. Berry Nappies, 1½ doz. Berry Nappies } 3 Berry Sets
- ¼ doz. 8½-in. Deep Berry Bowls, 1½ doz. Berry Desserts } 3 Berry Sets
- ⅓ doz. 6½-inch Covered Footed Bowls
- ¼ doz. Tall Celeries
- ⅓ doz. 8½-in. Pickle Dishes
- ¼ doz. 10¼-in. Celery Dishes
- ¼ doz. Covered Footed Jelly Bowls
- ¼ doz. Molasses Cans
- ⅛ doz. 9-in. Cake Stands

10 doz. in bbl.; wt. 150 lbs. .... Doz. **$1.15**

"2 STYLE" CRYSTAL GLASS DINING SETS

AO2014—Crystal glass, smooth edges. Asst. comprises the following:
4 only 4-pc. Table Sets (1 Sugar, 1 Cream, 1 Spoon Holder and 1 Covered Butter to set).
4 only 7-pc. Lemonade Sets (1 large Jug and 6 Tumblers to set).
4 only 7-pc. Salad Sets (1 large Bowl and 6 Nappies to set).
½ doz. sets of each style. 1 doz. sets in bbl. Wt. 110 lbs. .... Doz. **$6.75**

"4 STYLE" BERRY BOWLS.

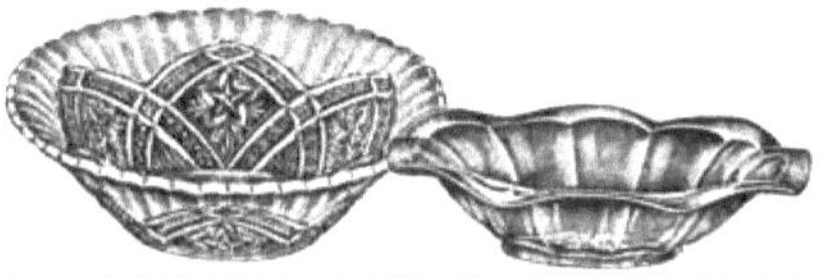

AO2023—Average size 8½ inches, fire polished crystal glass; 1½ doz. of each style, total, 6 doz. in barrel; weight 120 pounds, ... Doz. **$1.75**

2-STYLE" GLASS BERRY NAPPIES

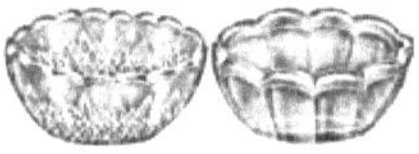

AO2193—Diam. 4¾ in., heavy crystal glass. 6 doz. of each style. 12 doz. asstd. in case. Wt. 75 lbs. .... Doz. **42c**

"3-STYLE" GLASS BERRY NAPPIES

AO2005—Diam. 4½ in., crystal glass, well finished. Asst. comprises 4 doz. of each style 6 doz. in bbl. Wt. 77 lbs. .... Doz. **45c**

"2 STYLE" COVERED BUTTERS AND SUGARS

AO2018—Crystal glass, smooth edges, asstd. 2 doz. covered butters and 2 doz. covered sugars. 4 doz. in bbl. Wt. 100 lbs. Doz. **$1.70**

"4-STYLE" COVERED SUGARS

AO2189—Ht. 7 in., heavy crystal glass, smooth edges. 1 doz. each as per illustration. 4 doz. asstd. in bbl. Wt. 100 lbs. Doz. **$1.60**

"3 STYLE" GLASS COVERED BUTTERS

AO2017—Crystal glass, smooth edges. Asstd. 1 doz. each style. 3 doz. in bbl. Wt. 90 lbs. Doz. **$1.85**

AO2020—As AO2017, 5 styles. 1 doz. each. 5 doz. in bbl. Wt. 120 lbs. .... Doz. **$1.78**

"3 STYLE" GLASS COVERED SUGARS

AO2011—Crystal glass, smooth edges. 1 doz. each style; total, 3 doz. in bbl., wt. 80 lbs. Doz. **$1.75**

AO2019—As AO2011, 5 styles. 1 doz. each. 5 doz. in bbl. Wt. 100 lbs. .. Doz. **$1.65**

"2 STYLE" FOUR-PIECE TABLE SETS

AO2016—Set comprises Covered Butter, Covered Sugar, Cream Pitcher and Spoon Holder. Crystal glass, fire polished. ½ doz. sets of each style. 1 doz. sets in bbl.; wt. 80 lbs. Doz. sets. **$5.45**

"4 STYLE" COVERED BUTTERS

AO2188—Diam. 7¼ in.; heavy crystal glass, smooth edges. 1 doz. each as per illustration. 4 doz. asstd. in bbl. Wt. 100 lbs. Doz. **$1.75**

"2 STYLE" GLASS BERRY SETS

Set consists of one 7¼ in. berry bowl and six 4¼ in. berry nappies to match.

AO2012—Heavy crystal glass, smooth edges, one-half dozen sets of each style; total, 1 doz sets in bbl. (wt. 70 lbs.). .... Doz. sets. **$4.25**

"2 STYLE" FOOTED BERRY SETS

Set consists of one 7½-in. bowl and six 4¾-in. berry nappies to match.

AO2013—Imitation cut crystal glass, smooth edges. ½ doz. sets of each style; total 1 doz. sets in bbl. Wt. 80 lbs. Doz. sets. **$4.75**

"2 STYLE" BERRY BOWLS

AO2024—Diam. 10 in., fire polished crystal glass. 2 doz. asstd. in bbl. Wt. 85 lbs. Doz. **$2.75**

"2-STYLE" HIGH FOOT COVERED BOWLS

AO2009—Average ht. 9¾ in., crystal glass, smooth edge. Asstd. 1 doz. each of 2 styles. 2 doz. in bbl. Wt. 106 lbs. Doz. **$3.10**

PLAIN CRYSTAL HIGH FOOT COVERED BOWLS

AO2010—Crystal glass, smooth edges. Asstd. as follows: ½ doz. 9 in., ½ doz. 10¼ in., ½ doz. 11½ in. high. 1½ doz. in bbl. Wt. 100 lbs. Doz. **$3.75**

"2 STYLE" FOOTED COVERED PRESERVE BOWLS

AO2008—Ht. 7½ in., fire polished crystal glass. 2 doz. each of 2 styles. 4 doz. in bbl. (wt. 110 lbs.) Doz. **$1.75**

CRYSTAL WEDDING GLASS COVERED BOWLS

AO177—Heavy crystal, full finished, fire polished. Asstd. as follows: 1 doz. ht. 9½ in., ½ doz. ht. 10½ in. 1½ doz. in bbl. Wt. 90 lbs. Doz. **$8.15**

CRYSTAL GLASS FOOTED COVERED HONEY DISH

AO2021—2 styles. Size 6x5½x5½ in. crystal glass, smooth edges. 3 doz. in bbl. Wt. 115 lbs. Doz. **$2.25**

PLAIN OIL OR VINEGAR CRUETS

AO2194—Capacity 8½ oz., heavy crystal glass. 2 doz. in carton. Doz. **$1.75**

GLASS BUTTER MOLDS

AO123—Bomer butter mold, crystal glass, fire polished, size 4¾ in. (inside measurement), height 2¾ in., hardwood handle, with glass imprint of sheaf of wheat and cow, 2 stamps with each mold, 2 doz. in case. Doz. **$3.25**

COLONIAL STYLE CRYSTAL GLASS CELERY HOLDERS

AO2186—Size 6x4¾ in., heavy crystal glass, fire polished. 5 doz. in bbl. Wt. 150 lbs. Doz. **$1.75**
Less than bbl. Doz. **$1.95**

SANITARY CRYSTAL GLASS DIPPERS

AO2077—Heavy annealed glass, patent attachment for wood handle; 2 doz. in case. Wt. 16 lbs. Doz. **$1.30**

AO2078—Graduated 4 and 8 ozs., heavy annealed crystal glass, patent attachment for wood handle; 2 doz. in case. Wt. 16 lbs. Doz. **$1.30**

SANITARY GLASS ROLLING PINS

AO2025—Length 16 in., open end, 1 pc. crystal. (To prevent dough from sticking, fill open end with cold water.) 1 doz. in carton. Wt. 32 lbs. Doz. **$2.65**

STAR CUT GLASS CREAMS AND SUGARS

A2281—Creams, size 2½ x 3 in., crystal glass, cut star center. Doz. **$1.75**

A2282—Sugars, size 3½x3¼ in., crystal glass, cut star center. Doz. **$1.75**

GLASS CANDY TRAYS

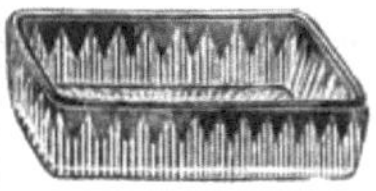

AO2085—7¾x4⅝x1⅜ in., plain pressed clear crystal, star bottom, 5½ doz. in bbl. Doz. **$1.30** (Total, **$7.15**)
A2085½—As AO2085, less quantity than bbl. Doz. **$1.50**
AO2086—8¾x5x2 in., same pattern as AO2085. 4 doz. in bbl. Doz. **$1.60** (Total, **$6.40**)
A2086½—As AO2086, less quantity than bbl. Doz. **$1.75**

CANDY TRAYS

AO2087—Size 5¼x8¼ in., plain pressed crystal glass, smooth edges, star bottom. 5 doz. in bbl. Wt. 100 lbs. Doz. **$1.50**
Less than bbl. Doz. **$1.75**

COVERED DISPLAY JARS

Heavy crystal glass.

AO2175—Capacity 1 gallon, ht. 9 in., diam. at top 6¾ in. 1 doz. in barrel. Doz. **$4.95**
AO2176—Capacity 2 gallons, ht. 11 in., diam. at top 8 in. Each in carton. Doz. **$10.20**
★**AO2177**—Capacity 3 gallons, ht. 12 in., diam. at top 9¼ in. Each in carton. Doz. **$13.75**

HANGING FISH GLOBES

AO2179—Crystal glass, smooth edges, asstd as follows:
2 only ½-gallon
2 only 2-gallon
1 only 1-gallon
1 only 3-gallon
Total, 6 globes in bbl. for **$3.25**

No Charge for Package on Any Goods. . . . .

SYRUP PITCHERS

Removable Patent Sanitary Tops. Clear crystal glass.

AO2169 AO2171

AO2169—2 styles. 10 oz., plain and optic flute design, glass lip. 1 doz. asstd. 2 doz. in carton. Wt. 37 lbs. Doz. **$2.00**
AO2171—25 oz., plain swell shape, heavy crystal, glass lip. 1 doz. in pkg. Wt. 27 lbs. Doz. **$3.25**

CRYSTAL MOLASSES CANS

Removable patent spring metal top.

A2229—Capacity 11 oz. heavy crystal glass. 1 doz. in case. Weight 20 lbs. Doz. **$3.00**

DECORATED CRYSTAL GLASS MOLASSES CANS—GLASS LIP, REMOVABLE TOP

AO2173—Capacity 22 oz., crystal glass, raised strawberry and vintage, decorated in bright colors. 1 doz. in carton, wt. 28 lbs. Doz. **$4.00**

SYRUP PITCHERS

Removable Patent Sanitary Tops—Clear crystal glass.

AO2172—13 oz., height 5¼ in., brilliant crystal, fluted design, patent nickeled top, lipped, 1 doz. in pkg. Weight 22 lbs. Doz. **$3.50**

SANITARY SYRUP PITCHERS

Polished Metal Patented Slip-on Top.

A3002 A3003

A3002—Capacity 12 ozs. Heavy crystal glass, smooth edges. Doz. **$3.15**
A3003—Capacity 16 ozs. Heavy crystal glass, smooth edges. Doz. **$3.95**

OPAL DECORATED MOLASSES CANS WITH REMOVABLE TOP

AO2174—3 styles, average capacity 17 oz., white opal glass, decorated and tinted in bright colors. 1 doz. asstd. in pkg. Wt. 28 lbs. Doz. **$3.95**

OPAL GLASS NEST EGGS

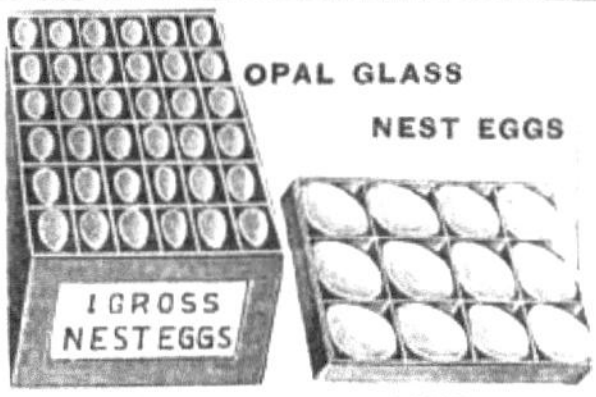

A5015 A5016

A5015—Opal nest eggs, pkd. 12 doz. in crate. Gro. **$1.75**
A5016—Opal glass nest eggs, regular size, pkd 1 doz. in box. Doz. **16**

NICKEL NUT BOWLS

A9930—Diam. 7½ in., heavily nickel plated, pierced design border, with nickel plated nut cracker and 6 nut picks. Each, **$2.00**
A9931—Same as A9930, diam. 8½ in. Each, **$2.50**

MAHOGANY FINISH NUT BOWLS

A9932—Diam. 8½ in., felt bottom, with nickel nut cracker and 6 nut picks. Each, **$1.25**

A9933—Diam. 8½ in., depth 2 in., with silver plated nut cracker and 6 nut picks. Each, **$2.10**

RED CLAY FLOWER POTS AND SAUCERS—Molded clean smooth finish. Best grade red clay.

AO738—Asst. contains—
3 doz. 4-in. | 3 doz. 5-in. | 3 doz. 6-in. | 1 doz. 7-in. | ½ doz. 8-in.
10½ doz. in pkg., wt. 350 lbs. Total for asst. **$8.35**
AO739—Asst. contains—
1 doz. 8-in. | 1 doz. 9-in. | 1 doz. 10-in. | ½ doz. 12-in.
3½ doz. in pkg., wt. 395 lbs. Total for asst. **$11.65**

Lemonade or Water Sets—
Each set comprises pitcher and 6 tumblers to match, mirror serving tray with Mahogany finished wood frame size 15½x11½ in. These sets are suitable for wedding gift purposes.

A1781—Crystal glass, wide gold band top. Set, **$2.15**

A1784—Crystal glass, gold band top. Set, **$2.25**

A1785—Crystal glass, thin blown, grape cutting. Set, **$2.25**

A1786—Crystal glass, thin blown, poinsettia cutting .... Set, **$2.25**

A1789—Crystal glass, thin blown, deep cut star with rays .... Set, **$2.75**

A1790—Crystal glass, thin blown, deep cut daisy and foliage .... Set, **$2.75**

A1795—Crystal glass, heavy gold band edge. Set, **$3.15**

A1792—Crystal glass, thin blown, deep grape and vintage cutting .... Set, **$3.45**

A1794—Crystal glass, deep cut floral and hobnail .... Set, **$4.95**

PLAIN GLASS WATER OR LEMONADE SETS

AO2000—Fire polished crystal glass, star bottom, 8½-in. jug and six 4-in. tumblers. 8 sets in case .... Set 57c

SUN BURST LEMONADE OR WATER SETS

Set comprises 1 large Jug and 6 Tumblers to match.

AO2003—Jug, ht. 8½ in., tumbler, ht. 4 in.; fire polished crystal glass; 3 sets in case, wt 26 lbs .... Set 82c

IMITATION CUT CRYSTAL GLASS
Fire polished. Open stock

A2098—Tumbler, capacity 8½ oz.... Doz. 94c
A2097—Jug, ½-gal. size, height 8½ in. .... Doz. $4.00
A2099—Goblet, capacity 8½ oz.....Doz. $1.15

CRYSTAL GLASS JUGS

AO2006—2 styles, ½ gal. capacity, ht. 8½ in., fire polished glass star bottom. 1½ doz each style, 2½ doz. in bbl., 120 lbs... Doz. $3.50

"2 STYLE" IMITATION CUT CRYSTAL GLASS JUGS

AO2007—Ht. 8½ in. ½ gal. size, clear crystal fire polished glass. 1½ doz. each of 2 styles. 2½ doz. in bbl. (Wt. 120 lbs.) ... Doz. $3.50

"2 STYLE" CRYSTAL GLASS JUGS

AO2181—Heavy crystal glass, fire polished, asstd. as follows:
1 doz. imitation cut, capacity 50 ozs.
1 doz. Colonial style, capacity 48 ozs.
Total 2 doz. in bbl., wt. 130 lbs.... Doz. $3.75

GLASS COVERED JUGS

AO2180—Heavy crystal glass, smooth edges, 1 doz. squat shape, capacity 50 oz.; 1 doz. tall shape, capacity 59 oz.; 2 doz. in bbl., wt. 115 lbs..... Doz. $3.95

SANITARY ALL GLASS COOLERS AND DISPENSERS

These coolers are ideal for Grape Juice, Iced tea, coffee and water.
The tight fitting top makes them extremely sanitary. Each has a separate compartment for Ice. Cannot dilute or mix with beverage. Metal parts are non-corrosive.

AO1—Capacity 1 gal., clear crystal glass; each packed in case. Wt. 38 lbs. Each, $7.25
AO2—Capacity 2 gal. clear crystal glass; each packed in case. Wt. 45 lbs. Each, $8.50

Page 10

TABLE TUMBLERS, Etc.

STAPLE TABLE TUMBLERS

The best tumbler made to sell at these low prices. Machine made, clear crystal, free from air bubbles, smooth edges and bottoms, fire polished.

AO100 – Capacity 9 ounces, 3 styles equally asstd.; packed 20 doz. in bbl.—no less sold (wt. 165 lbs.) .... Doz. **39c**

AO102 – Capacity 9 ounces, 3 styles equally asstd.; packed 20 doz. in bbl.—no less sold (wt. 165 lbs.)........ Doz. **39c**

AO101 AO104

Horseshoe Bottom – Clear crystal glass, smooth edges. No less than carton sold.

AO101 – Capacity 8 oz. 22 doz. in bbl., wt. 165 lbs. .... Doz. **39c**

AO104 – 9 oz. 6 doz. in dustproof carton, 40 lbs. Doz. **42c**

AO105 AO106

Fluted Star Bottom – Clear crystal glass, smooth edges. No less than carton sold.

AO105 – 9 oz. 6 doz. in dustproof carton, 40 lbs.. .... Doz. **42c**

Colonial Shape – Clear crystal glass, smooth edges, star bottom.

AO106 – 8½ oz. 6 doz. in carton, 40 lbs. Doz. **42c**

AO107 AO110

Light Hotel – Plain clear crystal glass, smooth edges, light bottom.

AO107 – 8½ oz. 6 doz. in dustproof carton, 40 lbs. No less sold. .... Doz. **42c**

Low Iced Tea or Lemonade – Plain, clear crystal, smooth edges and bottom.

AO110 – 12 oz., ht. 4½ in., diam. top 3¾ in. 6 doz. in dustproof carton, 50 lbs. No less sold. .... Doz. **57c**

AO111½ AO111

Tall Iced Tea or Lemonade – Plain clear crystal, smooth edges and bottom.

AO111½ – 12 oz., height 5¼ in., diam. top 3¼ in. 16 doz. in bbl. 150 lbs. No less sold. Doz **55c**

AO111 – 12 oz., height 5¼ in., diam. top 3¼ in. 6 doz. in dustproof carton, 50 lbs. No less sold Doz. **57c**

AO112 AO113

Fluted Iced Tea or Lemonade – Smooth edge and bottom.

AO112 – 12 oz., height 5 in., diam. top 3¾ in. 6 doz. in dustproof carton, 60 lbs. No less sold .... Doz. **75c**

AO113 – 12 oz., height 5 in., diam. top 3¾ in. 6 doz. in carton 60 lbs. No less sold Doz. **82c**

COLONIAL TABLE TUMBLERS

★ **AO103** – Capacity 8½ oz., 20 doz. in bbl.—no less sold (weight 165 lbs.) Doz. **39c**

HEAVY HOTEL TABLE TUMBLERS

AO108 AO109

AO108 – Capacity 9 oz., heavy bottom; packed 6 doz. in dustproof carton—no less sold, wt. 40 lbs. .... Doz. **57c**

AO108½ – As AO108, 18 doz. in bbl. wt. 155 lbs.. .... Doz. **54c**

AO109 – Capacity 9 oz., heavy round bottom, 6 doz. in carton, wt. 40 lbs. .... Doz. **57c**

COLONIAL ICED TEA OR LEMONADE GLASSES

Clear crystal glass, full finished, highly fire polished, smooth bottom.

AO119 AO2029

AO119 – Colonial style, capacity 11 oz., ht. 5 in., smooth edges. 15 doz. in bbl., wt. 155 lbs .... Doz. **75c**
Less than bbl. **90c**

AO2029 – Capacity 11½ oz., ht. 5 in., diam. at top 2¾ in.; 8 doz. in carton, wt. 60 lbs. Doz. **$1.10**

AO2030 AO2031

AO2030 – Capacity 12 oz., ht. 5½ in.; diam. at top 3⅝ in.; 6 doz. in carton, wt. 60 lbs. Doz. **$1.25**

AO2031 – Capacity 12 oz., ht. 5½ in., diam. at top 3¾ in.; 6 doz. in carton, wt. 60 lbs. Doz. **$1.35**

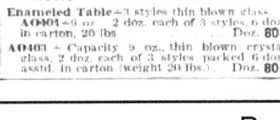

THIN BLOWN PLAIN AND ENGRAVED TABLE TUMBLERS

AO400 AO401 AO402

Thin Blown Table – Not made from chimney ends. Plain smooth melded edges. Each wrapped in tissue.

★ **AO400** – 9 oz. 20 doz. in bbl., 80 lbs. Doz. **58c**

AO401 – 9 oz. 6 doz. in shipping carton 20 lbs.. .... Doz. **64c**

Thin Blown Banded – 3 styles crystal glass.

★ **AO402** – 9 oz. 2 doz. each of 3 styles, 6 doz. in carton, 20 lbs .... Doz. **78c**

AO404 AO403

Enameled Table – 3 styles thin blown glass.

AO404 – 9 oz 2 doz. each of 3 styles, 6 doz. in carton, 20 lbs .... Doz. **80c**

AO403 – Capacity 9 oz., thin blown crystal glass, 2 doz. each of 3 styles, packed 6 doz. asstd. in carton (weight 20 lbs.) Doz. **80c**

BLOWN TAPER-SHAPED TUMBLERS

Thin blown glass, fire polished, smooth finished edges. Each tumbler wrapped in paper.

A1417 – Capacity 5 oz. Doz. **65c**

A1418 – Capacity 7 oz. Doz. **72c**

A1419 – Capacity 8 oz. Doz. **78c**

A1420 – Capacity 10 oz. Doz. **90c**

A1421 – Capacity 12 oz. Doz. **$1.20**

A1422 – Capacity 14 oz. Doz. **$1.35**

A1423 – Capacity 16 oz. Doz. **$1.45**

THIN BLOWN CRYSTAL GLASS BELL SHAPED TABLE TUMBLERS

Each tumbler wrapped in tissue paper.

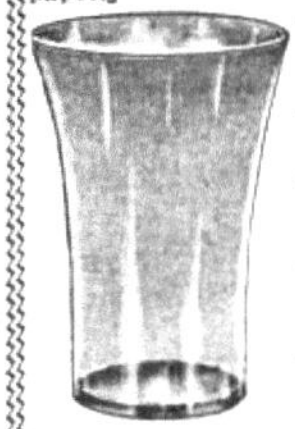

AO412 – Capacity 7 oz., 31 doz. in bbl. Wt. 115 lbs. Doz. **72c**

A1412 – As AO412, but sold less than bbl. Doz. **80c**

AO412½ – Capacity 10 oz. 18 doz. in bbl Doz. **87c**

A1412½ – As AO412½, but sold less than bbl. Doz. **96c**

AO413 – Capacity 12 oz.; 15 doz. in bbl (wt. 100 lbs.), Doz. **$1.10**

A1413 – As AO413, but sold less than barrel .... Doz. **$1.25**

BLOWN WHISKEY GLASSES

A1106 – Capacity 1 oz. Doz. **50c**

A1108 – Capacity 2 oz. Doz. **52c**

A1109 – Capacity 2½ oz. Doz. **55c**

A1110 – Capacity 3 oz. Doz. **55c**

THIN BLOWN GLASSES

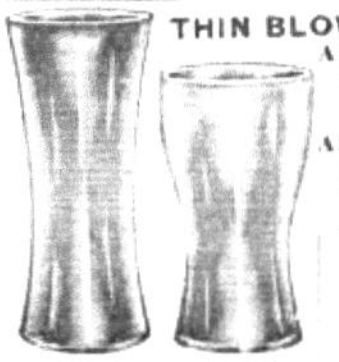

A1416 A1415

A1416 – Ginger Ale Glasses, capacity 7 oz., crystal glass. Doz. **85c**

A1415 – Coca Cola Glasses, capacity 7 oz., crystal glass. Doz. **85c**

THIN BLOWN STRAIGHT SODA GLASSES

A1414 – Capacity 7 oz., crystal glass .... Doz. **75c**

PRESSED BELL SODAS

Crystal full finished, smooth bottom and edge.

AO424 – 7 oz., Ht. 4 in., packed 22 doz. in bbl. .... Doz. **65c**

AO424½ – Same as AO424, sold less than bbl.. Doz. **80c**

AO425 – 8-oz., ht. 4¼ in. packed 19 doz. in bbl. .... Doz. **70c**

AO425½ – Same as AO425, sold less than bbl. .. Doz. **85c**

AO426 – 10-oz., ht. 4¼ in., packed 17 doz. in bbl. .... Doz. **75c**

AO426½ – Same as AO426, sold less than bbl .. Doz. **95c**

PRESSED BAND HEAVY HOTEL GOBLETS

AO2196 – Capacity 9 oz., ht. 5½ in.; 10 doz. in bbl. Wt. 155 lbs. .... Doz. **85c**

HOTEL GOBLETS

Clear crystal glass, fire polished and finished.

AO2197 AO2198 AO2199

AO2197 – Capacity 9 oz., ht. 5¾ in. 10 doz. in bbl. Wt 135 lbs. Doz. **98c**

AO2198 – Capacity 10 oz., ht. 5¾ in. 9 doz. in bbl. Wt 150 lbs Doz. **$1.15**

AO2199 – Capacity 10 oz., ht 5¾ in. 9 doz. in bbl Wt 150 lbs Doz **$1.25**

ST. LOUIS HANDLED BEER MUGS

AO2026 – Capacity 5 oz., ht. 4 in., crystal glass smooth edges. 10 doz in case. Wt 65 lbs. Doz. **67c**

AO2027 – Capacity 6 oz. ht. 4¼ in., heavy crystal glass, smooth edges. 8 doz. in case. Wt. 85 lbs. Doz. Out

AO2028 – Capacity 8 oz., ht. 4½ in., heavy crystal glass, smooth edges. 8 doz. in case. Wt. 75 lbs........ Doz. **84c**

FLUTED JELLY GLASSES

AO117 – Capacity 6½ oz. height 3⅝ in., diameter at top 2¾ in. packed 24 doz. in bbl. no less sold (weight 150 lbs.) .... Doz. **37c**

AO118 – Capacity 7 oz. height 3½ in., diameter at top 2¾ in.; packed 21 doz in bbl.—no less sold (weight 150 lbs.)........ Doz. **39c**

JELLY CLASSES

Measurements and capacity are actual—not trade sizes.

None better made

Clear crystal smooth edges and bottom, tight fitting tin covers.

AO114 – Capacity 6½ oz., height 3⅝ in., diameter at top 2¾ in. packed 21 doz in bbl. no less sold (weight 150 lbs.) .... Doz. **37c**

PRESSED BAND CAPPED JELLY TUMBLERS

AO120 – Capacity 7½ ozs., smooth edges, crystal glass, packed 25 doz. in bbl. Wt. 150 lbs .... Doz **37c**

WHITE CROWN VACUUM MASON JAR CAPS

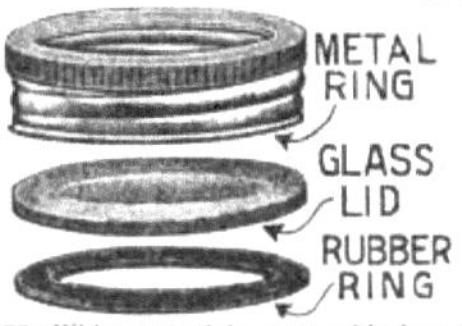

A7020 – White porcelain cap, with lacquered metal rim, red rubber seal; 1 doz. in carton. Gro. **$1.95**

MASON'S FRUIT JAR CAPS

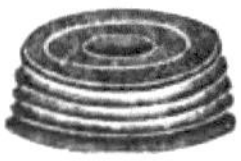

★ **A7007** – Genuine Boyd patent top of heavy zinc and porcelain lined; fits standard size jars; without rubbers. Gro. **$3.05**

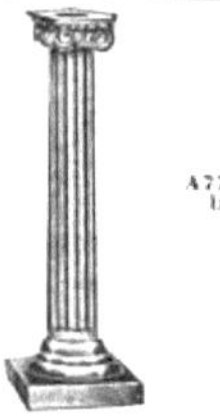

CANDLESTICK

A7741 – Ht. 10½ in., painted in bronze .... Each. **50c**

HIGH GRADE FIRE POLISHED GLASS CANDLESTICKS

A1442 – Height 6¼ in. Doz. **$1.30**

CRYSTAL EYE CUP

A1047 – Ht. 2½ in., clear crystal, full finished, fire polished, correct shape 1 doz. in box........ Doz **60c**

GLASS CASTERS

Will save the wear and tear of carpets, rugs and polished floors. Heavy Crystal Glass. Smooth edges

A1049 A1050 A1051

A1049 – Diam. 2 in., for tables. Doz. **35c**

A1050 – Diam. 3 in., for beds .... Doz. **42c**

A1051 – Diam. 4 in., for stoves Doz **72c**

Open Stock Glassware

Crystal Glass Wine Glasses

A2080 A2081 A2082 A2084 A2079

A2084 A2068

A2080—Capacity 2 oz., crystal glass. Doz. **42c**

A2081 — Capacity 3 oz. imitation cut crystal glass.......Doz. **45c**

A2082—Capacity 3 oz., imitation Rock Crystal, fire polished. Doz. **64c**

A2084—Capacity 2½ oz., Star Bottom. Doz. **65c**

A2079—Capacity 2½ oz., fire polished crystal glass.......Doz. **62c**

A2083—Capacity 3 oz., imitation cut Sun Burst Star, fire polished. Doz. **65c**

A2068 — Capacity 2½ oz., Colonial style, fire polished.......Doz. **58c**

High Grade Polished Glass Handled Custards

A1461 A1458

A1461—3x2¼ in., plain star bottom. (Gro. $8.50); Doz. **72c**

A1458 — 3½x2⅛ in., plain bell shape, star bottom.......(Gro. $8.50); Doz. **72c**

Crystal Glass Handled Sherbets

A2052 — 2¼x3¼ in., plain glass, star bottom. Doz. **55c**

Crystal Glass Sundaes or Sherberts

A2075 A2069

A2075—Size 2½x3¼ in.......Doz. **55c**

A2069—Size 3x3¾ in.......Doz. **88c**

A2076 A2072

A2076—Size 3x3½ in. Doz. **65c**

A2072—Size 2¾x2¾ in. Doz. **92c**

A2074 A2073

A2074—Size 4x3¼ in.......Doz. **$1.05**

A2073—Size 4¼x4⅛ in.......Doz. **$1.10**

Colonial Style Sundae

A2230—Size 3¼x3½ in., crystal glass, smooth molded edges. Doz. **82c**

Crystal Glass Handled Sherbets

A2092—2¼x2¾ in., imitation cut glass. Doz. **55c**

Fire Polished Glass Sundaes or Sherbets

A1460 A1457

A1460—3x2¾ in., Colonial, star foot. Doz. **68c**

A1457—3¼x2⅛ in., plain bell, star foot. Doz. **72c**

Star Cut Glass Sherbets

A2278—Crystal glass, smooth edges, star cutting. Doz. **$1.35**

Star Cut Glass Custards

A2280 — Size 2 x 3 in. crystal glass, smooth edges, star cutting.......Doz. **$1.35**

Crystal Glass Handled Olives

A2095—Size 5½ in., imitation cut fire-polished glass. Doz. **82c**

Crystal Glass Footed Nut Dishes

A2096—Size 5½ in., imitation cut crystal, fire-polished.......Doz. **80c**

Crystal Glass Heart-Shape Bonbons

A1303—Size 6 in., imitation cut crystal glass.......Doz. **65c**

Crystal Glass Berry or Salad Nappies

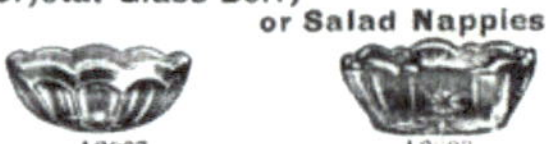

A2067 A2097

A2067—Size 4¾ in., colonial fire-polished glass. Doz. **40c**

A2094

A2093—Size 4¼ in., imitation cut sun burst star. Doz. **45c**

A2094—Size 4¼ in., imitation cut crystal glass. Doz. **60c**

Crystal Glass Vinegar Cruets or Oil Bottles in Open Stock

A2070 A2071

Heavy crystal glass, fire-polished, smooth edges.

A2070—Capacity 7 ounces. Doz. **$1.95**

A2071—Capacity 6½ ounces. Doz. **$1.95**

Colonial Style Finger Bowl

A2066 — Size 4½x2½ in., crystal fire-polished glass, ground bottom. Doz. **$1.15**

High Grade Fire Polished Glass Table Salt

A1440 — Size 3½x1½ in., plain oblong, star bottom. (Gro. $4.80); Doz. **42c**

High Grade Fire Polished Crystal Glass Individual Salts

A1437 A1438 A1439

A1437—Size 2x1 in., plain oblong, star bottom. (Gro. $4.00); Doz. **35c**

A1438 — Size 1¾x1 in., footed, imitation cut glass.......(Gro. $4.50); Doz. **40c**

A1439 — Size 1¼x¾ in., round, imitation cut glass.......(Gro. $4.50); Doz. **40c**

Crystal Glass Salts and Peppers with Aluminum and Nickel Tops

A1043 A1040 A1041

A1043 — Ht. 3 in., **nickel top**, heavy crystal, shell pattern. 1 doz. in spaced box. Doz. **45c**

A1040—Ht. 3 in., crystal glass, block pattern. 1 doz. in spaced box.......Doz. **45c**

A1041—Ht. 3¼ in., crystal glass, Colonial pattern. 1 doz. in box.......Doz. **45c**

A1042 A1045 A1044

A1042—Ht. 3½ in., heavy crystal glass, plain pattern. 1 doz. in spaced box.......Doz. **45c**

STAR VALUE ★ **A1045** — Ht. 4½ in., heavy crystal glass, Colonial pattern. 1 doz. in spaced box.......Doz. **60c**

A1044 — Ht. 4½ in., crystal glass, ribbed pattern. 1 doz. in spaced box.......Doz. **60c**

TABLE GLASSWARE—OPEN STOCK

Full finished, fire polished; an entirely new clear crystal imitation cut pattern; no rough edges.

A2043 A2044

A2043—Cream Pitcher, ht. 5 in.......Doz. **$1.50**

A2044—Spoonholder, ht. 4¼ in.......Doz. **$1.25**

A2042 A2041

A2042—Covered Sugar, ht. 6½ in. Doz. **$2.35**

A2041—Covered Butter, 7¼-in.......Doz. **$2.75**

A2046 A2047

A2046—Covered Sugar, ht. 6½ in.......Doz. **$2.15**

A2047—Cream Pitcher, ht. 5 in.......Doz. **$1.25**

A2045 A2048

A2045—Covered Butter, 7¾ in.......Doz. **$2.25**

A2048—Spoonholder, ht. 4¼ in.......Doz. **$1.05**

AO2040—Berry Bowl, 10-in. 3½ doz. in bbl. Doz. **$2.25**

A2040½—As AO2040, sold less than bbl. Doz. **$2.50**

A2049 A2050

A2049—Tall Jugs (½ gal. capacity). Doz. **$3.85**

A2050—Berry Nappy, 4¼-in.......Doz. **50c**

A2051—Berry Nappy, 4¾-in.......Doz. **60c**

A2052—Handled Sherbet, size 2¼x3¼. Doz. **55c**

Crystal fire polished, smooth edges, star bottom.

AO2039—½ gal. Jug, 2¼ doz. in bbl. Doz. **$3.95**

A2039½—As AO2039, sold less than bbl. Doz. **$4.50**

Metal Top Sugar Shaker

A2201 — Ht. 5 in., heavy crystal glass. 1 doz. in spaced box. Doz. **75c**

Crystal Glass Toothpick Holders

A2089—Size 2x2 in., imitation cut crystal glass. 1 doz. in spaced box.......Doz. **45c**

High Grade Fire Polished Glass Toothpick or Match Holder

A1444—Size 2½x1¾ in. (Gro. $6.00); Doz. **52c**

Handled Spoonholders

In open stock

A2184 A2185

A2184 — Size 4x3¾ in., heavy crystal glass, smooth edges.......Doz. **$1.10**

A2185—Size 4x3¾ in., Colonial style, heavy crystal glass, smooth edges.......Doz. **$1.25**

High Grade Fire Polished Glass Optic Sugar and Cream

A1447 A1448

A1447—Sugar, size 5x2⅛ in., star bottom. Doz. **90c**

A1448—Cream, size 4½x2⅛ in., star bottom. Doz. **95c**

High Grade Fire Polished Glass Coasters

Used as plates for Iced Tea, Cup and Sundae Glasses.

A1443 A2088

A1443—Diam. 3½ in., star bottom.......Doz. **40c**

A2088—Diam. 4 in., heavy fire polished crystal glass.......Doz. **42c**

Cut Glass Coasters

A2279 — Diam. 3½ in., crystal glass, star cutting and polished center. Doz. **88c**

Percolator Top

Will fit any percolator.

★ **A2200**—Diameter 2¾ in., crystal glass. (Gro. $4.20); Doz. **37c**

Crystal Glass Measuring Cups

Graduated ¼, ½, ¾ and 1 cup.

A1462 A2202 and A1463

A1462—Smooth edges.......Doz. **72c**

A2202—Side lip, smooth edges.......Doz. **74c**

A1463—Side lip, smooth edges.......Doz. **82c**

Crystal Glass Lemon Juice Extractors

Heavy crystal glass, fire polished. One turn of lemon extracts every drop of juice. Used as plates for Iced Tea, Cup and Sundae Glasses.

A2091 A2090

★ **A2091**—5½ in. Doz. **75c**

★ **A2090**—6 in. Doz. **96c**

A1046

A1046 — 2-pc. combination, 3½x4 in., crystal, smooth edges. 1 doz. in pkg. Doz. **$1.25**

AMERICAN CUT GLASS

Heavy lead glass blanks, brilliant luster finish. New shapes and deep rich cutting

BERRY AND FRUIT BOWLS

A3800—Diam. 7 in., ht. 3½ in., combination floral and jewel cutting, satin petals .... Each. $1.65

A3801—Diam. 8 in., ht. 4 in., combination floral and jewel cutting, satin petals, cut scalloped edge. Each. $2.10

A3802—Diam. 8 in., ht. 3 in., satin finish, pin-wheel, fan and strawberry cutting ...... Each. $2.25

A2801 — Diam. 8 in., ht. 3¾ in., combination floral and jewel cutting, satin petals .. Each. $3.25

A3806—Diam. 9 in., ht. 4 in., combination floral and jewel cutting. Each. $3.25

Berry and Fruit Bowls—Continued

A3805—Diam. 8 in., ht. 3½ in., large floral cutting, jeweled center .... Each. $3.50

A3810—Diam. 9 in., ht. 4¼ in., deep hob-star, fan and diagonal cutting .... Each. $7.50

OVAL ORANGE OR SALAD BOWLS

A3811—Size 9¾x6½x4 in., combination jewel and floral cutting, satin petals .... Each. $2.50

A3812 — Size 11½x7½x4¼ in., same cutting as A3811 .... Each. $3.50

A3813—Size 11½x8x4 in., combination jewel, hob-star, diagonal and floral cutting, satin petals. Each. $4.50

SAUCE DISHES

A2812—Size 5 in., satin finish, pin-wheel, strawberry and star cutting .... Each. 85c

HANDLE NAPPIES

A2816—Size 5 in., satin finish, pin-wheel, hob-star and fan cutting. Each. $1.00

A2818—Size 6 in., same cutting as A2816 .... Each. $1.20

A3818—Size 6 in., polished floral cutting, satin finished petals, jewel centers ...... Each. $1.50

FOOTED NUT DISHES

A3855—Size 6x2¾ in., combination jewel and floral cutting, satin petals .... Each. $1.50

A3856—Size 7x3¼ in., same cutting as A3855 ..... Each. $2.00

COVERED BUTTER DISHES

A3859—Plate 8 in., ht. 6 in., combination floral and jewel cutting, satin petals, cut scalloped edge and knob .... Each. $3.50

SPOON AND OLIVE DISHES

A3819—Size 7¾x3¾ in., satin finish, pin-wheel and hob-star cutting .... Each. 95c

A3822—Size 7¾x4¾ in., combination satin finish, pin-wheel, jewel and fan cutting ... Each. $1.25

CELERY TPAYS

A3824 — Size 10¾x4¾ in. satin finish, pin-wheel, strawberry and fan cutting. Each. $1.65

A3825 — Size 10¾x4½ in., combination jewel and floral cutting, satin petals Each. $1.85

A3827—Size 11½x4½ in., combination floral and jewel cutting, jeweled satin petals ... Each. $2.10

ICE CREAM TRAYS

★A3860—Size 14x7½ in., combination jewel and floral cutting, satin finished petals, jewel center, polished leaves Each. $3.75

SUGAR AND CREAM SETS

A3839—Sugar, 6½x4x3 in.; Cream, 5¾x3½x3¼ in.; combination jewel and floral cutting, satin finished petals, cut scalloped edge and handles .... Set $2.45

A3840—Sugar, 6½x4x3 in.; Cream, 5¼x3½x3 in.; combination satin pin-wheel, jewel and fan cutting, satin pin-wheel cut bottom, cut scalloped edge and handles. Set. $3.10

TUMBLER OR WATER GLASSES

A2887—Tumblers .... Doz. $3.25

A3836—9 ozs., ht. 4 in., whirling star and fan cutting, cut star bottom .... Doz. $5.50

A3837—9 ozs., ht. 4 in., combination jewel and floral cutting, satin petals jewel centers cut star bottoms .... Doz. $6.75

MAYONNAISE BOWL AND PLATE

A3844—Plate 6 in., bowl 5x3 in.; combination jewel and floral cutting, satin petals Set. $2.25

WATER PITCHERS

A2886—½-gal. Jug .. Each. $2.00

A3830—3-pt. size, ht. 8½ in., pin-wheel, hob-star and strawberry cutting, cut bottom, notched top and handle .... Each. $2.50

A3831—4-pt. size, ht. 11 in., same cutting as A3830 .. Each. $3.65

A3832 — 3½-pt. size, ht. 9¼ in., combination jewel and floral cutting, satin petals, jewel centers, cut bottom, notched top and handle .... Each. $3.95

ICE TUBS

A3842—Size 4¾x5½ in., combination jewel, strawberry, fan and satin pin-wheel cutting, satin pin-wheel cut bottom .. Each. $2.25

A3843—Size 5½x7 in., combination jewel and floral cutting, satin petals Each. $3.25

FLOWER OR CANDY BASKETS

Deep combination jewel, hob-star and floral cutting, 3 satin petals, polished leaves, scroll handle, cut scalloped edge.

A3851—Size 5½x3½ in. Each. $1.50

A3852—Size 6x3½ in. Each. $2.10

A3853—Size 7x4½ in. Each. $2.85

A3854—Size 8x4½ in. Each. $3.45

HIGH FOOTED COMPORTS

Combination Jewel and Floral Cutting—Polished leaves, satin petals, cut scalloped edge, notched stem, cut floral bottom.

A3848—Ht. 7½ in., diam. 5 in., satin petals ..... Each. $2.00

A3849—Ht. 7¾ in., diam. 6 in., satin petals ..... Each. $2.50

A3850—Ht. 9 in., diam. 7 in., satin petals ...... Each. $3.50

CONCAVE VASES

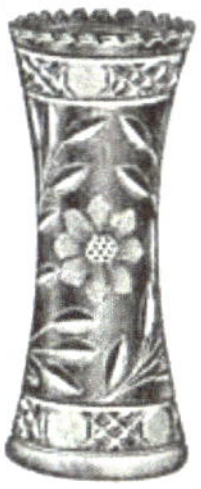

Combination jewel and floral cutting, polished leaves, satin petals, jewel center, notched top, star bottom

A3871—Ht. 8 in. Each. $1.75

A3872—Ht. 10 in. Each. $2.85

A3873—Ht. 12 in. Each. $3.75

A3874—Ht. 14 in. Each. $4.75

BELL-SHAPED VASES

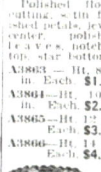

Polished floral cutting, satin finished petals, jewel center, polished leaves, notched top, star bottom

A3863 — Ht. 8½ in. Each. $1.65

A3864—Ht. 10½ in. Each. $2.65

A3865—Ht. 12 in. Each. $3.50

A3866—Ht. 14 in. Each. $4.50

CYLINDER SHAPED VASES

Combination jewel, diagonal and floral cutting, poinsettias with jewel centers, satin finished buds star cut bottom.

A3875—Ht. 8 in. Each. $2.10

A3876—Ht. 10 in. Each. $3.25

A3877—Ht. 12 in. Each. $4.25

A3878—Ht. 14 in. Each. $6.00

FIGURES

Statuary, Busts and Vases

Figures—Continued.

DECORATED VASES

HISTORIC BUSTS

DECORATED VASES

A7714
A7715

A7714—Cherry boy, height 20 in., painted features, costume in bright colors. Each, **$1.00**

A7715—Cherry girl, height 20 in., painted features, costume in bright colors. Each, **$1.00**

A7726—Cherry boy, height 26 in., painted features, costume in bright colors. Each, **$1.95**

A7727—Cherry girl, height 25 in., painted features, costume in bright colors. Each, **$1.95**

A7711
A7720

A7711—Water carrier, Ht. 19½ in., painted in colors. Each, **$1.05**

A7720—Red Riding Hood, Ht. 17 in., painted features, costume in bright colors. Each, **$1.25**

JUVENILE FIGURES

A7731
A7732
A7735

A7731—"Shakespeare," height 12 in., old ivory finish. Each, **60c**

A7732—"General Robert E. Lee," height 13 in., bronze finish. Each, **60c**

A7735—"Wagner," height 11½ in., old ivory finish. Each, **60c**

BUSTS

A7701
A7702

A7701—Ht. 15 in., Red Berries and foliage in bright colors, vase in gray. Each, **$1.00**

A7702—Ht. 17½ in., pears and foliage in bright colors, vase in old ivory. Each, **$1.00**

A7703
A7706

A7703—Ht. 15½ in., cherries and foliage in bright colors, vase in brown. Each, **$1.00**

A7706—Ht. 15 in., apples and foliage in bright colors, vase in Nile green. Each, **$1.25**

A7712
A7713
A7718

A7712—"Rebecca at the Well," ht. 18½ in., painted in bronze. Each, **$1.05**

A7713—"Venus at Bath," ht. 17 in., old ivory finish. Each, **$1.05**

A7718—Colonial female, ht. 20 in., ivory features, costume in delicate colors. Each, **$1.25**

A9930—Juvenile figures, Boys and Girls, painted features, bright color costumes. Ht. 15 in. Asstd. subjects. Each, **65c**

COMIC FIGURES

A7761
A7729

A7761—Female bust, ht. 16 in., painted in bronze and oriental colors. Each, **$1.00**

A7729—"Indian Chief," ht. 20½ in., painted in bright colors. Each, **$1.95**

ANIMALS

A7762—Lion, 16 x 18 in., old ivory finish. Each, **$1.15**

A7737—As A7762, Size 7x6¼ in. Each, **50c**

ART TRUMPET VASE

A7707—Ht. 14 in., embossed roses and foliage in bright colors, vase in light green. Each, **$1.00**

A7719

A7719—Colonial male, ht. 19 in., features in ivory, costume painted in delicate colors. Each, **$1.25**

A7745—"Mutt," ht. 21 in., Ivory finish. Each, **85c**

A7746—"Jeff," ht. 15½ in., old ivory finish. Each, **85c**

A7740—Bull Terrier, ht. 15 in., painted in bright colors. Each, **$1.10**

A7736—Same as A7740, Size 6½x7½ in. Each, **50c**

CAT AND KITTENS

A7738—Size 7⅓x8⅓ in., painted in colors. Each, **50c**

For Flower Pots and Saucers See Page 326

JARDINIERES AND PEDESTALS

ART DECORATED JARDINIERES

Earthen body, hard fired, fancy raised floral, landscape and grape designs. Prettily decorated in delicate blended tints on ivory satin-finished background. Glazed on inside in old ivory.

Art Decorated Jardinieres - Continued

JARDINIERES AND PEDESTALS

AO1011—Size 8¼x9½ in. Packed 6 only in crate. Wt. 85 lbs. Each, **$1.50**

AO1008—Size 6x6¼ in. 1½ doz. in pkg. Wt. 74 lbs. Doz. **$3.25**

AO1012—Size 9½x10 in. 3 only in crate. Wt. 50 lbs. Each, **$2.25**

AO1020
AO1014

AO1020—Ht. of Jardiniere and pedestal 12½ in., jardiniere 6¾ x6 in.; rustic raised design, dark green blended glaze. 6 in crate. Wt. 70 lbs. Each, complete, **65c**

AO1009—Size 7x7 in. 1 doz. in crate. Wt. 101 lbs. Doz. **$6.25**

ART DECORATED JARDINIERES AND PEDESTALS

Attractive shape. Antique finish.

AO1013—Hard-fired earthen body, raised grape and vintage design, enriched with antique satin finish, old ivory and Nile green tints, glazed in old ivory on inside; ht. of Jardiniere and Pedestal 24 in.; size of Jardiniere 9x10 in. 1 in crate. Wt. 55 lbs. Jardiniere and Pedestal. **$4.50**

AO1011—Hard-fired earthen body, raised floral and foliage design, enriched with antique satin finish in old ivory and Nile green tints, glazed in old ivory on inside; ht. of Jardiniere and Pedestal 27½ in., size of Pedestal 11x15½ in. 1 in crate. Wt. 65 lbs. Jardiniere and Pedestal. **$6.00**

JARDINIERE AND PEDESTAL

AO1010—Size 8x8 in. ½ doz. in pkg. Wt. 65 lbs. Doz. **$12.00**

A7743—Ht. of jardiniere and pedestal 28½ in., old ivory finish. Complete. **$3.75**

Crystal Glass and Decorated Vases

IRIDESCENT GLASS VASES

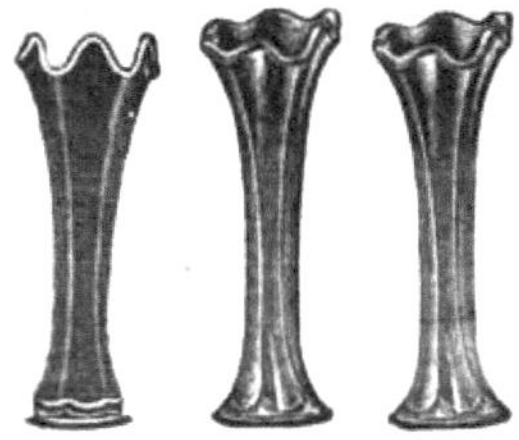

AO2263 AO2245 AO2247

AO2263—Ht. 9 in., golden and royal blue glass with oriental hues. 4 doz. asstd. in bbl. Wt. 55 lbs. .... Doz. **$1.38**

AO2245—Ht. 11¼ in., golden and blue colored glass with oriental hues, 3 doz. asstd. in bbl. Wt. 50 lbs. .... Doz. **$1.65**

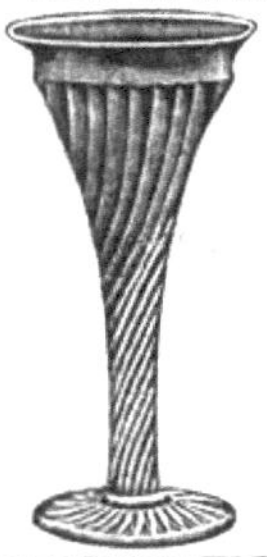

AO2246—As AO2245. 5 doz. in bbl. Wt. 80 lbs........ Doz. **$1.45**

AO2247—Ht. 11¼ in., crystal glass. 3 doz. in bbl. Wt. 50 lbs. Doz. **$1.65**

CLEAR CRYSTAL GLASS SPIRAL VASES

Full finished, fire polished. Used as supports for glass shelves in trimming windows.

A1171—Height 9 in. Doz. **$2.25**

A1172—Height 12 in. Doz. **$4.80**

IRIDESCENT TALL FLOWER VASES—WIDE TOP

Suitable for chrysanthemums and long stem flowers.

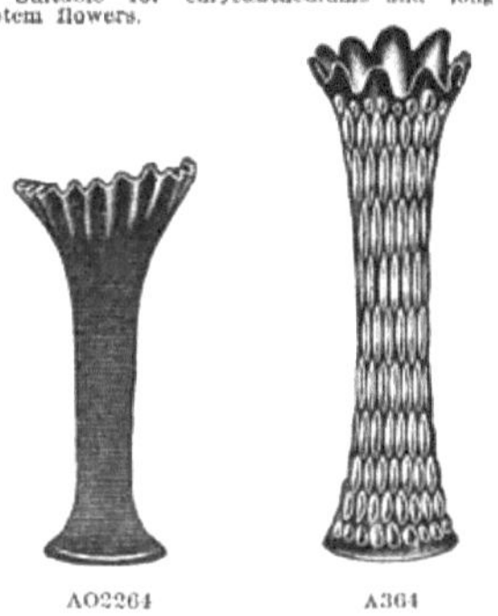

AO2264 A364

AO2264—Ht. 10 in., golden and royal blue glass, rustic design with oriental hues. 4 doz. asstd. in bbl. .... Doz. **$1.52**

A364—Ht. 21 in., royal blue and golden glass, blended with oriental colors. 1 doz. asstd. in bbl. Wt. 100 lbs .... Doz. **$6.00**

DECORATED VASES

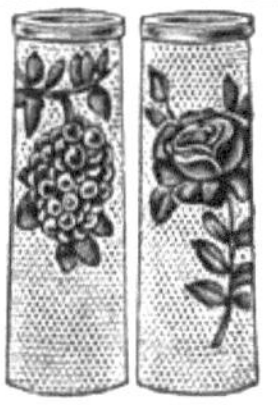

AO2154 — Ht. 9 in., crackled crystal glass, raised floral and fruit designs, decorated in bright Red and Green, gold top. 6 doz. in bbl. Wt. 80 lbs.................. Doz. **$1.42**

Total for asst. **$8.52**

AO340 AO341

★**AO340** — Ht. 9½ in., stained all over: Pink, Blue, Purple and Green; embossed panels, grapes, and vines, decorated with gold bronze. 2 doz. in carton. Wt. 30 lbs. Doz. **$1.75**

AO341 — Ht. 9½ in., stained all over; Pink, Blue, Purple and Green; embossed bird and foliage, decorated in gold and colors. 2 doz. in carton. Wt. 30 lbs.................. Doz. **$1.95**

No Charge for Package on Any Goods

Decorated Vases—Contd.

AO2113—2 styles, ht. 9½ in., asstd. tints, deep floral and panel embossing, decorated in red and green, clou ed with gold. 2 doz. asstd. in carton. Wt. 30 lbs............ Doz. **$2.05**

Total for asst. **$4.10**

AO2161—3 styles, Ht. 10½ in., asstd. tints raised grapes, flowers and foliage designs illuminated with bronze, gold clouded all over. 1 doz. in bbl. Wt. 60 lbs. . Doz. **$4.35**

CRACKLED GLASS ROSE BOWLS

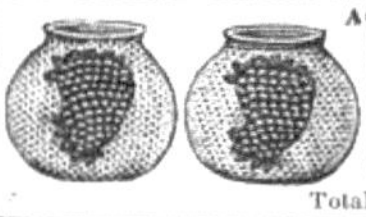

AO2168 — Ht. 3½ in., asstd. green, blue, canary and pink tints, decorated red and green luster. 3 doz. asstd. in pkg. Wt. 30 lbs Doz. **75¢**

Total for asst., **$2.25**

Sanitary White Crockery Ware—With Colored Bands

White as Porcelain, extra high gloss, underglaze blue band decoration; strong and durable; will not craze.

Pitchers—

A3109—Ht. 4 in., capacity ¾ pt. Doz. **$1.50**

A3110—Ht. 4¾ in., capacity 1 pt. Doz. **$1.85**

A3111—Ht. 5¼ in., capacity 1½ pts. Doz. **$2.40**

A3112—Ht. 5¾ in., capacity 2½ pts. Doz. **$2.85**

A3113—Ht. 6½ in., capacity 4 pts. Doz. **$3.75**

A3114—Ht. 7 in., capacity 5 pts. Doz. **$4.85**

Bowls—

A3100—Diam. 4¾ in.. Doz. **$0.90**
A3101—Diam. 5¾ in.. Doz. **$1.15**
A3102—Diam. 6¾ in.. Doz. **$1.50**
A3103—Diam. 7¾ in.. Doz. **$2.00**
A3104—Diam. 8¾ in.. Doz. **$2.60**
A3105—Diam. 9¾ in.. Doz. **$3.35**
A3106—Diam. 10¾ in.. Doz. **$4.50**
A3107—Diam. 11¾ in.. Doz. **$6.50**

WHITE CROCKERY DECORATED CUSPIDORS

A3116—Size 7x4½ in., wide and narrow gold band decorations. Doz. **$4.25**

A3117—Size 7½x4¾ in., wide and narrow green colored band decoration Doz. **$4.25**

WHITE CROCKERY "HALL BOY" JUGS

Stnadard 24 size

A3115—Ht. 6¾ in., capacity 2¾ pts Doz. **$3.75**

UNDERGLAZE BLUE BAND WHITE CROCKERY CUSTARD CUPS

A3108—Size 3½x2¼ in..... Doz. **60c**

STONEWARE SLOP JAR OR COMBINET

A3087—Ht. 12 in., with wire bail. 1 doz. in crate. Wt. 200 lbs. Doz. **$8.25**

A3087½—Same as A3087, ½ doz. in crate. Wt. 100 lbs..... Doz. **$8.75**

ROYAL BLUE MIXING BOWLS

White gloss finish inside and outside. Decorated with 2 narrow and 1 wide blue band.

A3048—Size 4½ in........ Doz. **90c**
A3049—Size 5¼ in...... Doz. **$1.20**
A3050—Size 6¼ in...... Doz. **$1.50**
A3051—Size 7¼ in...... Doz. **$2.00**
A3052—Size 8¼ in...... Doz. **$2.75**
A3053—Size 9¼ in...... Doz. **$4.00**
A3054—Size 10¼ in...... Doz. **$5.40**

TERRA-COTTA MILK PANS

Brown glazed inside and out.

AO1006—Hard fired, raised figured patterns; two staple sizes; 3 doz. ½-gal. size 4¼x8¼ in., 3 doz. 1-gal. size 5x10 in.; total, 6 doz. packed in crate (wt. 306 lbs.) Doz. **$1.95**

WHITE CROCKERY OYSTER BOWLS

A3133—Diam. 5¾ in., size 30s. Doz. **$1.80**

BLUE & BROWN COLOR GLAZED STONE PITCHERS

Water Pitchers—Ht. 8 in., capacity 2 qts.

A3125—3 doz. in crate. Doz. **$2.25**
A3125½—1 doz. in crate. Doz. **$2.40**

GLAZED STONEWARE SPITTOONS

A3085—Diam. 7½ in..... Doz. **$2.35**
A3085½—3 doz. in crate.. Doz. **$2.15**

Cuspidors—Size 7¼x6 in.

A3126—4 doz. in crate. Doz. **$2.25**
A3126½—1 doz. in crate. Doz. **$2.40**

STONEWARE CHAMBERS

AO3088—Size 9¼x5½ in., 3 doz. in crate. Wt. 140 lbs..... Doz. **$2.75**
Less than crate lots.... Doz. **$3.00**

EMBOSSED WHITE CROCKERY UNCOVERED CHAMBERS

Extra large 9s size

A3118—Size 7¾x10 in., large handle. Doz. **$4.50**

WHITE CROCKERY COVERED CHAMBERS

A3119—Large size (7¾x10 in.); hard glazed white body, large grip handle Doz. **$6.75**

AMERICAN MADE JET BLACK TEA POTS

Hard rock body, glazed inside and outside. 2 doz. asstd. in crate, giving an excellent variety of sizes for a small investment.

AO2240—Asstd. as follows: ½ doz. 8 oz., ½ doz. 16 oz., ½ doz. 24 oz., ½ doz. 46 oz., 2 doz. in crate. Wt. 80 lbs.................. Doz. **$4.25**

AO2241—Asstd. as follows: 1 doz. 16 oz., ½ doz. 24 oz., ½ doz. 46 oz., 2 doz. in crate. Wt. 100 lbs. Doz. **$4.10**

AO2242—Asstd. as follows: 1 doz. 16 oz., ½ doz. 24 oz., ½ doz. 46 oz., 2 doz. in crate. Wt. 100 lbs....Doz. **$4.50**

COLONIAL PANEL AMERICAN TABLE GLASSWARE—In Open Stock—

Select clear crystal glass, fire polish finish, medium weight.

A2061—Handled Dishes, size 6½x5½ in. Doz. $1.25

A2055—Creamers, ht. 4½ in. Doz. $1.65

A2053—Covered Butters, ht. 5¼ in. Doz. $3.00

A2051—Covered Sugars, ht. 6½ in. Doz. $2.15

A2067—Berry Dishes, size 4¾x4¼ in. Doz. 45c

A2063—Berry Dishes, size 4¼x4¾ in. Doz. 77c

A2064—Berry Bowls, size 6½x6½ in. Doz. $1.30

A2062—Berry Dishes, size 8½x8½ in. Doz. $2.35

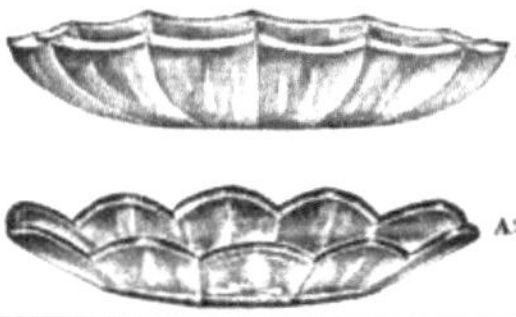

A2060—Celery Trays, size 10¼x5 in. Doz. $1.75

A2059—Pickle Dishes, size 7½x4 in. Doz. 90c

A2066—Finger Bowls, size 4½x2½ in. Doz. $1.15

A2069—Sundaes, size 3½x3¼ in. Doz. 88c

A2056—Spoonholders, ht. 4 in. Doz. $1.25

A2070—Oils, capacity 7 oz. Doz. $1.85

A2068—Wines, capacity 2¼ oz. Doz. 58c

A2058 A2057

A2058—Tumblers, ht. 4¼ in. Doz. $1.10

A2057—Goblets, ht. 6¼ in. Doz. $1.35

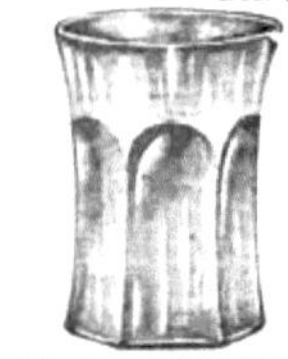

A2065—Iced Tea Tumblers, size 5 in. Doz. $1.40

Rockingham Ware

Mottled brown, high gloss, hard glaze. Measurements are actual.

A3030—Size 4¼ in.	Doz.	60c
A3031—Size 5¼ in.	Doz.	85c
A3032—Size 6½ in.	Doz.	Out
A3033—Size 7¾ in.	Doz.	Out
A3034—Size 8¾ in.	Doz.	$2.15
A3035—Size 9¾ in.	Doz.	$2.75
A3036—Size 10½ in.	Doz.	$3.60

Baking Dishes—

A3045—Size 7¼ in.	Doz.	$1.55
A3046—Size 8¼ in.	Doz.	$2.15
A3047—Size 9¼ in.	Doz.	$2.40

Covered Butter Jars—
A3037—Capacity 2 lbs. Doz. $3.25

Custards.
A3044—Size 3¾x2¾ in. Doz. 54c

Covered Salt Boxes—
A3038—Size 6x4½ in. Doz. $3.25

Pitchers or Jugs.
A3039—Capacity 3 pts. Doz. $2.15

A3040—Capacity 4 pts. Doz. $3.60

Cuspidors.
A3042—Size 7x4½ Doz. $2.25

"Pyrex" Transparent Oven Glassware

For baking and serving. High thermal endurance. Quickly absorbing and retaining, causing foods to bake rapidly and thoroughly. Solves the problem of serving foods direct from the dish. Easy to clean, greaseproof and odorproof. Don't fail to order "Pyrex" ovenware, as it is the coming cooking utensil and will repeat sales.

Round Covered Casseroles—
A1700—Capacity 2 qts. Each, $1.55
A1701—Capacity 2½ qts. Each, $1.75

Round Covered Casseroles—Fits all standard mountings.
A1702—Capacity 1 qt. Each, $1.10
A1703—Capacity 1½ qts. Each, $1.35

Oval Baking Dishes—
A1716—Capacity 10 oz. 6 in pkg. Each, 40c
A1717—Capacity 12½ oz. 6 in pkg. Each, 42c
A1718—Capacity 18½ oz. 6 in pkg. Each, 48c

Custard Cups—
A1719—Capacity 4 oz. 6 in pkg. Doz. $1.50

This Catalog is our ONLY Traveling Representative.

Round Pudding or Baking Dishes—
A1704—Capacity 2½ qts. 3 in pkg. Each, $1.00
A1705—Capacity 2 qts. 3 in pkg. Each, 90c
A1706—Capacity 1½ qts. 3 in pkg. Each, 78c
A1707—Capacity 1 qt. 3 in pkg. Each, 65c

Round Shallow Pudding Dishes—
A1708—Capacity 1 qt. 3 in pkg. Each, 65c
A1709—Capteity 1½ qts. 6 in pkg. Each, 78c

Wide Flange Pie Plates—
A1710—Size 8½ in. 6 in pkg. Each, 68c

Ramekin—
A1720—Capacity 3½ in. 6 in pkg. Doz. $1.35

Round Pie Plates—
A1711—Size 8 in. 6 in pkg. Each, 58c
A1712—Size 9 in. 6 in pkg. Each, 68c

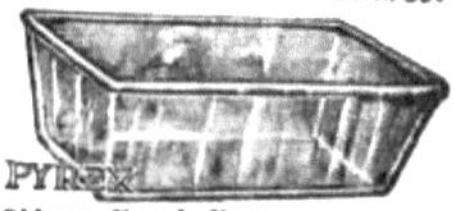

Oblong Bread Pans—
A1713—Size 8½x4½x2⅝ in., 3 in pkg. Each, 68c

Round Cake Dishes—
A1714—Size 8½x1 in. 3 in pkg. Each, Out

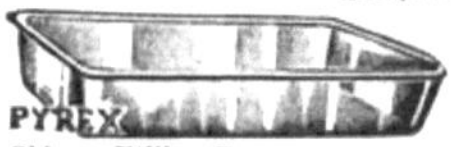

Oblong Utility Pans—
A1715—Size 10x6x1¾ in. 3 in pkg. Each, 85c

Percolator Tops—
A1721—Diam. 2¼ in., ht. 1¼ in. 2 doz. in pkg. Doz. $1.30

"PYREX" GIFT SETS

A useful present when a gift of distinction is desired.

A1722 — Set comprises the following pieces:
1 only 1½ qt. Covered Casserole.
1 only Au Gratin Dish.
1 only Bread Pan.
1 only Pie Plate.
1 only Shirred Egg Dish.
6 only Ramekins.
1 set packed in attractive box. Set, $4.00

CASSEROLES

A9907—Round, 7-in., Brown Guernsey fireproof baking dish, white lined covered casserole heavy metal nickel plated frame, size 7x3½ in. Complete, 95c

A9907½—As A9907, but Pyrex glass covered casserole. Complete, $1.55

NICKEL PLATED CASSEROLES

A9920—With White Lined Brown Fireproof Cooking Dishes. Ht. 4 in., diameter 7 in. Each, $1.50

A9921—As above, but ht. 4½ in., diam. 8 in. Each, $2.00

DECORATED GLASS CUSPIDORS

AO2223—Size 7x4 in., crystal and opal glass tinted in colors, decorated with flowers in colors and gold bands. 3 doz. in bbl. Wt. 100 lbs. Doz. $2.40

AO2224—Size 7¼x5½ in., crystal and opal glass, tinted and decorated with roses and gold bands. 3 doz. in bbl. Wt. 110 lbs. Doz. $3.25

YELLOW WARE IN OPEN STOCK

Standard sizes, hard yellow ware body, glazed inside and out.

Yellow Ware Mixing Bowls–

- A3055–Size 4¼ in. ..... Doz. 54c
- A3056–Size 5¼ in. ..... Doz. 60c
- A3057–Size 6¼ in. ..... Doz. 85c
- A3058–Size 7¼ in. ..... Doz. $1.20
- A3059–Size 8¼ in. ..... Doz. $1.80
- A3060–Size 9¼ in. ..... Doz. $2.40
- A3061–Size 10¼ in. ..... Doz. $3.00
- A3062–Size 11¼ in. ..... Doz. $4.50

Yellow Ware Nappies or Baking Dishes–

- A3065–Size 6¼ in. ..... Doz. $1.20
- A3066–Size 7¼ in. ..... Doz. $1.50
- A3067–Size 8¼ in. ..... Doz. $1.80
- A3068–Size 9¼ in. ..... Doz. $2.40

Yellow Ware Pie Plates–
A3064–Size 9 in. ..... Doz. $1.45

Open Butter Jars–

- A3069–Capacity 2 lbs. . Doz. $1.80
- A3070–Capacity 3 lbs. . Doz. $2.15

Covered Butter Jars–

- A3072–Capacity 3 lbs. Doz. $3.60
- A3073–Capacity 5 lbs. Doz. $4.50
- A3074–Capacity 10 lbs. Doz. $6.00

Custard Cups–
A3082–Size 3¾x3¾ in. Doz. 60c

Rolling Pins–
A3080–Length 15 in. . . Doz. $3.60

Spice Jars–
Ginger, Allspice, Nutmeg, Cinnamon, Pepper and Cloves.
A3081–Size 4½x2¾ in. Doz. $1.50

Covered Jars–

- A3076–Size 7½x5 in., Tea Jar. Doz. $3.60
- A3077–Size 7½x5 in., Coffee Jar. Doz. $3.60
- A3078–Size 7½x5 in., Sugar Jar. Doz. $3.60
- A3079–Size 7½x5 in., Rice Jar. Doz. $3.60

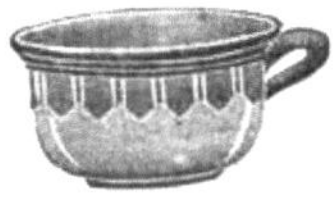

Chambers–

- A3083–Size 7½x4 in. Doz. $2.40
- A3084–Size 9½x5½ in. . Doz. Out

COOKING AND SERVING DISHES

Open Stock.

Famous "Guernsey" Brown White Lined Ware—Fireproof, light weight, hard fired, glazed outside rich brown, inside cream white, each piece trade marked. Sizes given are actual.

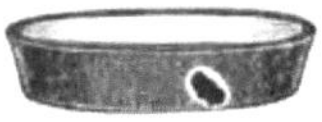

Bakers or Open Vegetable Dishes

- A8807–Length 5½ in. . . Doz. $1.10
- A8808–Length 6 in. . . Doz. $1.45
- A8809–Length 7 in. . . Doz. $1.75

Round Casserole with Covers

- A8812–7½x5 in. ...... Doz. $7.00
- A8813–8¼x5½ in. ...... Doz. $8.00

Custard
A8800–Diam. 3¼ in. ...... Doz. 82c

"Guernsey" Jet Black Teapots–Light weight, hard fired and fireproof, glazed on inside and outside in rich dark brown gloss.

A8817–8-oz. capacity . . Doz. $1.50

WHITE CROCKERY

Dishes or Platters–Hotel thick. Actual Size.

- A193–2½-in., 5⅜-in. . . Doz. $1.00
- A194–3 -in., 6⅜-in. . . Doz. $1.10
- A195–4 -in., 7¼ in. . . Doz. $1.20

Hotel Bakers—Double thick. Actual Size.

- A180–2½-in., 5¼-in. . Doz. $1.20
- A181–3 -in., 5½-in. . Doz. $1.25
- A182–4 -in., 6¼-in. . Doz. $1.30

Fluted Chambers—Covered–

- A208–Size 9s .... Doz. $7.50
- A209–Size 6s. ...... Doz. $9.00

Fluted Chambers—Uncovered–

- A205–Size 12s .... Doz. $3.65
- A206–Size 9s .... Doz. $4.85
- A207–Size 6s .... Doz. $6.10

FIREPROOF PRESERVING KETTLE ASSORTMENT

AO1015–Hard fireproof clay, natural finish outside, blue inside, extra deep, wire bail handle with enameled wood grip; assortment consists of the following: ½ doz. 2-qt., 1 doz. 4-qt., ½ doz. 6-qt.; total, 2 doz. in crate (wt. 150 lbs.) Doz. $3.00

For Sanitary White Crockery Ware With Colored Bands See Page 332. . . . . .

STAPLE WHITE CROCKERY DINNER AND CHAMBERWARE

Assortments of 12 and 24 Doz.

Good quality of white ware. All full size pieces. Comprises none but every-day sellers.

AO613–Asst. made up of the following quantities and pcs.

- 4 doz. Teas, 3x3¼ in.; Saucers 5 in.
- 4 doz. Teas, 2½ x 3¼ in. Saucers 5¼ in.
- 3 doz. 6-in. Plates, act. 8½ in.
- 4 doz. 7-in. Plates, act. 9¼ in.
- ½ doz. 6-in. Bakers, act. 8¼ in.
- ½ doz. 7-in. Bakers, act. 9¼ in.
- ½ doz. 7-in. Nappies, act. 8¼ in.
- ½ doz. 8-in. Dishes, act. 11 in.
- ½ doz. 10-in. Dishes, act. 13 in.
- ½ doz. Jugs, cap. 3½ pts.
- ½ doz. Creams, cap. 18 ozs.
- ½ doz. 7-in. Covered Dishes, act. 9 in.
- 3 doz. 4-in. Fruits, act. 5¼ in.
- ½ doz. Ewers and Basins, 12s.
- ½ doz. Chambers, 9s.
- ½ doz. Bowls, 30s (capacity 1½ pts.)
- ½ doz. Bowls 42s (capacity ¾ pt).

Total, 24 doz. ..... Doz. $2.10

AO612–Asst. made up of the following quantities and pcs.

- 2 doz. Teas, 3x3¼ in.; Saucers 5 in.
- 2 doz. Teas, 2½ x 3¼ in. Saucers 5¼ in.
- 1½ doz. 6-in. Plates, act. 8½ in.
- 2 doz. 7-in. Plates, act. 9¼ in.
- ¼ doz. 6-in. Bakers, act. 8¼ in.
- ¼ doz. 7-in. Bakers, act. 9¼ in.
- ¼ doz. 7-in. Nappies, act. 8¼ in.
- ¼ doz. 8-in. Dishes, act. 11 in.
- ¼ doz. 10-in. Dishes, act. 13 in.
- ¼ doz. Jugs, cap. 3½ pts.
- ¼ doz. Creams, cap. 18 ozs.
- ¼ doz. 7-in. Covered Dishes, act. 9 in.
- 1½ doz. 4-in. Fruits, act. 5¼ in.
- ¼ doz. Ewers and Basins, 12s.
- ¼ doz. Chambers, 9s.
- ¼ doz. Bowls, 30s (capacity 1½ pts.)
- ¼ doz. Bowls, 42s (capacity ¾ pt.)

Total, 12 doz. ..... Doz. $2.15

AMERICAN WHITE CROCKERY CHAMBERWARE

Ewers and Basins, Cable.

- A70–12s .... Doz. $19.80
- A71–12s, Ewers only, Doz. 9.90
- A72–12s, Basins only, Doz. 9.90

Ewers and Basins, Fancy.

- A73–9s .... Doz. 23.75
- A74–9s, Ewers only . . Doz. 11.88
- A75–9s, Basins only . . Doz. 11.88

Chambers, Covered, Cable.

- A76–12s .... Doz. 7.90
- A77–9s .... Doz. 10.20

Chambers, Open, Cable.

- A78–12s .... Doz. 5.40
- A79–9s .... Doz. 7.20

Chambers, Covered, Fancy.

- A80–9s .... Doz. 10.20

Combinets, Fancy.

- A81–Full size .... Doz. 21.00

Bed Pans.

- A82–1s, Large size .... Doz. 16.50

Soap Slabs.

- A84–3¾x4½ in. ...... Doz. 1.25

Dinner Set Compositions

Composition of "42-piece" Dinner Set

6 Plates, 5-in	6 pieces.
6 Plates, 7-in	6 pieces.
6 Fruit Saucers, 4-in	6 pieces.
6 Cups and Saucers	12 pieces.
6 Individual Butter Dishes	6 pieces.
1 Dish, 10-in	1 piece.
1 Covered Dish	2 pieces.
1 Baker, 7-in	1 piece.
1 Sauce Boat	1 piece.
1 Pickle Dish	1 piece.
	42 pieces.

Composition of "45-piece" Dinner Set

6 only Plates, 5-in	6 pieces.
6 only Plates, 7-in	6 pieces.
6 only Plates, 7-in., deep	6 pieces.
6 only Fruits, 4-in., deep	6 pieces.
6 only Individual Butters	6 pieces.
6 only Cups and Saucers	12 pieces.
1 only Dish, 10-in	1 piece.
1 only Baker, 7-in	1 piece.
1 only Salad	1 piece.
	45 pieces.

Composition of "51-piece" Dinner Set

6 Plates, 5-in	6 pieces.
6 Plates, 7-in	6 pieces.
6 Plates, 7-in., deep	6 pieces.
6 Fruits	6 pieces.
6 Individual Butters	6 pieces.
6 Cups and Saucers	12 pieces.
1 Dish, 8-in	1 piece.
1 Dish, 10-in	1 piece.
1 Baker, 7-in	1 piece.
1 Covered Dish, 7-in	2 pieces.
1 Boat	1 piece.
1 Sugar	2 pieces.
1 Cream	1 piece.
	51 pieces.

Composition of "56-piece Dinner Set

6 Plates, 5-in	6 pieces.
6 Plates, 6-in	6 pieces.
6 Plates, 7-in	6 pieces.
6 Fruits, 4-in	6 pieces.
6 Individual Butters	6 pieces.
6 Teacups and Saucers	12 pieces.
1 Dish, 8-in	1 piece.
1 Dish, 10-in	1 piece.
1 Baker, 7-in	1 piece.
1 Covered Dish, 7-in	2 pieces.
1 Covered Butter	3 pieces.
1 Sauce Boat	1 piece.
1 Pickle Dish	1 piece.
1 Bowl	1 piece.
1 Sugar	2 pieces.
1 Cream	1 piece.
	56 pieces

Composition of "100-piece" Dinner Set

12 Plates, 6-in	12 pieces
12 Plates, 7-in	12 pieces
12 Soup Plates, 7-in	12 pieces
12 Fruit Saucers, 4-in	12 pieces.
12 Individual Butters	12 pieces
12 Teacups and Saucers	24 pieces
1 Dish, 10-in	1 piece
1 Dish, 12-in	1 piece.
1 Baker, 7-in	1 piece.
2 Covered Dishes, 7-in	4 pieces
1 Covd. Butter and Drainer	3 pieces
1 Sauce Boat	1 piece.
1 Pickle Dish	1 piece
1 Bowl	1 piece.
1 Sugar Bowl and Cover	2 pieces
1 Cream Pitcher	1 piece.
	100 pieces

American Decorated Semi-Porcelain Dinner Sets—

Semi-vitrified body, will not crack. Light in weight, strong and durable. Each piece with the maker's trademark.

Homer Laughlin's White Semi-Porcelain Dinner Sets

OPEN STOCK

"Hudson" shape in White Crockery is the most largely sold shape that has ever been produced. Hard white Semi-Porcelain body, cream white glaze, will wear longer than others and always looks clean and new.

Equal to any Imported Porcelain made.

"Hudson" White Semi-Porcelain Dinner Sets

A133—45-piece Dinner Set	Set,	$4.85
A134—51-piece Dinner Set	Set,	$6.65
A132—100-piece Dinner Set	Set,	$13.30

For composition see page 334.

"Hudson" White Semi-Porcelain Dinnerware in Open Stock

Teas and Saucers, "Fancy Shape.		
A100—Teas 3½x2½ in., saucers 6 in.	Doz.	$2.30
Coffee Cups and Saucers, "Fancy".		
A102—Coffee Cups 3¾x2¾ in., saucers 6¼ in.	Doz.	2.60
Plates.		
A103—4 in., actual 6½ in.	Doz.	.95
A104—5 in., actual 7¼ in.	Doz.	1.07
A105—6 in., actual 8¼ in.	Doz.	1.31
A106—7 in., actual 9¼ in.	Doz.	1.65
A107—8 in., actual 9¾ in.	Doz.	2.01
Soup Plates.		
A108—7 in. deep rim, actual 9 in.	Doz.	1.90
A109—7 in. Coupe	Doz.	1.65
Cake Plate.		
A110—10 in.	Doz.	3.40
Bakers or Open Vegetable Dishes.		
A111—7 in., actual 6¾x9 in.	Doz.	2.85
Fancy Bowls.		
A112—5½x5¼ in., capacity 23 oz.	Doz.	2.38
Individual Butters.		
A113—3½ in.	Doz.	.48
Fruit or Individual Dishes, Round.		
A117—4 in., actual 5½ in.	Doz.	.71
Dishes or Meat Platers.		
A114—8 in., actual 8½x11¼ in.	Doz.	$2.38
A115—10 in., actual 10¼x13½ in.	Doz.	4.28
A116—12 in., actual 11¾x15½ in.	Doz.	7.13
Oatmeal Bowls.		
A118—6 in.	Doz.	1.07
Pickle Dishes, Oblong.		
A119—3½x6¾ in.	Doz.	3.60
Bone Plates.		
A120—3½x6¾ in.	Doz.	1.27
Salad Dishes, Deep, Round.		
A121—7 in., actual 8¼ in.	Doz.	2.85
Covered Butter Dishes.		
A122—8 in.	Doz.	8.55
Covered Vegetable Dishes.		
A123—6x8 in.	Doz.	9.98
Cream Pitchers.		
A124—Ht. 4½ in.	Doz.	2.38
Jugs, Tall Shape.		
A125—Ht. 7½ in., 24s	Doz.	4.75
Soup Tureens, Round.		
A126—8x3½ in.	Each,	1.65
Sauce or Gravy Boats.		
A127—6½ in.	Doz	3.80
Sugar Bowls and Covers.		
A128—Ht. 5 in.	Doz.	5.70
Tea Pots and Covers.		
A129—Ht. 8½ in.	Doz.	6.80

HOMER LAUCHLIN'S ORIENTAL BORDER DINNERWARE

With coin gold handles.

"Empress" shape, decorated with neat Oriental Border in 4 colors, linked with small pink flowers and foliage, gold striped edge, extra gold band on all hollow pieces, Mat coin gold covered handles.

"Empress" Oriental Border Dinner Sets

A382—45-Piece Dinner Set	Set,	$7.50
A383—51-Piece Dinner Set	Set,	11.25
A381—100-Piece Dinner Set	Set,	22.15

For composition see page 334.

"Empress" Oriental Border Dinnerware In Open Stock

A350—Tea cups 3½x2½ in; saucers 5½ in.	Doz.	$4.15
A351—Coffee cups 3¾x2½ in.; saucers 6 in	Doz.	4.95
Plates.		
A352—4-in., actual 6 in.	Doz.	1.38
A353—5-in., actual 7 in.	Doz.	1.55
A354—6-in., actual 8 in.	Doz.	1.90
A355—7-in., actual 8¾ in.	Doz.	2.40
A356—8-in., actual 9¼ in.	Doz.	2.92
Soup Plates.		
A357—7-in., Deep Rim, actual 8¼ in.	Doz.	2.75
A358—7-in., Coupe, actual 8 in.	Doz.	2.41
Bakers or Open Vegetables.		
A360—7-in., actual 6½x8¾ in.	Doz.	4.13
Fancy Bowls.		
A361—3x5½ in., capacity 33 ozs.	Doz.	3.44
Individual Butters.		
A362—3¼-in	Doz.	.69
Dishes or Meat Platters.		
A363—8-in., actual 7¾x11¼ in.	Doz.	3.44
A364—10-in., actual 8¾x13¼ in.	Doz.	6.19
A365—12-in., actual 10x15½ in.	Doz.	10.31
Fruit Saucers or Individual Dishes, Round.		
A366—4-in., actual 5½ in.	Doz	1.04
Oatmeal Bowls.		
A367—6-in.	Doz.	$1.55
Pickle Dishes.		
A368—5½x8½ in.	Doz.	7.85
Bone Plates.		
A369—6½x3¼ in.	Doz.	2.25
Salad Dishes, Deep, Round.		
A370—7-in., actual 8½ in.	Doz.	4.13
Covered Butter Dishes.		
A371—7¾ in.	Each,	1.25
Covered Vegetable Dishes.		
A372—7-in., actual 5½x7¾ in.	Each,	1.50
Cream Pitchers.		
A373—Height 2½ in., capacity 9 ozs.	Doz.	6.68
Jugs—		
A374—Ht. 6¼ in., capacity 3 pints.	Doz.	10.48
Soup Tureen.		
A375—7¾x7¾ in.	Each,	2.60
Sauce or Gravy Boats—		
A376—5¾ in.	Doz.	7.74
Sugar Bowls and Covers.		
A377—Height 3 in.	Each,	1.15

"Avona" Thistle Dinner Sets

Decorated all over, thistles and foliage in natural color, gold traced edge, gold striped handle

A2982—100-pc. Dinner Set. Set, **$15.00**

For composition see Page 334.

"Verona" Pink Rose Border Dinner Sets

Decorated, small pink roses in bloom on double gold-traced edge. Gold striped handles. Colored hair lines with orange background

A2983—45-pc. Dinner Set. Set, **$7.50**

A2985—100-pc. Dinner Set........Set, **$21.00**

For composition see Page 334.

"Verona" Pink Dresden Rose Border Dinner Sets

Decorated, clusters of pink roses and foliage border effect inserted between 2 lines of gold. Gold striped handles.

A2986—45-pc. Dinner Set. Set, **$7.50**

For composition see Page 334.

AMERICAN SEMI-PORCELAIN DINNER SETS

A0620—Delicate pink rose border, gold traced handles. Set, **$14.25**

100 Piece—See Composition Page 334.

Likes B. B. H. Packing.

Fremont, N. C., Dec. 16, 1918.

Baltimore Bargain House:

Gentlemen—Just a word to tell you about the glassware I ordered from you. It came in perfect condition. I never saw anything so nicely packed. It was in a subsantial barrel and I think would have gone around the world in good shape.

Yours truly, J. R. SHORT.

Homer Laughlin's (American) Semi-Porcelain Dinner Ware

Pure white decorated semi-porcelain, light in weight, strong and durable, guaranteed against crazing. Has a densely hard body, glazed so that it will not readily break, chip or show crisscross scratches like ordinary table ware.

WHITE AND GOLD DECORATED DINNER WARE

A02500/205—12 doz. asstd. in bbl. .... Doz. $2.05
See composition below.

WHITE AND GOLD DECORATED DINNER WARE

A05001/215—12 doz. asstd. in bbl. .... Doz. $2.15
See composition below.

WHITE AND GOLD DECORATED DINNER WARE

A05506/210—12 doz. asstd. in bbl. .... Doz. $2.40
See composition below.

"HUDSON" WHITE SEMI-PORCELAIN DINNER WARE
Equal to any Imported Porcelain made.

A0100/180—12 doz. asstd. in bbl. .... Doz. $1.80
See composition below.

HOMER LAUGHLIN "JUNE ROSE" DINNER WARE

A0210/235—12 doz. asstd. in bbl. .... Doz. $2.35
See composition below.

GOLD BAND DINNER WARE

A0400/235—12 doz. asstd. in bbl. .... Doz. $2.35
See composition below.

GOLD DECORATED DINNER WARE
The most popular and best selling pattern produced in America

A0450/245—12 doz. asstd. in bbl. .... Doz. $2.45
See composition below.

COMPOSITION OF DINNER WARE

3 doz. Hd. Cups and Saucers.	1 doz. Rim Soups, actual 9 in.	1/6 doz. Covd. Dishes, 10x7 in.	1/6 doz. Creams.
2 doz. Plates 6 in., actual 8 in.	1 doz. Coupe Soups, actual 8½ in.	1/6 doz. Bakers, 9x7 in.	1/6 doz. Dishes, 10x11 in.
3 doz. Plates 7 in., actual 9 in.	1 doz. Fruits, 5 in.	1/6 doz. Sugars.	1/6 doz. Bowls, 5x3½ in.

White and Gold Dinner Sets

A Good Set for Premium Use.

Decorated with small flowers and fresco designs in gold. Set consists of the following:

6 only Breakfast Plates.
6 only Tea Cups.
6 only Tea Saucers.
6 only Dessert Cups.
6 only Individual Butters.
1 only Meat Platter.
1 only Open Vegetable Dish.

A601—Each packed in carton .... Set. $2.65
A0601/6—Packed 6 sets in barrel .... Set. $2.45
A0601/12—Packed 12 sets in barrel .... Set. $2.40

WHITE AND GOLD 56-PIECE DINNER SET

A0605—Decorated with gold hairline center, enriched with fancy gold designs, gold traced edges and handles; each set in carton .... Set. $8.15

See composition page 334.

A0601 6

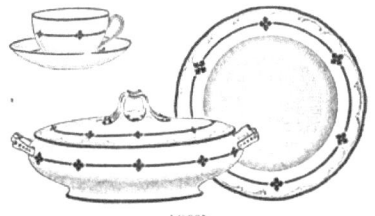

AO605

HOMER LAUGHLIN Decorated American SEMI-PORCELAIN DINNERWARE

OPEN STOCK Pure white decorated semi-porcelain, light weight, strong and durable, guaranteed against crazing. Has densely hard body, glazed so it will not readily break, chip or show criss-cross scratches as ordinary ware. HOMER LAUGHLIN

WHITE AND GOLD FLORAL DECORATED

New "Republic" shape, pure White Semi-Porcelain, rich cream white glaze, light weight, decorated with gold floral design on all edges. A good set at a very low price.

DETAIL OF DESIGN

Republic" White and Gold Dinner Sets—Composition see page 334

A2532—45-Piece Dinner Set....... Set. $5.15 | A2533—51-Piece Dinner Set........ Set. $7.00
A2531—100-Piece Dinner Set.................. Set. $14.00

"Republic" White and Gold Dinnerware in Open Stock

A2500—Tea cups 3½x2⅜ in., saucers 6 in. Doz. $2.40
A2501—Coffee Cups 3¾x2¾ in., saucers 6¼ in. Doz. 2.60

Plates.
A2502—4-in., act. 6¼ in. ...... Doz. 1.00
A2503—5-in., act. 7¼ in. ...... Doz. 1.13
A2504—6-in., act. 8⅓ in. ...... Doz. 1.38
A2505—7-in., act. 9¼ in. ...... Doz. 1.75
A2506—8-in., act. 10 in. Doz. 2.12

Soup Plates.
A2507—7-in., Deep Rim, act. 9 in. ...... Doz. 2.00
A2508—7-in., Coupe, act. 8¼ in. ...... Doz. 1.75

Bakers or Open Vegetables.
A2510—7-in., act. 6¾x9 in. ...... Doz. 3.00

Fancy Bowls.
A2511—3½x5¼ in., cap. 23 ozs. ...... Doz. $2.50

Ind. Butters.
A2512—3⅛ in. ... Doz. .50

Dishes or Meat Platters
A2513—8-in., act. 8½x11¼ ...... Doz. 2.50
A2514—10-in., act. 10¼x13½ ...... Doz. 4.50
A2515—12-in., act. 11¾x15½ ...... Doz. 7.50

Fruit or Ind. Dishes, Round.
A2516—4-in., act. 5½ in. ...... Doz. .75

Oatmeal Bowls.
A2517—6-in. ...... Doz. 1.13

Pickle Dishes, Oblong.
A2518—Act. 5¾x8¼ in. Doz. 3.75

Bone Plates.
A2519—Act. 6½x3½. Doz. 1.40

Salad Dishes Deep Round.
A2520—7-in., act. 8½ in. Doz. $3.00

Covered Butter Dishes
A2521—7⅛ in. ... Doz. 9.00

Covered Vegetable Dishes.
A2522—7-in., act. 6x8 in. ...... Doz. 10.50

Cream Pitchers.
A2523—Ht. 4½ in. Doz. 2.50

Jugs. Tall Shape.
A2524—Ht. 7½ in. Doz. 5.00

Soup Tureens.
A2525—8x8½ in. Each. 1.65

Sauce or Gravy Boats.
A2526—7-in. ..... Doz. 4.00

Sugar Bowl and Cover.
A2527—Ht. 4½ in. Doz. 6.00

WHITE AND GOLD DECORATED

New "Republic" shape pure White Semi-Porcelain, rich cream white glaze, light weight, decorated with gold edge on all pieces and fancy scroll design in gold. Handles have gold stripe.

DETAIL OF DESIGN

'Republic" White and Gold Dinner Sets—Composition see page 334

A5033—45-Piece Dinner Set......... Set. $5.40 | A5034—51-Piece Dinner Set......... Set. $7.35
A5032—100-Piece Dinner Set.................. Set. $14.75

"Republic" White and Gold Dinnerware in Open Stock

A5001—Tea cups 3½x2⅜ in., saucers 6 in. Doz. $2.50
A5002—Coffee Cups, 3¾x2¾ in., saucers 6¼ in. Doz. 2.75

Plates.
A5003—4-in., act. 6¼ in. ...... Doz. 1.05
A5004—5-in., act. 7⅛ in. ...... Doz. 1.18
A5005—6-in., act. 8⅛ in. ...... Doz. 1.44
A5006—7-in., act. 9⅛ in. ...... Doz. 1.84
A5007—8-in., act. 10 in. Doz. 2.23

Soup Plates.
A5008—7-in., deep rim, act. 9 in. ...... Doz. 2.10
A5009—7-in., coupe, act. 8¼ in. ...... Doz. 1.84

Bakers or Open Vegetables.
A5011—7-in., act. 6¾x9 in. ...... Doz. 3.15

Fancy Bowls.
A5012—3½x5¼ in., cap. 23 ozs. ...... Doz. $2.63

Ind. Butters.
A5013—3⅛ in. ... Doz. .53

Dishes or Meat Platters.
A5014—8-in., act. 8½x11¼ ...... Doz. 2.63
A5015—10-in., act. 10¼x13½ ...... Doz. 4.73
A5016—12-in., act. 11¾x15½ ...... Doz. 7.88

Fruit or Ind. Dishes, Round.
A5017—4-in., act. 5½ in. ...... Doz. .79

Oatmeal Bowls.
A5018—6-in. ...... Doz. 1.18

Pickle Dishes, Oblong.
A5019—Act. 5¾x8¾ in. ...... Doz. 3.96

Bone Plates.
A5020—Act. 6½x3½ in. ...... Doz. 1.50

Salad Dishes, Deep Round.
A5021—7-in., act. 8½ in. ...... Doz. $3.15

Covered Butter Dishes
A5022—7⅛ in. ... Doz. 9.45

Covered Vegetable Dishes.
A5023—7-in., act. 6x8 in. ...... Doz. 11.00

Cream Pitchers.
A5024—Ht. 4½ in. Doz. 2.63

Jugs. Tall Shape.
A5025—Ht. 7½ in., cap. 9 ozs. ...... Doz. 5.25

Soup Tureens.
A5026—8x8½ in. Each. 1.75

Sauce or Gravy Boats.
A5027—7-in. ..... Doz. 4.20

Sugar Bowls and Covers
A5028—Ht. 4½ in. Doz. 6.30

"JUNE ROSE" DECORATED DINNERWARE

"Hudson" shape, decorated all over with sprays of pink June roses and green foliage, heavy gold edge on all pieces, striped gold handles.

DETAIL OF DESIGN

"Hudson" June Rose Dinner Sets—Composition see page 334

A582—45-Piece Dinner Set....... Set. $5.75 | A583—51-Piece Dinner Set........ Set. $7.85
A581—100-Piece Dinner Set.................. Set. $15.75

"Hudson" June Rose Dinnerware in Open Stock

A550—Tea cups 3½x2 in., saucers 5½ in. Doz. $2.60
A551—Coffee Cups 3¾x2½ in., Saucers 6 in. Doz. 2.95

Plates.
A552—4-in., act. 6 in. Doz. 1.13
A553—5-in., act. 7 in. Doz. 1.27
A554—6-in., act. 8 in. Doz. 1.55
A555—7-in., act. 8¾ in. Doz. 1.97
A556—8-in., act. 9¾ in. Doz. 2.39

Soup Plates.
A557—7-in., deep rim, act. 8¾ in. ...... Doz. 2.25
A558—7-in., Coupe, act. 8-in. ...... Doz. 1.97

Bakers or Open Vegetables.
A560—7-in., act. 6½x8¾ in. ...... Doz. 3.38

Fancy Bowls.
A561—3x5 in., cap. 33 ozs. ...... Doz. $2.82

Ind. Butters.
A562—3⅛-in. ... Doz. .57

Dishes or Meat Platters.
A563—8-in., act. 7¼x11¼ ...... Doz. 2.81
A564—10-in., act. 8¾x13¼ ...... Doz. 5.06
A565—12-in., act. 10x15½ ...... Doz. 8.44

Fruit Saucers or Ind. Dishes, Round.
A566—4-in., act. 5½ in. Doz. .84

Oatmeal Bowls.
A567—6-in. ...... Doz. 1.27

Pickle Dishes.
A568—5½x8½ in. Doz. 4.20

Bone Dishes.
A569—6½x3¼ in. Doz. 1.69

Salad Dishes, Deep Round.
A570—7-in., act. 8½ in. Doz. $3.38

Covered Butter Dishes
A571—7⅛-in. ... Doz. 10.13

Covered Vegetable Dishes.
A572—7-in., act. 5¼x7¾ in. ...... Doz. 11.82

Cream pitchers.
A573—Ht. 2½ in., cap. 9 ozs. ...... Doz. 2.81

Jugs.
A574—Ht. 6¼ in., cap. 3 pts. ...... Doz. 5.63

Soup Tureens.
A575—7¾x7¾. Each. 1.90

Sauce or Gravy Boats.
A576—5¼ in. ...... Doz. 4.50

Sugar Bowls and Covers.
A577—Ht. 3 in. ... Doz. 6.75

PLAIN GOLD BAND DINNERWARE

Plain shape, decorated with ⅛-in gold band, gold striped handles, extra gold band on tall and covered pieces. Staple good selling patterns.

DETAIL OF DESIGN

Plain Gold Band Dinner Sets—Composition see page 334

A432—45-Piece Dinner Set......... Set. $5.85 | A433—51-Piece Dinner Set........ Set. $8.00
A431—100-Piece Dinner Set.................. Set. $16.00

Plain Gold Band Dinnerware in Open Stock

A400—Tea cups 3½x2 in., saucers 5½ in. Doz. $2.65
A401—Coffee Cups 3¾x2½ in., saucers 6 in. Doz. 3.00

Plates.
A402—4-in., act. 6 in. Doz. 1.15
A403—5-in., act. 7 in. Doz. 1.30
A404—6-in., act. 8 in. Doz. 1.58
A405—7-in., act. 8¾ in. Doz. 2.00
A406—8-in., act. 9¾ in. Doz. 2.45

Soup Plates.
A407—7-in., deep rim, act. 8¾ in. ...... Doz. 2.30
A408—7-in., coupe, act. 8 in. ...... Doz. 2.00

Bakers or Open Vegtables.
A410—7-in., act. 6½x8¾ in. ...... Doz. 3.45

Fancy Bowls.
A411—3x5½ in., cap. 33 ozs. ...... Doz. $2.85

Ind. Butters.
A412—3⅛-in. ... Doz. .58

Dish or Meat Platters.
A413—8-in., act. 7¼x11¼ ...... Doz. 2.88
A414—10-in., act. 8¾x13¼ ...... Doz. 5.20
A415—12-in., act. 10x15½ ...... Doz. 8.65

Fruit Saucers or Ind. Dishes, Round.
A416—4-in., act. 5½ in. Doz. .86

Oatmeal Bowls.
A417—6-in. ...... Doz. 1.30

Pickle Dishes.
A418—5½x8½. Doz. 4.20

Bone Plates.
A419—6½x3¼ in. Doz. 1.75

Salad Dishes, Deep Round.
A420—7-in., act. 8½ in. Doz. $3.45

Covered Butter Dishes.
A421—7⅛-in. ... Doz. 10.35

Covered Vegetable Dishes.
A422—7-in., act. 5½x7¾ in. ...... Doz. 12.00

Cream Pitchers.
A423—Ht. 2½ in., cap. 9 ozs. ...... Doz. 2.83

Jugs.
A424—Ht. 6¼ in., cap. 3 pts. ...... Doz. 5.75

Soup Tureens.
A425—7¾x7¾. Each. 1.95

Sauce or Gravy Boats.
A426—5¼ in. ...... Doz. 4.60

Sugar Bowls and Covers.
A427—Ht. 3 in. ... Doz. 6.90

HOMER LAUGHLIN Decorated American SEMI-PORCELAIN DINNERWARE

OPEN STOCK Pure white decorated semi-porcelain, light weight, strong and durable, guaranteed against crazing. Has densely hard body, glazed so it will not readily break, chip or show criss-cross scratches as ordinary ware. HOMER LAUGHLIN

FANCY WHITE AND GOLD DECORATED

New "Republic" Shape, decorated with ¼-in. gold band and fancy design on all edges. Extra gold band and fancy design on covered pieces. Gold striped handles. Attractive pattern.

DETAIL OF DESIGN

Republic" Fancy Design Dinner Sets—Composition see page 334.

A5538÷45-Piece Dinner Set.....Set. **$5.95** A5539÷51-Piece Dinner Set.......Set. **$8.25**
A5537÷100-Piece Dinner Set.......................Set. **$16.75**

'Republic" Fancy Design White and Gold Dinnerware in Open Stock

A5506÷Tea cups 3½x-2⅝ in., saucers 6 in. Doz. **$2.70**
A5507÷Coffee cups, 3⅝-x2⅝ in., saucers, 6¼ in..........Doz. **3.15**
Plates.
A5508÷4-in., act. 6¼ in............Doz. **1.20**
A5509÷5-in., act. 7¼ in............Doz. **1.35**
A5510÷6-in., act. 8⅛ in............Doz. **1.65**
A5511÷7-in., act. 9½ in............Doz. **2.10**
A5512÷8-in., act. 10 in. Doz. **2.50**
Soup Plates.
A5513÷7-in., Deep rim. act. 9 in.......Doz. **2.40**
A5514 ÷ 7-in., Coupe. act. 8¼ in.....Doz. **2.10**
Bakers or Open Vegetables.
A5516÷7-in., act. 6¼-x9 in.........Doz. **3.60**
Fancy Bowls.
A5517÷5½x5¼ in., cap. 23 ozs.........Doz. **$3.00**
Ind. Butters.
A5518÷3¼ in....Doz. **.60**
Dishes or Meat Platters.
A5519÷8-in., act. 8½-x11¼.........Doz. **3.00**
A5520 ÷ 10-in., act. 10¼x13½.....Doz. **5.40**
A5521 ÷ 12-in., act. 11¾x15½.....Doz. **9.00**
Fruit or Ind. Dishes, Round.
A5522÷4-in., act. 5½ in............Doz. **.90**
Oatmeal Bowls.
A5523÷6-in......Doz. **1.35**
Pickle Dishes, Oblong.
A5524 ÷ Act. 5¼x8¾ in............Doz. **4.50**
Bone Plates.
A5525 ÷ Act. 6½x3½ in............Doz. **1.73**
Salad Dishes, Deep Round.
A5526÷7-in., act. 8¼ in............Doz. **$3.60**
Covered Butter Dishes
A5527÷7¾-in....Doz. **10.80**
Covered Vegetable Dishes.
A5528÷7-in., act. 6x8 in. Doz. **12.60**
Cream Pitchers.
A5529÷Ht. 4¼ in. Doz. **3.00**
Jugs, Tall Shape.
A5530÷Ht. 7½ in., cap. 9 ozs...........Doz. **6.00**
Soup Tureens.
A5531 ÷ 8x8½ in. Each. **2.00**
Sauce or Gravy Boats.
A5532÷7-in......Doz. **4.80**
Sugar Bowls and Covers
A5533÷Ht. 4½ in. Doz. **7.20**

GOLD SPRIG DECORATED DINNERWARE

"Hudson" shape, decorated with small sprigs in gold on border, heavy gold edge. Tall and covered pieces have extra gold border on bottom. Handles gold striped. Popular pattern.

DETAIL OF DESIGN

Hudson" Gold Border Dinner Sets—Composition see page 334.

A482÷45-Piece Dinner Set.......Set. **$6.35** A483÷51-Piece Dinner Set.......Set. **$8.70**
A481÷100-Piece Dinner Set.......................Set. **$17.50**

"Hudson" Gold Border Dinnerware in Open Stock

A450÷Tea cups 3½x2 in., saucers 5½ in. Doz. **$2.80**
A451÷Coffee Cups 3¾x-2½ in., saucers 6 in. Doz. **3.25**
Plates.
A452÷4-in., act. 6 in. Doz. **1.25**
A453÷5-in., act. 7 in. Doz. **1.41**
A454÷6-in., act. 8 in. Doz. **1.72**
A455÷7-in., act. 8¼ in. Doz. **2.19**
A456÷8-in., act. 9¾ in. Doz. **2.65**
Soup Plates.
A457÷7-in., Deep Rim, act. 8¼ in.....Doz. **2.50**
A458 ÷ 7-in., Coupe, act. 8 in........Doz. **2.19**
Baker or Open Vegetable.
A460÷7-in., act. 6½x8¾ Doz. **3.75**
Fancy Bowls.
A461÷3x5½ in., cap. 33 ozs.........Doz. **$3.13**
Ind. Butters.
A462÷3¼ in.....Doz. **.63**
Dishes or Meat Platters
A463÷8-in., act. 7¼x-11¼...........Doz. **3.13**
A464÷10-in., act 8¾-x13¼...........Doz. **5.63**
A465÷12-in., act. 10x-15½..........Doz. **9.38**
Fruit Saucers or Ind. Dishes.
A466÷4-in., act. 5½ in. Doz. **.94**
Oatmeal Bowls.
A467÷6-in.......Doz. **1.41**
Pickle Dishes.
A468÷5½x8½ in. Doz. **4.69**
Bone Plates.
A469÷6½x3¼ in. Doz. **1.91**
Salad Dishes, Deep Round.
A470÷7-in., act. 8½ in. Doz. **$3.75**
Covered Butter Dishes
A471÷7¾-in.....Doz. **11.25**
Covered Vegetable Dishes.
A472÷7-in., act. 5½x-7¾ in.........Doz. **13.15**
Cream pitchers.
A473÷Ht. 2½ in., cap. 9 ozs..........Doz. **3.13**
Jugs.
A474÷Ht. 6¼ in., cap. 3 pts..........Doz. **6.25**
Soup Tureens.
A475÷7¾x7¾ in. Each. **2.10**
Sauce or Gravy Boat.
A476÷5¼ in.....Doz. **5.00**
Sugar Bowls and Covers
A477÷Ht. 3 in...Doz. **7.50**

PERSIAN BORDER DINNERWARE

Empress shape, light weight, conventional medallion. Persian border, 6 delicate colors, gold traced edge and handles.

DETAIL OF DESIGN

"Empress" Persian Border Dinner Sets—Composition see page 334.

A9037÷45-Piece Dinner Set......Set. **$7.60** A9038÷51-Piece Dinner Set.....Set. **$10.45**
A9034÷100-Piece Dinner Set.......................Set. **$20.95**

Open Stock "Empress" Persian Border Dinnerware

A9005÷Tea cups 3½x-2½ in., saucers 5½ in. Doz. **$3.38**
A9006 ÷ Coffee Cups, 3¾x2½ in., saucers 6 in...........Doz. **3.95**
Plates.
A9007÷4-in., act. 6 in., Doz. **$1.50**
A9008÷5-in., act. 7 in. **1.68**
A9009÷6-in., act. 8 in. **2.06**
A9010÷7-in., act. 8¾. **2.63**
A9011÷8-in., act. 9¾. **3.20**
Soup Plates.
A9012÷7-in., Deep Rim, act. 8¾ in.....Doz. **3.00**
A9013 ÷ 7-in., Coupe, act. 8 in........Doz. **2.63**
Bakers or Open Vegetables.
A9015÷7-in., act. 6½-x8¾ in.........Doz **4.50**
Fancy Bowls.
A9016÷3½x5½ Doz. **$3.76**
Ind. Butters.
A9017÷3½-in....Doz. **.75**
Dishes or Meat Platters.
A9018÷8-in., act. 7¼-x11¼..........Doz **3.76**
A9019÷10-in., act. 8¾-x13¼..........Doz. **6.75**
A9020÷12-in., act. 10-x15½..........Doz. **11.25**
Round Fruit Saucers, or Ind. Dishes.
A9021÷4-in., act. 5¼ in...........Doz. **1.12**
Round Oatmeal Saucers
A9022÷6-in......Doz. **1.68**
Pickle Dishes.
A9023÷5½x8½. Doz. **5.64**
Bone Plates.
A9024÷6½x3¼ in. Doz. **2.35**
Deep Round Salad Dishes.
A9025÷7-in., act. 8½ in............Doz. **$4.50**
Butter and Cover.
A9026÷7¾-in. Doz. **13.50**
Covered Vegetable Dish.
A9027÷7-in., act. 5½-x7¾..........Each, **1.30**
Cream Pitchers.
A9028÷Ht. 2½ in., cap. 9 ozs..........Doz. **3.75**
Jugs.
A9029÷24s, ht. 6¼ in., 3 pts..........Doz. **7.50**
Soup Tureen and Cover.
A9030÷7¾x7¾.Each. **2.50**
Sauce or Gravy Boats.
A9031÷5¾ in....Doz. **6.00**
Sugar Bowl and Cover
A9032÷Ht. 3 in..Doz. **9.00**

GOLD BAND DECORATED DINNERWARE

Plain, neat and refined, 1/16-in. and 1 hairline gold band on edges. Extra gold band on tall and covered pieces. Mat finished coin gold handles. A high grade decoration.

DETAIL OF DESIGN

"Empress" White and Gold Dinner Sets—Composition see page 334.

A532÷45-Piece Dinner Set.......Set. **$6.40** A534÷51-Piece Dinner Set.......Set. **$9.70**
A531÷100-Piece Dinner Set.......................Set. **$18.85**

"Empress" White and Gold Dinnerware in Open Stock

A500÷Tea cups 3¼x2 in., saucers 5¼ in. Doz. **$3.70**
A501 ÷ Coffee Cups 3¼-x2½ in., saucers 6 in. Doz. **4.35**
Plates.
A502÷4-in., act. 6 in. Doz. **$1.15**
A503÷5-in., act. 7 in. **1.29**
A504÷6-in., act. 8 in. **1.58**
A505÷7-in., act. 8¾ in. **2.00**
A506÷8-in., act. 9¼ in. **2.45**
Soup Plates.
A507÷7-in. deep rim, act. 8¾ in......Doz. **2.30**
A508÷7-in., coupe, act. 8 in...........Doz. **2.00**
Bakers or Open Vegetables.
A510÷7-in., act. 6½x-8¾ in.........Doz. **3.45**
Fancy Bowls.
A511÷3x5½ in...Doz. **$2.88**
Ind. Butters.
A512÷3¼-in.....Doz. **.58**
Dishes or Meat Platters.
A513÷8-in., act. 7¼x-11½...........Doz. **2.88**
A514÷10-in., act. 8¾-x13¼..........Doz. **5.18**
A515÷12-in., act. 10x-15½..........Doz. **8.63**
Fruit Saucers.
A516÷4-in., act. 5¼ in. Doz. **.86**
Oatmeal Bowls.
A517÷6-in.......Doz. **1.29**
Pickle Dishes.
A518÷5½x8½. Doz. **7.00**
Bone Plates.
A519÷6½x3¼ in. Doz. **1.70**
Salad Dishes, Deep Round.
A520÷7-in., act. 8½ in. Doz. **$3.45**
Covered Butter Dishes.
A521÷7¾ in.....Doz. **11.60**
Covered Vegetable Dishes.
A522÷7-in., act. 5½x-7¾ in.........Doz. **15.00**
Cream Pitchers.
A523÷Ht. 2½ in., cap. 9 ozs..........Doz. **6.12**
Jugs.
A524÷Ht. 6¼ in., cap. 3 pts..........Doz. **9.35**
Soup Tureens.
A525÷7¾x7¾. Each. **2.25**
Sauce or Gravy Boats.
A526÷5¾ in.....Doz. **6.75**
Sugar Bowls and Covers.
A527÷Ht. 3 in...Doz. **12.30**
Tea Pots and Covers.
A528÷Ht. 4 in...Doz. **16.50**

Attractively Decorated American Semi-Vitreous Porcelain Dinner Sets

High-Grade Semi-Viterous Porcelain —Light weight, strong and serviceable. Guaranteed against crazing. All standard size pieces. Each set in bbl. Wt. 100 lbs.

EVERY-DAY SERVICE FOR 12 PERSONS

AO631—Decorated with large sprays of violets, white and pink roses, green and shadow foliage.............Set, **$14.50**

AO630—Decorated with wide gold band on all pieces. Set, **$14.50**

SET COMPRISES

12 only Dinner Plates	12 Pieces.	12 only Saucers	12 Pieces.	1 only Covered Butter & Drainer	3 Pieces.
12 only Breakfast Plates	12 Pieces.	1 only Covered Dish	2 Pieces.	1 only Pickle	1 Piece.
12 only Bread and Butter Plates	12 Pieces.	1 only Covered Casserole	2 Pieces.	1 only Sauce Boat	1 Piece.
12 only Coupe Soup Plates	12 Pieces.	1 only Medium Meat Dish	1 Piece.	1 only Covered Sugar	2 Pieces.
12 only Fruit Saucers	12 Pieces.	1 only Large Meat Dish	1 Piece.	1 only Cream Pitcher	1 Piece.
12 only Cups	12 Pieces.	1 only Open Vegetable Dish	1 Piece.	1 only Bowl	1 Piece.

Total, 100 Pieces

JAPANESE CHINAWARE

DECORATED THIN JAP CHINA CUPS AND SAUCERS

A17/1272—Cup 3¼x3 in., saucer 5½ in., decorated with large pink roses and foliage, brown edge, gold traced handle. 1 doz. in bundle................Doz. $2.25

A17/1294—Cup 3¼x2 in., saucer 5½ in., cobalt blue edge, illuminated with gold, bright floral center in natural colors. 1 doz. in bundle. Doz. $2.25

Decorated Thin Jap China Cups and Saucers—Contd.

A7—Cup 3¼x2 in., saucer 5½ in., oriental border decoration in bright colors, gold traced edge and handle. 1 doz. in bundle. Doz. $2.35

NIPPON THIN CHINA CUPS AND SAUCERS

★ A722—Cups 3½ x 2 in., saucers 5½ in., decorated with gold band on edge and handle. Doz. $2.40

HAND PAINTED JAP CHINA BERRY SETS

Set comprises large berry bowl and 6 nappies to match.

A3966—Diam. of bowl 8½ in., nappies 5 in., hand painted with bright flowers and foliage, cobalt blue border, illuminated with gold. Set, $1.25

A40363—Diam. of bowl 9½ in., nappies 5¼ in., hand painted with roses in 2-tone colors, lattice design, border in colors and gold. Set, $1.65

No Charge for Package on Any Goods

BRIGHT FLOWERED ROYAL NIPPON CHINA DINNER SETS

A1302—Bright floral decoration in 4-toned border effect, gold traced edges and handles. 100 pc. set in bbl. Wt. 100 lbs. Set, $27.50

BLUE FLORAL ROYAL NIPPON CHINA DINNER SETS

A1300—Thin transparent Royal Nippon China, decoration under glaze. Blue floral wreath border, blue traced edge, decorated handles. 100 pc. set in bbl. Wt. 100 lbs. Set $29.50

American Semi-Porcelain Decorated Salads or Berry Bowls

A6650—Diam. 8½ in., decorated with roses in bloom, gold floral border. Doz. $2.25

A6651—Diam. 8½ in., decorated in center with various fruits in bright colors, gold floral border. Doz. $2.25

A6652—Diam. 9 in., decorated in center with flowers and foliage in natural colors, gold floral border. Doz. $2.50

A6653—Diam. 9 in., decorated in center with various fruits in bright colors, gold floral border. Doz. $2.50

A6654—Diam. 9½ in., extra deep, decorated in center with asstd floral sprays and foliage in natural colors, gold floral stenciled border. Doz. $3.25

A6655—Diam. 9½ in., extra deep, decorated in center with fruits and flowers in natural colors, gold floral stenciled border. Doz. $3.25

A6656—Diam. 9½ in., decorated in center with grapes and vintage in bright colors, ½ in. gold band edge, enriched with fresco design. Doz. $4.25

A6657—Diam. 10¼ in., decorated in center with grapes and vintage in bright colors, ½ in. gold band edge, enriched with gold lace effect. Doz. $6.00

A6658—Diam. 10¼ in., decorated in center with poppies and foliage in bright colors, ½ in. gold band edge, enriched with lace effect. Doz. $6.00

A6659—Diam. 10 in., decorated with flowers in bright colors on asstd lustre background, gold lined edge. Doz. $6.00

No Charge for Package on Any Goods. . . . .

A6660—Diam. 10 in., decorated with grapes and vintage in delicate colors on asstd tinted lustre background, gold lined edge. Doz. $6.00

A6661—Diam. 10 in., decorated in center with flowers and fruits, 1½ in. gold covered edge, enriched with lace border effect. Doz. $10.50

A6662—Diam. 10 in., decorated in center with fruits and flowers in natural colors, 1½ in. gold band border, enriched with gold lace effect. Doz. $10.50

A6663—Diam. 10½ in., decorated in center with various fruits and flowers in bright colors, 1½ in. gold band border, enriched with lace border effect. Doz. $10.50

AMERICAN SEMI-PORCELAIN DECORATED CAKE PLATES

A6664—Diam. 10 in., decorated with grapes and vintage in bright colors, ¾ in. gold band edge, enriched with hairline and fresco border design in gold. Doz. $4.25

A6666—Diam. 10¾ in., decorated in center with asstd. fruits, flowers and foliage in natural colors, 1½ in. gold covered edge, enriched with gold fresco design in border effect. Doz. $10.50

We have NO Traveling Salesmen, or branches anywhere. . . . .

ELECTRIC DOMES

AO2400
AO1202

 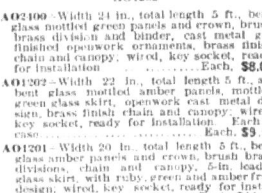

AO1201

AO2400—Width 24 in., bent glass mottled green panels and crown, brush brass division and binder, cast metal gilt finished openwork ornaments, brass finish chain and canopy, wired, key socket, ready for installation. . . . . Each, $8.00

AO1202—Width 22 in., total length 5 ft., art bent glass mottled amber panels, mottled green glass skirt, openwork cast metal design, brass finish chain and canopy, wired, key socket, ready for installation. Each in case. . . . . Each, $9.50

AO1201—Width 20 in., total length 5 ft., bent glass amber panels and crown, brush brass divisions, chain and canopy, 5-in. leaded glass skirt, with ruby, green and amber fruit design, wired, key socket, ready for installation. Each in carton. . . . . Each, $11.00

LINDSAY CAP GAS MANTLES

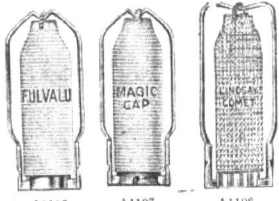

A1106   A1107   A1108

A1106—Fulvalu. Single weave, wire supports, each in tube. 1 doz. in box. . . . . Doz. 96c

A1107—Magic. Single weave, wire supports, each in tube. 1 doz. in box. . . . . . Doz. 96c

A1108—Comet. Single weave, corrugated cap, wire supports, powerful light and durable, each in tube; 1 doz. in box. . . . . Doz. 96c

A1109

★ A1109—Excelsior. Triple weave, corrugated cap, wire supports, each in tube; 1 doz. in box. . . . . Doz. $1.15

GAS MANTLES

LINDSAY INVERTED GAS MANTLES

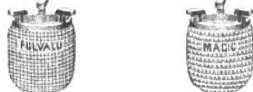

A1100

A1100—Lindsay Fulvalu, single weave, Ramie thread, magnesia ring, each in tube; 1 doz. in box. . . . . Doz. 96c

Lindsay Magic, triple weave, Ramie thread magnesia ring, each in tube; 1 doz. in box. . . . . . . Doz. Out

SAFETY GAS MANTLE.

★ A1129—Safety top, triple weave, magnesia ring; each mantle has white metal safety ring, which insures you against breakage in putting on or taking off mantle, each in box. . . . . Doz. 96c

LINDSAY SOFT INVERTED GAS MANTLE

With Magnesia Ring.

A1115—Lindsay Soft Inverted mantle on magnesia ring, single weave, can be used on any standard inverted burner, shapes itself after burning off coating, full directions with each mantle, each in box. 1 doz. in carton. . . . . Doz. $1.10

LINDSAY SOFT INVERTED GASOLINE MANTLES

A1118   A1117   A1116

A1118—Lindsay Junior, soft inverted Mantle, single weave, fits any standard pressure gasoline burner. Each mantle is enclosed in envelope, full directions with each mantle. 1 doz. in pkg. . . . . Doz. 77c

A1117—Lindsay Soft Inverted Mantle, for gasoline system, single weave, fits any standard burner. Each in envelope full directions with each mantle, strong and powerful light. 1 doz. in pkg. . . . Doz. 87c

★ A1116—Lindsay Duplex, soft inverted gasoline mantle, single weave, double fabric, extra strong, fits any standard gasoline burner. Each in envelope, full directions with each mantle. 1 doz. in pkg. . . . . Doz. 96c

For Gas Globes See Page 343

TOILET OR CHAMBER SETS

SEMI-PORCELAIN DECORATED TOILET OR CHAMBER WARE

Guaranteed not to craze.   All pieces full standard sizes.

A1607~Pink and yellow rose decoration. Comprises large pitcher, wash basin, covered chamber, covered soap dish, mug and large handle covered pail.................Set, $5.25

A1606~As A1607, without pail ....Set, $3.00

A1623~Decorations in center of pieces are in delicate bright colors, with 2 hairlines in gold, heavy gold-lined edge and handles, embossing gold traced: set comprises large pitcher, rolled-edge basin, small pitcher, covered chamber, covered soap dish, brush vase, mug and 2-handled covered pail. Set, $7.25

A1622~As A1623, but without jar.................Set, $4.50

A1611~Decorated with wide pink band, gold traced edge and handles; set comprises large pitcher, roll edge basin, small pitcher, covered chamber, covered soap dish and drainer, brush vase, mug and large 2-handled covered jar........Set, $8.00

A1610~Same as A1611, without covered jar. ......Set, $5.00

A1613~Decorated with wide blue band, otherwise same as A1611 ....Set, $8.00

A1612~Same as A1613, without covered jar.......Set, $5.00

Semi-Porcelain Decorated Toilet or Chamber Ware—Continued

A1609~Gold fresco decoration, gold traced edges and handles. Comprises large pitcher, wash basin, covd. chamber, covd. soap dish, water pitcher, brush vase, mug and large handled covd. pail........................Set, $3.00

A1608~As A1609, without pail.....................Set, $5.00

A1615~Pink Carnation and small blue flowers and foliage decorations with gold stippled edges and handles. Comprises large pitcher, wash basin, covd. chamber, covd. soap dish, water pitcher, brush vase, mug and large handle covd. pail. Set, $8.50

A1614~As A1615, without pail.................Set, $5.25

A1621~Springtime decoration with Pink Flowers. Green foliage and Pink Ribbon bowknot, heavy gold traced edges an' handles. Comprises large pitcher, wash basin, covd. chamber, covd. soap dish, water pitcher, brush vase, mug and large handle covd. slop jar.........................Set, $9.00

A1620~As A1621, but without jar.................Set, $5.25

COLONIAL WHITE AND GOLD CHAMBER SETS.

Decorated with flock of blue birds. Edge and handles traced in blue.

A1619~Set comprises large pitcher, roll edge basin, covd. chamber, covd. soap dish, mug and 2-handled covd. jar $7.50

A1618~As A1619, but without jar.......Set, $3.95

A1617~Gold traced decorations with gold star ped panels; set comprises large pitcher and roll edge basin, small pitcher, covd. chamber, covd. soap dish with drainer, brush vase, mug and covd. jar ....Set, $9.00

A1616~As A1617, but without covd. jar............Set, $5.25

DECORATED STONEWARE CHAMBER SETS

A1601~Underglazed Green Floral Print decorations. Comprises large pitcher, wash basin, covd. chamber, covd. soap dish, mug and large handle covd. pail. ....Set, $5.25

A1600~As A1601 without pail ....Set, $3.00

CEILING LIGHTS, ETC.

ELECTRIC PORCH LIGHT

A11045~6¾ in. brush brass ring, porcelain socket, 3¾ in. fitter, 8 in. white globe, frosted inside, complete. Each, $1.15

ELECTRIC CEILING LIGHT
For store or hall lighting.

A11046~5½ in. spun brush brass fixture, with porcelain socket, 3½ in. fitter, 8 in. white globe, frosted inside. Each, $1.50

Same Goods for Less Money
More Goods for Same Money

SEMI-INDIRECT CEILING LAMP
Wired Ready for Installation
About $4.75 Value for $3.85 Each

A10014~For Store or House Lighting; 14 in. white frosted glass bowl, embossed Roman design, brush brass finished chain and canopy; 1 keyless socket inside. Complete length 34 in.................Each, $3.85

SEMI-INDIRECT CEILING AND SHOWER LIGHT
Wired Ready for Installation
About $8.00 Value for $7.35 Each

A010012~14 in. white frosted glass bowl, embossed Roman design, brush brass finished chain, canopy and sockets; 1 keyless socket inside, 3 key socket shower, light and shades to match bowl. Complete length 37 in. ....Each, $7.25

Crystal Tungsten Reflectors

Clear crystal glass, brilliant diffuser of light, prismatic effect.

A10093~Diameter 6 in., depth 4½ in. 2¼ in. fitter, 25 to 40-watt..........Doz. $2.75

A10094~Diameter 7 in., depth 5 in., 2¼ in. fitter, 40 to 60-watt............Doz. $3.25

A10095~Diameter 7½ in., depth 5½ in., 2¼ in. fitter, 60 to 100-watt...Doz. $4.25

ELECTRIC FIXTURES— Wired Ready for Installation
Prices Quoted Include Glassware

Electric Fixtures—Extra heavy brass, brush brass finish and lacquered; will not tarnish. All prices quoted include embossed Roman design opal glassware. Wired ready for installation. Observe our low prices on these goods

A11031—1 light, length 36 in............................Each, **$2.15** | A11034—3 lights, length 36 in............................Each, **$5.50** | A11035—4 lights, length 36 in............................Each, **$7.25**
A11032—2 lights, length 36 in............................Each, **$4.50** | A11033—3 lights, length 24 in............................Each, **$5.75** | A11043—4 lights, length 42 in............................Each, **$12.75**

A11037—Complete length 31 in., 14-in. white frosted embossed opal glass bowl, brush brass finished chain and canopy; key socket inside. Each in case............Each, **$4.50**

A11038—Complete length 37 in., 14 in. white frosted glass bowl, brush brass finished chain, canopy, sockets and receptacles; with keyless socket, inside 3 key shower lights. Each in case....................Each, **$8.95**

A11041—Length 9 in., round curved tubing, 1 light, key socket, 2¼-in. fitter, spun brass wall plate.......................Each, **$1.35**

A11030—Length 9 in., round tubing, key socket, 2¼-in. fitter, spun brass wall plate. Each, **$1.75**

A11042—Round tubing, brush brass, 1 light key socket, 2¼-in. fitter, length 24 in. Each, **$1.75**

A11039—Complete length 36 in., spread 20 in., 2 key sockets.........................Each, **$3.95**

A11040—Complete length 36 in. spread 30 in., 3 lights complete.............Each, **$4.95**

Embossed Tinted Glass Ceiling Lights

A11026—Complete length 31 in., 14 in. deep, delicate white frosted bowl, decorated in blue, brush brass finished chain and canopy, wired, socket inside........Each, **$5.95**

A11028—As A11026, decorated in pink. Each, **$5.95**

A11027—Complete length 37 in., 14 in. deep, white frosted bowl, decorated in delicate blue, brush brass finished chain and canopy, sockets and receptacles, wire complete with inside keyless socket, 3 keyless shower lights. Each in case........Each, **$10.75**

A11029—As A11027, decorated in pink. Each in case. Wt. 20 lbs.........Each, **$10.75**

Round Tubing Electric Fixtures

Brush brass finish, covered key sockets, wired complete ready for installation, equipped with 6 in. crystal ribbed shade, 2¼ in. fitter. Price complete with glassware.

AO11048—Length 24 in..........Each, **$2.10**

AO11049—Length 6½ in..........Each, **$1.75**

AO11047—Complete length 22 in., spread 18 in., 2 lights.........Each, **$4.50**

ELECTRIC HALL LIGHT

A11044—Length 46 in., 10x5¼ in. white frosted globe.......Each, **$3.75**

Ornamental Cast Metal Electric Fixtures

Newest design. Massive construction, bronze gold finish and burnished, cast canopy and socket covers, 2¼ fitters, key socket, fancy chain, white frosted electric shades and bowls. Wired complete ready for installation.

A11050—Bracket, 1 light, heavy cast wall plate, complete with 4½ in. frosted shades........Each, **$4.00**

A11051—Bracket, 2 lights, heavy cast wall plate, complete with 4½ in. frosted shades........Each, **$5.00**

A11052—Chain drop, 1 light, length 36 in., complete with 4½ in. frosted shade........Each, **$2.25**

A11053—2 light shower, 36 in. long, spread 12 in., complete with 4½ in. white frosted shades........Each, **$5.75**

A11054—3 light shower, length 36 in., spread 16 in., 14 in. heavy gold bronze plate, complete with 4½ in. white frosted shades...Each, **$11.25**

A11055—Length 40 in., heavy gold bronze shade ring, 2 keyless inside lights........Each, **$8.25**

A11056—Length 40 in., spread 22 in., heavy gold bronze shade ring. Complete with white frosted bowl and four 4½ in. frosted shades........Each, **$13.50**

A11057—Ceiling light, heavy gold bronze shade ring. Complete with 14 in. white frosted bowl. Each, **$7.00**

For Other Electrical Fixtures See Pages 341 and 345

Page 25

LIME BEAD TOP CHIMNEYS

Unselected: packed in corrugated tubes.

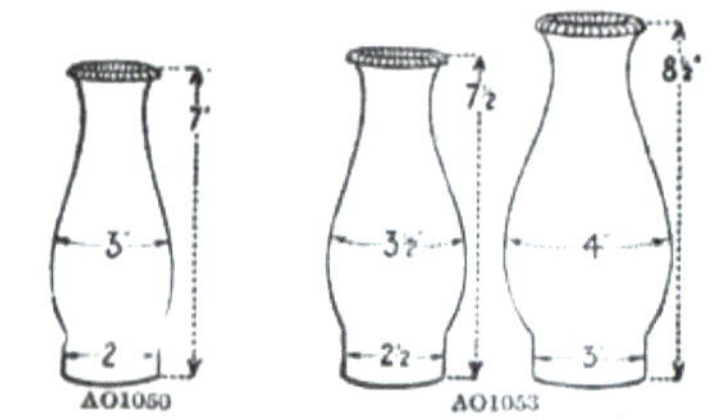

AO1050 AO1053

AO1050–Fits size No. 0 Sun Burner, height 7 in.; 6 doz. in case (weight 27 lbs.) .... Doz. 92c

AO1051–Fits size No. 1 Sun Burner, height 7½ in.; 6 doz. in case (weight 37 lbs.) .... Doz. 98c

AO1052–Fits size No. 2 Sun Burner, height 8½ in.; 6 doz. in case (weight 45 lbs.) .... Doz. $1.15

AO1053–2 doz. fit size No. 1 Sun Burner, height 7½ in.; 4 doz. fit size No. 2 Sun Burner, height 8½ in.; total, 6 doz. in case, asstd. (weight 45 lbs.) .... Case, $6.65

EMBOSSED GLOBE CRYSTAL LAMP CHIMNEYS

Will fit No. 2 Sun or Climax burner.

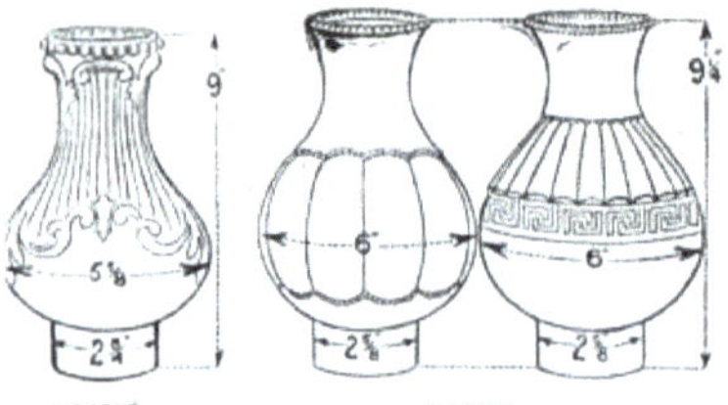

AO2222 AO2221

AO2222–Ht. 9 in., diam. at bottom 3 in. 1 doz. in case. Wt. 30 lbs. .... Doz. $1.75

AO2221–9¼ in., diam. at bottom 3 in. ½ doz. each style. 1 doz. in case. Wt. 40 lbs. .... Doz. $2.25

HAND-PAINTED LARGE BULB CRYSTAL FLINT CHIMNEYS

AO1072–Fits size No. 2 Sun or Climax Burner; 3 doz. in case (wt. 45 lbs.)..Doz. $2.00

LEAD GLASS NIGHT LAMP CHIMNEYS

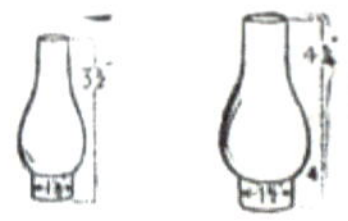

A534 A535

A534–Nutmeg chimney, fits Nutmeg burner, height 3½ in., diameter at bottom 1½ in. 1 doz. in pkg....Doz. 60c

A535–Gem chimney, fits Hornet or Gem burners, height 4¾ in., diameter at bottom 1½ in. 1 doz. in package. Doz. 65c

No Package Charge On Any Goods.

Hand-Made Flint Glass Lamp Chimneys

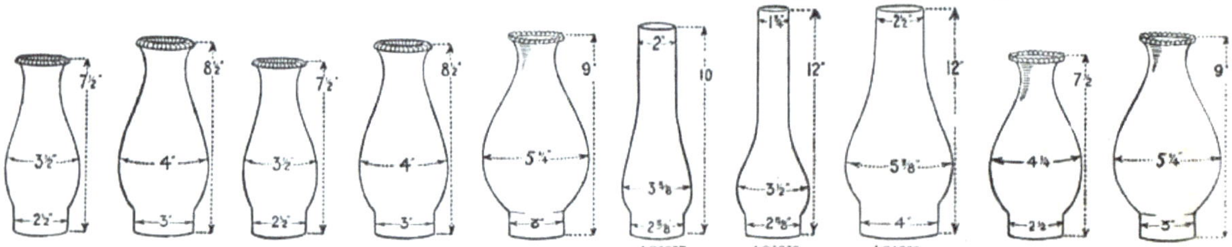

AO1057 AO1059 AO1060

Selected Crystal Flint Bead Top–Wrapped in tissue paper, packed in tubes.
AO1054–Fits size No. 1 Sun Burner, 6 doz. in case (weight 37 lbs.) .... Doz. Cut
AO1055–Fits size No. 2 Sun Burner, 6 doz. in case (weight 45 lbs.) .... Doz. $1.45

Asstd. Selected Flint Bead Top–
AO1056–2 doz. fit size No. 1 burners, 4 doz. fit size No. 2 burners; total 6 doz. asstd. in case. (weight 45 lbs.). Case, $8.00

Large Bulb Crystal Flint Chimneys–Packed in straw.
AO1066–Fits size No. 2 Sun or No. 3 Climax Burner, ht. 9 in., diam. of bulb 5 in.; 3 doz. in case (weight 45 lbs.) Doz. $1.85
AO1067–Same as AO1066, 6 doz. to case (weight 70 lbs.) Doz. $1.75

Rochester No. 2–Packed in corrugated tubes.
AO1057–No. 2 Rohester; fits No. 2 Royal, Rochester and Bristol Center draft burners. 3 doz. in case (wt. 27 lbs.) .... Doz. $1.65
AO1057½–As AO1057, but 1 doz. to case (wt. 10 lbs.) Doz. $1.75
AO1058–Same as AO1057, 6 doz. to case (weight 50 lbs.) Doz. $1.55

Rochester No. 2 and 3–Packed in corrugated tubes.
AO1059–No. 2 Rochester; for large globe Parlor Lamps; 1 doz. in case (weight 12 lbs.) Doz. $2.25
AO1060–No. 3 Rochester; fits No. 3 Burner Rochester or Juno Store Lamps. 1 doz. in case (wt. 22 lbs.)..Doz. $2.50

Asstd. Large Bulb Crystal Flint–
AO1068–2 doz. fit size No. 1 burner; 4 doz. fit size No. 2 burner; total, 6 doz. asstd in case (weight 70 lbs.) Doz. $1.75

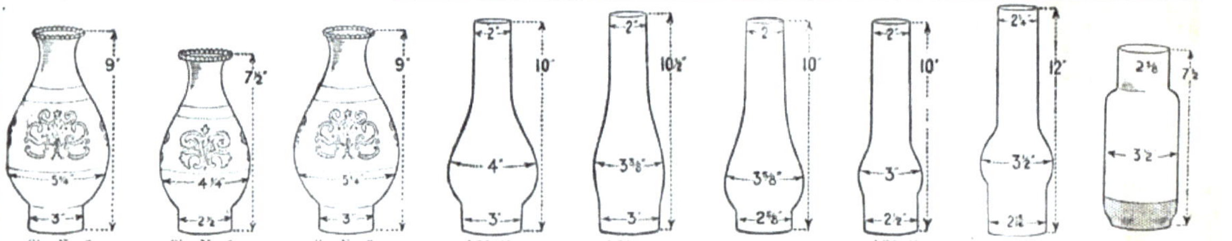

Size No. 3 Size No 1 Size No. 2 AO1061 AO1062 AO1065 AO1065½

Large Bulb Enameled–Wrapped in tissue paper, packed in straw.
AO1069–Fits size No. 2 Sun or Climax Burner, height 9 in., diam. of bulb 5 in.; 3 doz. in case (weight 42 lbs.) Doz. $1.95
AO1070–Same as AO1069, packed 6 doz. to case (weight 70 lbs) .... Doz. $1.85

Asstd. Large Bulb Enameled–
AO1071–2 doz. fit size No. 1 Burner; 4 doz. fit size No. 2 Burner; total, 6 doz. in case (weight 75 lbs.)..Doz. $1.90

Electric No. 2–Packed in corrugated tubes.
AO1061–Size 2 Electric, fits any No. 3 flat wick burner, and No. 2 Sun, 3 doz. in case (weight 34 lbs.) Doz. $1.65
AO1062–Size 2 Electric, Slim Bulb, to go through Parlor Lamp Globes, 3 doz. in case (weight 32 lbs.)..Doz. $1.65

No. 2 B. & H. or Rayo–Packed in corrugated tubes.
AO1063–Size No. 2 B. & H., fits our A190 Rayo Lamp, 3 doz. in case (weight 30 lbs.) Doz. $1.65
AO1064–Same as AO1063, packed 6 doz. in case (weight 55 lbs.) .... Doz. $1.55

Belgian or Success–Packed in corrugated tubes.
AO1065–Size No. 1 Belgian, fits Belgian or Success centre draft burner, 1 doz. in case (weight 12 lbs.)..Doz. $1.85
AO1065½–Size 00 Belgian, fits No. 3 Plumwood or Success Store Lamp, 1 doz in case (weight 16 lbs.)..Doz. $2.50

Combination Gas Crystal Flint Chimneys–
AO1081–Frosted bottom, 3 doz. in case (weight 34 lbs.) Doz. $1.25
Less than case...Doz. $1.50

LANTERN GLOBES

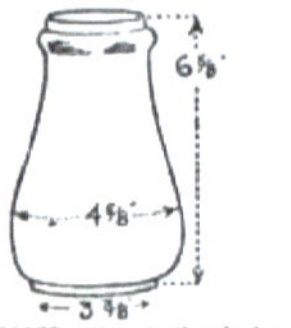

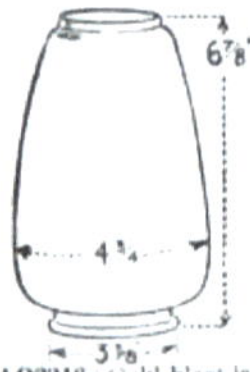

★ AO1169–Size "0" tubular, fits all regular makes of tubular lanterns, ground top and bottom, first quality, packed 5 doz. in bbl. Weight 77 lbs .... Doz. 96c

★ AO1170–Same as AO1169, packed 2 doz. in case. Doz. $1.15

★ AO2216–Cold blast lantern globe, fits our "Blizzard Lantern," packed 5 doz. in bbl. Wt. 78 lbs. Doz. $1.10

AO2217–Same as AO2216, packed 2 doz. in case. Doz. $1.50

"D-LITE" AND "NU-STYLE" LANTERN GLOBE

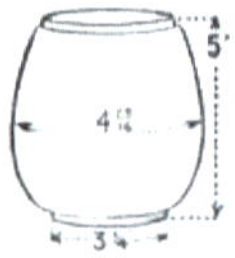

AO2218–Fits D-Lite and Nu-Style lanterns; packed 5 doz. in bbl. Weight 75 lbs. Doz. $1.45

AO2218½–Same as AO2218; packed 2 doz. in case. Doz. $1.50

RUBY STAINED "O" LANTERN GLOBES

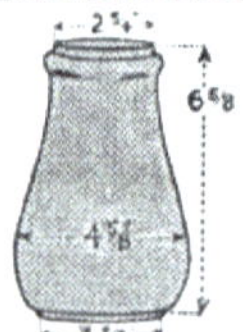

AO2220–Fits all regular makes of Tubular Lanterns, crystal glass, ruby stained; 2 doz. in case .... Doz. $1.70

BULLSEYE "O" LANTERN GLOBES

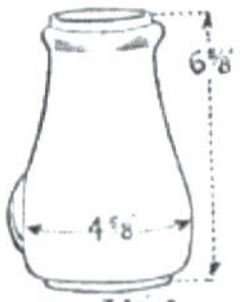

AO2219–Crystal glass, with heavy molded bullseye; 1 doz. in carton .... Doz. $2.10

OPAL Q AIR HOLE GAS GLOBES

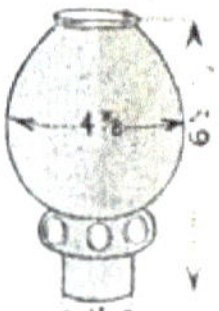

AO1232–Fine quality fireproof opal glass, height 6½ in., bottom 2 in., 5 doz. packed in bbl. Weight 55 lbs. Doz. $1.75

Less than bbl... Doz. $2.10

INNER CHIMNEYS FOR INVERTED LIGHTS

A4430–Crystal, height 4¾ in. fitter 3½ in., open at bottom Doz. 42c

WHITE OPAL SHADE

AO2236–10 in., good quality milk white, fits Rayo nickel lamp and our Power lights. 1½ doz. in bbl .... Doz. $7.00

Less than bbl .... Doz. $7.50

LINEN ELECTRIC LIGHT SHADES

AO141–Length 4 in., asstd. 1 doz. each rose, green and old gold–3 doz. asstd. in carton. Doz. 85c

AO142–Same as AO141. asstd. 1½ doz. each red and pink–3 doz. asstd. in carton. Doz. 85c

ELECTRIC SHADE HOLDERS

Fits all Standard Sockets.

A10019–Diam. 2½ in., solid brass, 3 brass screws .. Doz. 65c

This Catalog is our ONLY Traveling Representative.

GLASS LAMP ASSORTMENTS—With Burners and Chimneys

ONE-PIECE LAMPS WITH PATENT GLASS COLLAR

AO162—3 styles, 1-piece crystal glass, embossed pattern, square feet, No. 1 burner and chimney. No wicks. Asstd. as follows.
1 doz. Stand Lamps, ht. 15½ in.
1 doz. High Foot Stand Lamps, ht. 14½ in.
1 doz. Footed Hand Lamps, ht. 12¼ in.
3 doz. in bbl., wt. 97 lbs.   Doz. **$4.50**

CRYSTAL GLASS STAND LAMPS
With No. 2 Burners and Globe Chimneys, Shrunk on collars. No Wicks.

AO2209—Ht. 18 in., 3 styles heavy clear crystal glass, wide feet, packed 1½ doz. lamps ½ doz. each style; complete in bbl., wt. 100 lbs.   Doz. **$5.15**

CRYSTAL GLASS SEWING LAMPS
No. 2 burners, globe chimneys, brass shrunk on collars. No Wicks.

AO2212 — Ht. 17½ in., heavy crystal glass, wide feet. 1¾ doz. complete in bbl. Wt. 80 lbs.   Doz. **$6.00**

I-PIECE JUMBO CRYSTAL GLASS LAMPS
With No. 2 Burners and large Globe Chimneys. Brass shrunk on collars (no plaster.) No wick

AO2211—Ht. 19 in., extra heavy crystal glass wide foot, will hold nearly ½ gal. of oil 2 styles, 6 each; total, 12 complete in bbl., wt. 83 lbs.   Each, **72c**

ONE-PIECE CRYSTAL GLASS LAMP ASSORTMENT
Complete with patent glass collars, burners and chimneys—no wicks.

ONE PIECE WONT BREAK

AO167—5 styles, hand, stand and sewing, clear crystal glass, round base. Asst. comprises—
½ doz. Low ft. hand lamps, No. 1 burner and chimney, ht. 12 in.
½ doz. High ft. hand lamps, No. 1 burner and chimney, ht. 14¼ in.
½ doz. Stand lamps, No. 1 burner and chimney, ht. 16 in.
½ doz. Stand lamps, No. 2 burner and chimney, ht. 18 in.
½ doz. Sewing lamps, No. 2 burner and chimney, ht. 17½ in.
2 doz. lamps complete in bbl., wt. 93 lbs. (Total for asst., $9.00). Doz. **$5.75**

ONE-PIECE CRYSTAL GLASS LAMP ASSORTMENT
Patent glass collars with burners and chimneys—no wicks.

ONE PIECE WONT BREAK

AO163—Clear crystal, sq. feet, asstd. as follows.
½ doz. footed Hand Lamps, No. 1 burner and chimney, ht. 12 in.
½ doz. Stand Lamps, No. 1 burner and chimney, ht. 15½ in.
1 doz. Stand Lamps, No. 2 burner and chimney, ht. 18 in.
½ doz. Stand Lamps, No. 2 burner and chimney, ht. 18½ in.
½ doz. Sewing Lamps, No. 2 burner and chimney, ht. 17 in.
Tot. 1, 2½ doz. pkd. in bbl., wt. 122 lbs   Doz. **$5.75**

CRYSTAL GLASS TABLE LAMPS
No Wick.
With Burners and Chimneys.

AO164—One-piece heavy crystal glass, wide foot, clinched on brass collar (no plaster). No. 2 brass burner and chimney. ht. 17½ in., will hold 16 oz. oil. 2 doz. in bbl.; wt. 150 lbs. Doz. **$6.00**

CRYSTAL GLASS SEWING LAMPS
With No. 2 Burner and Globe Chimney.
No Wick.

AO2210—Ht. 18½ in., shrunk-on brass collar. 1 doz. complete in bbl. Wt. 77 lbs. Doz. **$7.25**

For Gas Mantles See Page 340. . .

GLASS LAMP ASSORTMENT
With Burners and Chimneys. Packed complete in barrel, for which we make no charge. Gold Brand Decorated Lamp.
No Wicks

AO2109 — Crystal glass shrunk-on collar, complete with No. 2 burners and chimneys, wie not Asstd. as follows.
½ doz. Stand Lamps, ht. 18½ in.
½ doz. Stand Lamps, ht. 19½ in.
½ doz. Stand Lamps, ht. 20 in.
½ doz. Sewing Lamps, ht. 17½ in.
Packed 12 in bbl, Wt. 85 lbs   Each, **78c**

ONE PIECE JUMBO CRYSTAL GLASS SEWING LAMPS
With patent glass collar. No plaster. Complete with No. 2 burner, chimney and wick.

AO3000—Ht. 19½ in., capacity 3 pts. 1 doz. in bbl., wt. 115 lbs. Doz. **$10.00**
AO3001—Ht. 19 in., capacity 3 pts. 1 doz. in bbl., wt. 115 lbs. Doz. **$10.00**

DECORATED CRYSTAL GLASS SEWING LAMPS
With burners and chimneys. No wick.

AO2107—Ht. 19 in., decorated embossed crystal foot, shrunk-on collar, complete with No. 2 burner and embossed globe chimney, packed 6 in bbl. Each, **80c**

NICKEL PLATED KEROSENE LAMPS
Ht. 20 in. Nickel plated, center draft burner, complete with tripod, 10-in. opal shade, wick and No. 2 Rochester chimney.
AO1240—1 doz. in case. Doz. **$24.50**
AO1240½—½ doz. in case. Doz. **$25.50**

2½ DOZ. ASST. ONE-PIECE CRYSTAL GLASS LAMPS

Without Burners and Chimneys.

ONE PIECE
WONT BREAK

AO166—With shrunk on collars, without burners and chimneys. Heavy plain crystal glass, wide foot. Assortment comprises the following:

½ doz. No. 1 collar flat hand lamps, ht. 3½ in.
½ doz. No. 1 collar stand lamps, ht. 8 in.
1 doz. No. 2 collar stand lamps, ht. 9 in.
¼ doz. No. 2 collar stand lamps, ht. 9½ in.
¼ doz. No. 2 collar stand lamps, ht. 10 in.

2½ doz. in bbl.; wt. 104 lbs. .... Doz. **$3.35**

ONE-PIECE LAMP ASST.

Patent Glass Collar. (Without Burners and Chimneys.)

ONE PIECE
WONT BREAK

AO160—Extra heavy crystal glass, embossed, square foot; assorted as follows:

½ doz. Footed Hand Lamps, No. 1 collar, ht. 4½ in.
½ doz. Stand Lamps, No 1 collar, ht. 8 in.
1 doz. Stand Lamps, No. 2 collar, ht. 9 in.
¼ doz. Stand Lamps, No. 2 collar, ht. 10 in.
¼ doz. Sewing Lamps, No. 2 collar, ht. 8½ in.

2½ doz. in bbl.; wt. 106 lbs. .... Doz. **$3.25**

"2 STYLE" CRYSTAL GLASS LAMPS

Without Burners and Chimneys.

One piece, wide foot. No. 2 patent glass collar. Will not come off.

AO178—Ht. 8½ in., capacity 24 oz. oil, 1 doz. each 2 styles; total, 2 doz. wt. 103 lbs. .....Doz. **$4.35**

PIECE CRYSTAL GLASS STAND LAMPS

No. 2 patent glass collar, without burners and chimneys.

AO169

AO169—Ht. 9 in., heavy crystal glass, wide foot. 3 doz. in bbl. Doz. **$3.35**

A1169—Same as AO169, less than bbl. Doz. **$3.85**

AO170

AO170—Ht. 8½ in., heavy crystal glass, large wide foot. 2 doz. in bbl. .... Doz. **$4.35**

A1170—Same as AO170, less than bbl. Doz. **$4.75**

CRYSTAL GLASS CLINCH-ON COLLAR STAND LAMPS

AO2101—All No. 2 collars, good crystal glass. Asstd. as follows:
⅔ doz. Standard Lamps. Height 10¾ in.
⅔ doz. Standard Lamps. Height 10¼ in.
⅔ doz. Sewing Lamps. Height 9 in.
2 doz. in bbl. Weight 81 lbs. .... Doz. **$3.15**

ASST. CRYSTAL SEWING LAMPS

AO2103—**Asstd. in 3 styles,** height 8½ in. No. 2 Brass Shrunk-on Collars. 2 doz. asstd. in bbl .... Doz. **$3.15**

CRYSTAL GLASS STAND LAMPS

AO2208—Without Burners and Chimneys. No. 2 Brass Shrunk-on Collar. No plaster. Ht. 9 in., oil capacity 14 oz., 3 doz. in bbl.; wt. 95 lbs. .... Doz. **$2.25**

ONE PIECE CRYSTAL GLASS LOW FOOTED HAND LAMP

A168—With patent No. 1 glass collar, without burners and chimneys, ht. 4½ in. .... Doz. **$1.95**

NIGHT LAMPS

A2239/40—Height 8 in., crystal glass, ruby and green raised flowers, decorated with gold bronze, brass burner and tripod complete with chimney; each in carton ..Doz. **$3.25**

WALL BRACKET LAMP

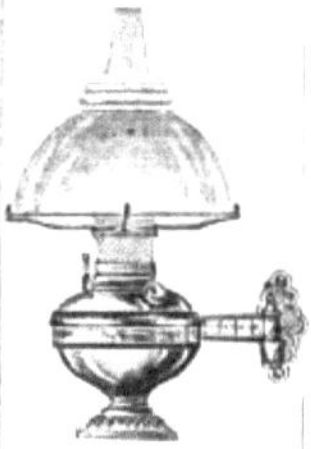

A1242—No. 2 nickel royal fount and bracket, complete with tripod, 10 in. porcelain shade and chimney, complete.. Each. **$2.85**

GLASS KITCHEN OR SIDE LAMP FOUNTS

Without Burners and Chimneys.

AO2203

A2205

AO2203—Crystal glass founts. No. 2 brass collar, fits our A43 Kitchen and Queen Anne. Doz. **96c**

A2204—Flat filler founts with heavy No. 2 brass collar and side filler. Fits any B ring or cup bracket .... Doz. **$1.75**

A2205—Handled flat filler founts with heavy No. 2 brass collar and side filler. Heavy glass handle, serviceable fount for bracket or kitchen use .... Doz. **$2.50**

CRYSTAL GLASS HAND LAMPS

Without Burners and Chimneys.

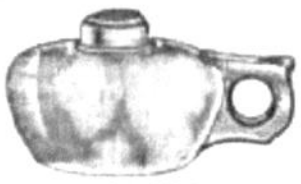

AO2206

AO2207

AO2206—Oil capacity 15 oz., clear crystal glass, heavy brass shrunk-on collar, no plaster, 10 doz. in bbl., wt. 110 lbs. Doz. **$1.40**

A2206½—Same as AO2206, sold less than bbl. Doz. **$1 50**

AO2207—Ht. 6 in., oil capacity 12 oz., clear crystal glass, heavy brass shrunk-on collar, no plaster. 6½ doz. in bbl. Wt. 120 lbs. Doz. **$1.65**

A2207½—Same as AO2207, sold less than bbl. Doz. **$1.75**

BRONZE BRACKET LAMPS—COMPLETE

No Wick.

A891—Bronze Bracket Lamp, complete with No. 2 filler fount, No. 2 Sun Burner, No. 2 Sun Chimney and 7-in. Silvered Glass Reflector. ½ doz. in case. .Doz. **$9.45**

A892—No. 2 filler fount, No. 2 Sun Burner, No. 2 Sun Chimney and 7-in. Silvered Glass Reflector; adjustable reflector throws light up or down. ½ doz. in pkg. Doz. **$10.50**

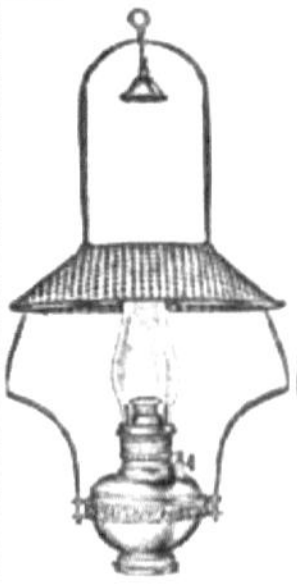

AO1238

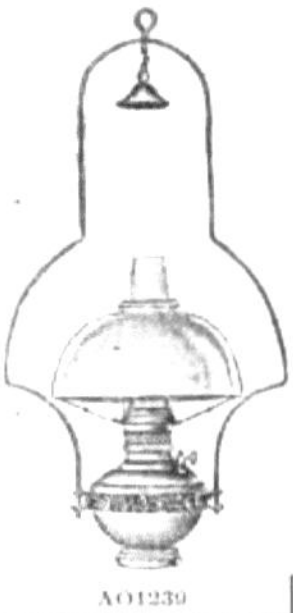

AO1239

NO. 2 NICKEL ROYAL STORE LAMPS

AO1238—Length 28 in. No. 2 royal center draft burner with oil drip cup, 15 in. embossed tin shade, smoke bell, wick and chimney. Each in case. Wt. 19 lbs. .... Each. **$3.00**

AO1239—Length 28 in. 6 in. solid brass fount, No. 2 royal center burner, oil drip cup, 10 in. opal shade, smoke bell, wick and chimney. Each in case. Wt. 20 lbs. .... Each. **$3.75**

No. 3 MAMMOTH BANNER LAMPS

Brass finish. Can be lighted without removing chimney.

AO1236—**No. 3 Banner,** embossed 1 gal. brass fount, burns 7½ hours, improved ratchet wick lift and oil indicator, complete with 14 in. dome shade, harp, smoke bell and chimney. Each in case. Wt. 21 lbs. .... Each. **$6.15**

AO1237—**"Plumwood."** Ht. 33 in. spread 15 in. 1 gal. solid brass fount, improved ratchet wick lift and oil indicator, complete with 14 in. dome shade, harp, smoke bell and chimney. Each in case. Wt. 20 lbs. .. Each. **$6.15**

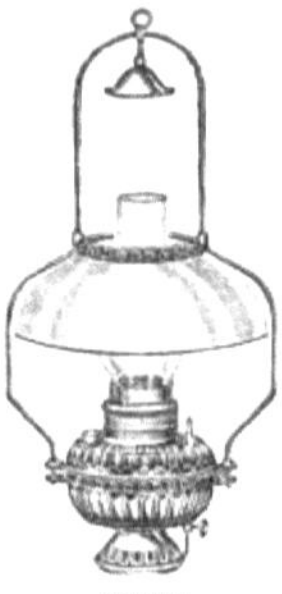

AO1236

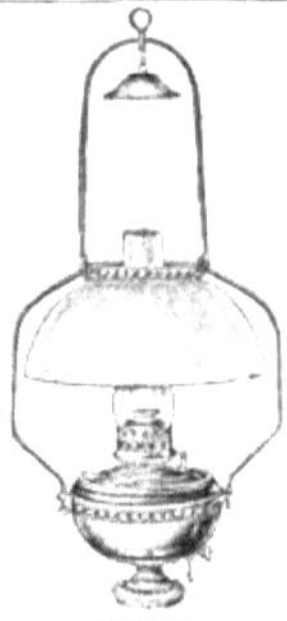

AO1237

"RAYO" EXTENSION LAMPS

AO2599½—Length (closed) 28 in., spring extension, **heavy brass** "Rayo" center draft front chimney, smoke bell and 14-in. white dome shade; each in case. Each. **$7.95**

BRASS EXTENSION FIXTURE FOR OUR Nos. 1236, 1237, 1238 AND 1239 LAMPS

Extends 39 in., length over all when fully extended 49 in. Wt. 11 lbs.

A1243—Ratchet stop, heavy cast yoke and safety hook, works smoothly, positive stop. Each in box. Each. **$1.65**

A1243½—As A1243, but nickel plated. Each. **$1.75**

DECORATED CRYSTAL GLASS PARLOR LAMPS

AO2110—Ht. 26 in., crystal glass, raised grapes, roses and vintage, decorated in bright colors, on gold bronze back-ground. No. 2 brass shrunk-on collar, No. 2 sun burner, bulb chimney to match; 6 complete in bbl. Wt. 65 lbs. Each. **85c**

DECORATED PARLOR LAMP

AO153—Height 26 in., 10-in. globe, gilt metal foot and trimmings, lift-out fount, center draft burner and chimney, decorated with large American beauty roses in bloom, Georgia green background; 1 lamp complete in bbl. Wt. 36 lbs. .Each. **$5.00**

MARVEL ELECTRIC LAMP

Can be used anywhere and everywhere—on desk, table, piano or wall, in home or office.

STAR VALUE

A4—Brush brass base and socket, **Green Aluminum Linen Metal Shade,** complete with 6 ft. of silk cord and plug attachment **ready to connect** .... Each. **$1.55**

"DIM-A-LITE" ELECTRIC PORTABLES

Saves current from 20% to 80%.

Regulates same as gas. Universal holder. Can be hung on bed, chair, bureau, in fact, anyplace.

PULL CHAIN FOR
FIVE CHANGES OF
LIGHT

A4444—Brushed brass, 8 ft. of cord, and plug, ready to attach to any socket; will take lamp as large as 40-watt, but 20 or 25-watt are recommended, **price does not include bulb.** Each. **$2.85**

MORE GOODS FOR SAME MONEY

SAME GOODS FOR LESS MONEY

Baltimore Price Reducer

The Merchant's Best Buying Guide

Merchants Everywhere Turn To A. W. C.

For December Needs—

—because it is well known that we have greater resources in goods and values wanted in December than any other wholesaler in America. Extraordinary attractions and unmatchable values herein will help you do a big Holiday business and make a strong finish for the year.

See Our Lines Of Toys, Dolls And Holiday Goods On Pages 6 to 85

See Our "Monthly Dozen" On Pages 2 and 3

DECEMBER, 1926

PRICES herein are Guaranteed against advance until Dec. 24th, inclusive. Any reduction in the meantime will go into effect at once and you will get the benefit of same, regardless of quotations in Catalog.

American Wholesale Corporation

Established in 1881

PAID IN CAPITAL OVER FOURTEEN MILLION DOLLARS

MANUFACTURERS OF CLOTHING OVERALLS, SHIRTS & NECKWEAR

Baltimore, Md.

COPYRIGHT 1926 BY AMERICAN WHOLESALE CORPORATION

WHOLESALERS OF GENERAL MERCHANDISE

TERMS : NET 60 DAYS

OUR LIBERAL TERMS: ALL BILLS OF GOODS bought from American Wholesale Corporation and shipped between December 26th and April 1st, which together total *$1000*, or more, are payable June 1st.

It is not necessary to buy $1000, or more, at any one time. The above Liberal Terms apply to a number of smaller purchases as well, if added together they total $1000, or more, and are shipped between December 26th and April 1st.

All Bills of Goods bought from the American Wholesale Corporation and shipped between June 25th and October 1st, which together total $1000, or more, are payable December 1st.

ALL OTHER BILLS PAYABLE IN 60 DAYS, NET

Strictly One Price — No Discounts, No Interest Allowed For Anticipation

Our Sales In 1925 Were

$28,681,702.24

SEE SWORN STATEMENT BELOW

Our Cost of Securing Orders Through Catalog, For The Year 1925, Was a "Fraction Under 2%"

We, Bartels & Spamer, Certified Public Accountants, do certify under oath that we have examined the books of the American Wholesale Corporation with the statement of their Selling Cost and Sales and find same to be correct and true.

Sworn before me
Witness my hand
and seal

Ernest E Braes
Notary Public

Signed *Bartels & Spamer.*
Certified Public Accountants

NOTE:—The cost of selling by drummers is $7\frac{1}{2}\%$ to 12%. Our cost of securing orders through Catalog is a fraction under 2% as shown above by sworn statement of Certified Public Accountants. In buying of us you save the difference in selling expenses as well as other economies in our modern methods of wholesaling.

We have no connection, or INTEREST, whatsoever in any other wholesale or retail stores anywhere.

We will, as a rule, fill all orders for usual and reasonable quantities, but we positively refuse to sell to wholesalers either directly or indirectly, as we are not catering to the wholesale trade. We sell to retail merchants exclusively.

AWC STIMULATORS

METAL ELECTRIC BRIDGE LAMP

About **$3.25** Value for **$2.75** Each

Six Lamps and Six Shades Complete in Case (NO LESS SOLD)

Wired, 6-ft. cord, 2-pc. plug, ready for use, bulbs not included. Ht. 56 in., cast metal openwork base, diam. 9 in., allover bronze finish, key socket, adjustable shade holder. 12-in. parchment shade, asstd. designs covered with small transparent beads edged with gold and black braid.

AO3006X — 6 lamps and shades complete.. Each, **$2.75** No less sold. Total, **$16.50**

'VOLSTEAD PUP' DECANTER

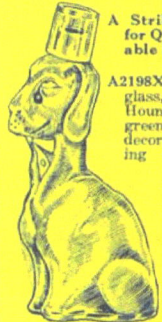

A Striking Novelty for Quick and Profitable Holiday Selling.

A2198X — Heavy molded glass, weeping Beagle Hound, asstd. crystal, green and rose features decorated in contrasting enameled colors, cap. 1 pt., 2 oz. smoothly finished tumbler forms cover as well as novel hat. 2 of each color in carton. Total ½ doz.

Doz. **$8.00**

DECORATED ORANGE COLOR GLASS CONSOLE SET

About **$2.10** Value for **$1.87** Set

POPULAR HOLIDAY SELLER

Burnt-in Colors — Will Not Wash Off

Comprises 9-in. orange color bowl, black detachable foot, two orange color candlesticks with red candles and 12 pcs. asstd. artificial fruit. AO1184/1X — Decorated all-over orange color, complete with candles and asstd. fruits in natural colors. 1 doz. in bbl. and case. Doz. sets. **$19.25** Less than doz. sets.. Set, **$1.87**

GOLDEN LUSTER GLASS

About **$1.95** Value; **$1.82** Set

AO2251X — Iced Tea Set, 70-oz. covered Colonial shape jug, bright golden luster finish, Topaz handle, attractive spiral design, six 12-oz. tumblers to match. Each set in carton. 4 in reshipping carton. Set, **$1.82**

PYREX MOUNTED WARE

Heavy gauge solid brass mountings, nickel plated, perforations, carved designs, metal feet and handles, fitted with Pyrex insets.

Pie Baker
A9892X — Round, 8 in. (Doz. $13.50); Each **$1.20**
A9893X — Round, 9 in. (Doz. $16.50); Each **$1.45**

Casserole
A9890X — Round, 7 in., cap. 2 pts. (Doz. $19.50); Each, **$1.85**
A9891X — Round, 8 in., cap. 3 pts. (Doz. $27.00); Each, **$2.40**

IMPORTED BEVERAGE SETS
Great For Holiday Selling

Big Selling Gift Items. Blown glass barrels and glasses, ground and polished stoppers. Mounted with four polished nickel hoops, faucet and ring glass holders. Two kinds: ICY FROSTED AND SOLID ORANGE COLOR. GLOSSY FINISH GLASS. Each set complete in carton with six 1½-oz. blown glasses.

NICKEL TRIMMED—ON STAND
A602X — Frosted, cap. 1½ pt., ht. 8¾ in., nickel stand and handle .... Set, **$3.50**
A606X — Solid Orange, cap. 1½ pt., ht 8¾ in., nickel stand and handle .... Set, **$4.50**
A603X — Frosted, cap. 1 qt., ht. 10 in., nickel stand and handle .... Set, **$4.25**
A607X — Solid Orange, cap. 1 qt., ht. 10 in., nickel stand and handle .... Set, **$5.25**

A602 and A606

SEMI-PORCELAIN SALAD BOWL

About **$2.40** Value; **$2.25** Doz.

A5006X — Diam. 9½ in., asstd. orange, pink and green tinted edges, asstd. color rose and foliage center .... Doz. **$2.25**

EUROPEAN CHINA SALAD BOWL

About **$4.25** Value; **$4.05** Doz.

A6666X — Diam. 9 in., asstd. blue, tan and green shadow foliage borders, 3 asstd. large rose centers, bright colors. Doz. **$4.05**

BLUE LUSTER JAPANESE CHINA CUP AND SAUCER

About **$2.25** Value; Our Price **$1.87** Doz.

A6138X — Extra fine quality, pure white Japanese china body, solid blue luster outside, white inside. Cup 3⅜ x 2 in., saucer 5½ in. diam.

12 Cups and 12 Saucers make 1 dozen
2 doz. in carton. Doz. (24 pcs.) **$1.95**
12 doz. in case, Doz. (24 pcs.) **$1.87**

THIN-BLOWN SPIRAL TABLE TUMBLER

Big Holiday Seller

A1385/1X-9-oz. spiral shape, clear crystal, smooth edges. 6 in set. (Doz. sets, $3.60); Set of 6, **32c**

ELECTRIC BRIDGE LAMP

About **$5.75** Value for **$4.50** Each Complete

Six Lamps and Six Shades Complete In Case

(NO LESS SOLD)

Wired complete, 8-ft. extension cord, 2-pc. plug, ready for installation, bulbs not included. (For bulbs see page 532). AO3600X — Ht. 56 in., gold & black polychrome finish stand and cast metal base, gilt finish adjustable arm, pull-chain socket. Complete with 14-in. Old Rose, Blue and Gold plaited silk shade, 6-in. two-tone silk fringe and skirt, ornamented with gold cord and braid. 6 lamps and asstd. colored shades complete in case, no less sold. Each Complete, **$4.50** Total for 6 lamps & 6 shades, **$27.00**

IMPORTED BEVERAGE SET

About **$2.15** Value for **$1.95** Set

A624X — Tray 8 in.. bottle 10½ in. cap. 12 oz., wide solid blue band dged with gold, decorated with red, tan and white enamel, fancy shape footed glasses.

SET (8 pcs.) **$1.95**

ELECTRIC JUNIOR FLOOR LAMP

About **$10.00** Value for **$7.25** Each

For Complete Line of Lamps and Shades See Pages 92 & 93

Wired complete, 8-ft. extension cord, 2-pc. plug, ready for installation, bulbs not included (for bulbs see page 532). Ht. 58 in., gold and black polychrome finish stand and cast metal base, gilt finish ornamental top, fancy turned shaft, 2 pull-chain sockets. Complete with 22-in. chiffon silk plaited shades in asstd. Old Rose Blue and Old Gold colors, 6-in. 2-tone silk fringe and skirt, fancy gold braid trimmed. 6 lamps and 6 shades complete in case, no less sold. AO3700X — Lamp and shade complete .... **$7.25** Total for 6 lamps and 6 shades, **$43.50**

AWC AMERICAN WHOLESALE CORPORATION

STIMULATORS

17 AND 23-PC. JAPANESE CHINA TEA SETS

Allover Solid Luster Color (For composition see page 110)

Beautifully decorated with bright luster colors inside and outside. Each set securely packed in strong carton. 23-pc. set service for six.

A2618X—23 pcs., Orange luster outside, mother-of-pearl inside
A6100X—23 pcs., Blue luster outside, tan luster inside.......
A6101X—23 pcs., Tan luster outside, mother-of-pearl inside... Set $4.45

A6102X—17 pcs., Blue luster outside, tan luster inside. ....
A6103X—17 pcs., Tan luster outside, mother-of-pearl inside. Set, $2.95

23-PC. JAPANESE CHINA GEISHA GIRL TEA SETS

For composition see page 110

All Standard Size Pieces, Exceptional Value

A513X — 23 pcs. strong, light wt. clear white body, allover hand-decorated with foliage, flowers, landscape scenes and Geisha Girls in bright **red** and **green** combinations, neat red band edge..... SET (23 pcs.) $2.75

A513½X—23 pcs. as A513, 6 sets to case. SET (23 pcs.) $2.45

BIG VALUE IRIDESCENT GLASS ASSORTMENT

About 92c Value For 85c Doz.

Popular inexpensive gifts, extensively used for premiums, souvenirs, etc. Golden iridescent finish, embossed fruit and floral designs in radiant golden iridescent effect, fancy shapes.

AO615X—Asst. contains ½ doz. each of the following pieces:
- ½ doz. 5x4-in. footed tulip Bonbon.
- ½ doz. 5½x4-in. footed tulip Bonbon, fruit embossed.
- ½ doz. 10½-in. Vases.
- ½ doz. 5½-in. scalloped Nappy.
- ½ doz. 4¾-in. three-footed crimped Nappy.
- ½ doz. 6½-in. footed flared Nappy.
- ½ doz. 6¼-in. violet Vase.
- ½ doz. crimped edge Nappy.
- ½ doz. 5½-in. scalloped edge Bonbon.
- ½ doz. 7-in. double handled Tray.
- ½ doz. 5¾-in. Nappy, openwork Bonbon.
- ½ doz. 6-in. three-footed Bonbon.

Big Value To Sell From 10c Up To 25c

Total 6 doz. asstd. in bbl. (No less sold) Wt. 70 lbs. (Total, **$5.10**): Doz. 85c

SPIRAL AMBER COLOR GLASS ASST.

Big $1.00 to $1.50 Holiday Sellers

For $6.25 Asst.

Genuine amber color glassware, full polished finish. All popular sellers that retail quickly from $1.00 to $1.50.

AO266X—Asst. consists of ⅙ doz. 11-in. Footed Cabarettes. ⅙ doz. 11½-in. Handled Sandwich Trays. ⅙ doz. 7½-in. Blown Vases. ⅙ doz. 3-pc. Mayonnaise Sets. ⅙ doz. Handled 9-in. Console Bowls. ⅓ doz. 9-in. Candlesticks.... Total 14 pcs. in bbl., no less sold. Asst. (14 pcs.), $6.25

12¾-IN. TOKONOBE VASE ASST.

About $15.00 Value for $12.00 Doz.

Ht. 12¾ in., 4 asstd. shapes, light weight earthenware body, asstd. color rustic finish embossed flowers, birds and foliage, bright hand-painted colors, outlined with gold. ½ doz. asstd. in case.

AO401X—2 doz. in case............................Doz. $12.00

AO401/1X—1 doz. in case............................Doz. $13.50

ORANGE AND BLACK GLASS ASST.

Ribbed design, orange color glassware, fired black band decoration. Full polished finished.

AO267X—Asst. consists of:
- 5 only footed Mayonnaise Sets.
- 5 only ½-lb. Candy Jars and Covers.
- 5 only 6½-in. high Footed Comports.
- 5 only 8½-in. Footed Salad Bowls.
- 5 only 6½-in. Covered Bonbon Dishes.
- 5 only 8-in. tall shape Vases.

Total 2½ doz. pcs. in bbl., no less sold. (Total, **$10.62**); Doz. $4.25

9-PC. PYREX HOLIDAY GIFT ASST.

Worth 5% More

Nine of the most popular pieces in the Pyrex line, neatly packed in Holiday display box. Attractive and useful Holiday gifts.

AO1733X—Asst. consists of:
- 1 only 1½-qt. Casserole.
- 1 only 10½x6½-in. Utility Dish.
- 1 only 9-in. Pie Plate.
- 6 only 6-oz. Custard Cups.

Total 9 pcs. in attractive box. SET (9 pcs.) $3.25

ORANGE AND BLACK GLASS ASSTS.

Big $1.00 to $1.50 Holiday Sellers

Orange color glassware, decorated with wide black band and enameled floral sprays and foliage in colors, fired decorations, full polished finish.

AO2266X—Asst. consists of:
- 1 only 9-in. Footed Fruit Bowl.
- 1 only 1-lb. Candy Jar.
- 1 only 8½-in. Footed Comport.
- 1 only 5-in. Low Footed Bonbon.
- 1 only 8-in. Rolled Edge Vase.
- 1 only 9½-in. Footed Nappy.

Total, 6 pcs. in asst., in bbl., no less sold. Asst. (6 pcs.) $5.70

COMMERCIAL AND RESIDENTIAL LIGHTING UNITS

Each Unit Wired, Assembled and Packed Complete in Individual Carton Ready to Install—Bulbs Not Included.

Wired strictly according to specifications approved by the National Board of Fire Underwriters. Equipped with the Nationally known HYPERION GLASS-WARE, scientifically designed to produce a soft, mellow, evenly distributed light and to eliminate shadows. The finishes are of the highest quality and workmanship.

WHITE ENAMELED KITCHEN AND BATHROOM UNITS

Especially adapted for the proper lighting of kitchens and bathrooms.

A1267—Holder 4½ x 3 in., **Pull-Chain Socket**, shade 6x4½ in., extends 10½ in. from wall. Requires a 60-watt bulb. Complete in carton. Each, **$1.30**

A1270—Holder 4½ x 4 in., **Pull Chain Socket**, new tile design shade 6x1½ in., extends 10½ in. from wall. Requires 60-watt bulb. Complete in carton. Each, **$1.40**

A1265—Complete length 12 in., holder 6 in. diam., glass 9x6¾ in., keyless socket. Requires 100 to 150-watt bulb. Complete in carton. Each, **$1.70**

A1266 — Individual Pull-Chain Socket. Complete length 12 in., holder 6 in. diam., glass 9x6¾ in. Requires 100 to150-watt bulb. Complete in carton. Each, **$2.00**

A1269—Complete length 10 in., holder 6 in. diam., 9x6¾ in., efficient and decorative tile design glass, keyless socket. Requires 100 to 150-watt bulb. Complete in carton. Each, **$1.75**

A1268—Holder 6 x 4½ in., **Key Socket**, shade 5 x 4½ in., extends 6 in. from wall. Requires 40-watt bulb. Complete in carton. Each, **$1.10**

A1271—Holder 6 x 4½ in., **Key Socket**, new tile design shade 5x4½ in., extends 6 in. from wall. Requires 40-watt bulb. Complete in carton. Each, **$1.20**

WHITE ENAMELED OPEN TYPE CEILING UNIT

A1274 — Heavy gauge brass holder, 5½ in. Diam keyless socket, shade 6½ x2½ in. Requires 60-watt bulb. Complete in carton. Each, **90c**

WHITE ENAMELED KITCHEN OR BATH-ROOM PENDANT

Heavy gauge brass pendant, white enameled, shade 7x2¼ in., complete length 42 in. Requires 60-watt bulb. Complete in carton.

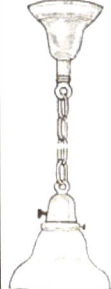

A1272 — Wired with key socket. Each, **$1.40**

A1273 — Wired with Pull-Chain Socket. Each, **$1.60**

STANDARD UNITS FOR STORES, OFFICES, SCHOOLS, CHURCHES, Etc.
Each Complete in Carton, Ready to Install. (For Bulbs, See Page 532)

Extensively used for efficient and uniform lighting of Stores, Offices and Public Buildings. Heavy gauge brass hanger, wired with No. 16 slow burning, silk covered wire, Edison base porcelain socket, 5-in. canopy suitably equipped for any type of electrical installation. Nationally known HYPERION UNITS, scientifically designed to eliminate shadows and produce a soft, mellow, evenly distributed light.

PLATED STATUARY BRONZE FINISH

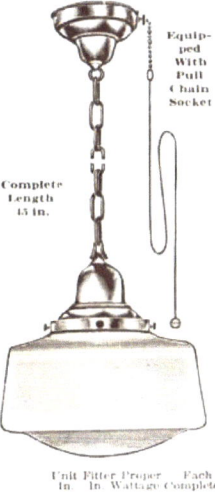

Equipped with Keyless Socket. Complete Length 45 in.

PLATED STATUARY BRONZE FINISH

Equipped With Pull Chain Socket. Complete Length 45 in.

ORNAMENTAL BRONZE AND GOLD FINISH

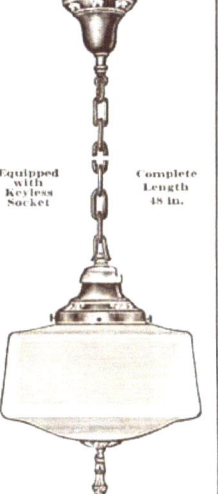

Equipped with Keyless Socket. Complete Length 48 in.

Unit Fitter Proper			Each
In.	In.	Wattage	Complete
A1279—10x6¾	4	100 to 150	$2.50
A1280—12x8½	6	150 to 200	3.25
A1281—14x9½	6	200	3.80

Unit Fitter Proper			Each
In.	In.	Wattage	Complete
A1282—10x6¾	4	100 to 150	$3.25
A1283—12x8½	6	150 to 200	4.00
A1284—14x9½	6	200	4.55

Unit Fitter Proper			Each
In.	In.	Wattage	Complete
A1291—48 12x8½	6	150 to 200	$3.71
A1295—48 14x9½	6	200	4.23

IVORY FINISH BEAM LIGHT
Complete with Frosted Bulb

A1241—Heavy spun brass, embossed and tinted, complete with 2-pc. socket and frosted bulb. Size 6x4 in., one light. Each, complete, **87c**

IVORY FINISH CEILING LIGHTS
Complete with Frosted Bulbs

Heavy spun brass, ivory finish, embossed and tinted, 2-pc. socket and frosted bulbs. Each complete in carton.

A1242—9x5½ in., 2-lt. Each, complete, **$1.75**

A1243—9½x5 in., 3-lt. Each, complete, **$2.50**

STANDARD UNITS FOR LOW CEILING STORES AND OFFICES

Each complete in carton ready to install. (For Bulbs See Page 532)

Heavy gauge brass holder with porcelain receptacle and crossbar, fitted with Hyperion Glassware.

PLATED STATUARY BRONZE FINISH

A1275 — Holder 6x4 in., glass 10x6¾ in., 100/150-watt bulbs. Each, complete, **$1.95**

A1276—Holder 8x6 in., glass 12x8½ in., 150/200-watt bulbs. Each, complete, **$2.80**

PLATED STATUARY BRONZE FINISH WITH INDIVIDUAL SWITCH CONTROL

A1277 — Holder 6x4 in., glass 10x 6¾ in., 100/150-watt bulbs. Each, complete, **$2.60**

A1278—Holder 8x6 in., glass 12x8½ in., 150/200-watt bulbs. Each, complete, **$3.60**

DECORATED ONE-LIGHT PENDANTS With Pull-Chain Socket

Heavy gauge brass decorated pendant, equipped with pull-chain socket 7½x8x2¼ in., shade tinted and decorated to match pendant. Complete length 45 in.

	Color	Proper Wattage	Each Comp.
A1285—Ivory and Pink		60	$2.30
A1286—Ivory and Blue		60	2.30
A1287—Ivory and Antique		60	2.30

DECORATED UNITS FOR LOW CEILINGS

Heavy gauge brass decorated holder, diam. 7 in., keyless socket, 9x6½ in., HYPERION Unit decorated and trimmed with imported drops to match coloring on holder and glass. Complete length 14 in.

	Color	Proper Wattage	Each Comp.
A1288—Ivory and Pink		100	$2.90
A1289—Ivory and Blue		100	2.90
A1290—Ivory and Antique		100	2.90

DECORATED BEDROOM OR SUN PARLOR UNITS

Heavy gauge brass pendant enameled and decorated, keyless socket, 9x9½ in., HYPERION Unit decorated and trimmed with imported drops to match coloring on holder and glass. Complete length 45 in.

	Color	Proper Wattage	Each Comp.
A1291—Ivory and Pink		100	$3.50
A1292—Ivory and Blue		100	3.50
A1293—Ivory and Antique		100	3.50

ELECTRIC BOUDOIR AND TABLE LAMPS

Newest Designs, High Grade Finishes. 6-ft. Silk Cord and 2-Pc. Plug. No Electric Bulbs.

NEW POPULAR SELLING BOUDOIR LAMPS

A3502—ht. 12½ in. embossed cast metal base and shade frame, old ivory enameled finish, rose tinted parchment inset.
Doz. **$12.00**
Each. **$1.25**

Ht. 13½ in., cast metal base, 6 in. satin frosted glass shade.
AO3500—Ivory finish base, white satin finish shade, hand-decorated inside with landscape scenes Each. **$1.75**
AO3501—Bronze finish base, salmon satin finish shade, hand-decorated inside with landscape scenes Each. **$1.75**

Ht. 12½ in., solid luster semi-porcelain base, floral border, ebony finish wood stand, 7½-in. floral oval silk shades with gold braid and silk flower.
A3503—Old Rose
A3504—Blue
A3505—Canary
Each. **$1.50**

Ht. 12½ in., solid color luster china base, white plum blossom decorated, ebony finish wood stand, 7½-in. oval silk shade with gold braid and silk flower.
A3506—Old Rose.
A3507—Blue.
A3508—Tan.
Each. **$1.75**

Ht. 12½-in., solid color luster china base, 8½-in. fancy oval beaded parchment shade, hand-painted designs, silk ruching.
A3100/2 — Jet Black base, ship on gold background
A3100 — Blue base, bird on blue background.
A3100/1 — Rose base, flowers on rose background.
Each. **$3.25**

Ht. 13½-in., solid color luster china base and figure, gold line trimmed, 8x7-in. oval beaded parchment shade, hand painted birds and flowers, silk ruching.
A3103 — Blue base, blue and rose shade.
A3103/1 — Rose base, rose and blue shade.
A3103/2 — Canary base, gold and blue shade.
Each. **$3.35**

Ht. 13½-in., solid color luster china base, oval shade 9½x6½-in. hand-painted designs, silk ruching.
A3101/2 — Jet Black base, ship on gold background.
A3101 — Blue base, bird on blue background.
A3101/1 — Rose base, flowers on rose background.
Each. **$3.75**

NEWEST CREATIONS IN TABLE LAMPS

AO1504—Bronze finish, ht. 22 in., 15-in. shade, 6 amber glass panels, 2 pull-chain sockets. Each. **$6.95**

AO1505—Jap gold finish, ht. 22 in., 17-in. shade, 6 amber glass panels, 2 pull-chain sockets. Each. **$9.50**

AO3041—Old ivory finish, ht. 22 in., 15-in. shade, 6 amber sunset dome panels, 2 pull-chain sockets. Each. **$9.75**

AO3049—Old gold finish, ht. 22 in., 15-in. shade, hand painted landscape scenes inside, frosted finish outside, 2 pull-chain sockets. Each. **$10.50**

AO3046—Old gold & Polychrome finish, ht. 24 in., one piece glass shade, hand-painted landscape scenes inside. Frosted finish outside, 2 silk pull-cords, amber glass finial. Each. **$14.50**

AO3067/70—Jet black china base, bronze metal foot, ht. 26 in., shade 20 in., old rose georgette lined and interlined, braid trimmed, 6-in. mixed gold bullion and silk fringe with skirt, 2 pull-chain sockets, amber glass finial. Each. **$14.25**

NEW IMPORTED ORIENTAL LAMPS

AO10   AO12   AO15

Hand dec. china base, raised scenes and floral designs, Matt gold and color enamel finish, hand carved teakwood base and top, solid metal harp, black & gold heavy Jap. silk shade, hand-painted, 3½-in. silk fringe. 6-ft. silk cord and 2-pc. plugs.

AO10—Ht 15 in., dark base, gold shade	Each.	$ 9.50
AO11—Ht. 19 in., light base, black & gold shade	Each.	11.95
AO12—Ht. 21 in., dark base, black & gold shade	Each.	13.50
AO13—Ht. 22 in., light base, gol sha e	Each.	17.50
AO14—Ht. 23 in., black & gold shade	Each.	18.50
AO15—Ht. 26 in., dark base, b'ack & gold shade	Each.	27.50

BOUDOIR LAMPS

Ht. 15 in., 8½-in. glass shade, hand-decorated and solid amber colors.

AO3037 — Ivory enameled base, frosted and hand-painted scenic shade. Each. **$3.85**

AO3038—Old gold base, frosted and hand-painted scenic shade.... Each. **$3.85**

AO3039—Old ivory finish, 8-in. shade, 4 amber sunset panels. Each. **$4.65**

AO3037-38

AO3039

AO3046 95—Polished metal footed base, ht. 28 in. old gold and polychrome finish, 16-in. beaded parchment shade, asstd. color ship scenes on gold background, silk ruching, 2 pull-chain sockets. Each. **$13.50**

AO3044—Gold finish, ht. 22 in., 18-in. six-panel shade, landscape decorated, illuminated 3-panel base, 2 pull-chain sockets. Each. **$16.75**

AO3045—Old gold finish, ht. 24 in., one-piece 16-in. hand-decorated landscape scene shade, illuminated 3-panel base, 2 silk pull-cords. Each. **$17.50**

Page 36

ELECTRIC METAL BRIDGE & FLOOR LAMPS

Latest patterns, artistic finishes. Choice selections of all the best makers. Shades of the newest colors, carefully selected to harmonize with stands. All metal bases wired complete with 8 ft. of silk cord and 2-pc. plug. Standard adjustable sockets.

AO3008 – Bridge Lamp, ht. 62 in. old gold finish, fancy ornamented base, decorated with Gold bronze.
Each, $3.75
Parchment Shades, 12x8¼ in., oval, beaded hand decorated, silk ruching.
AO3077 – Ship scene on Gold background.
AO3078 – Parrot on Pink background.
Each, $1.85
Complete Lamp and Shade $5.60

AO3002 – Bridge Lamp, ht. 58 in., bronzed, black & gold finish, heavy openwork base and ornament.
Each, $4.25
Silk Shades, 14x9 in., oval georgette, Jap silk lined, gold braid silk ruching, gold & black ornaments.
AO3115 – Black & Tangerine.
AO3116 – Blue & Rose.
AO3117 – Champagne & Rose.
Each, $2.95
Complete Lamp and Shade $7.20

AO3015 – Bridge Lamp, ht. 62 in., Spanish brass & polychrome finish, ornamental foot and arm.....Each, $4.95
Silk Shades, 14-in. octagon georgette, Jap silk lined and interlined, wide gold braid and 2-tone silk ruching, velvet flower ornament.
AO3118 – Black & Tangerine.
AO3119 – Blue & Rose.
AO3120 – Rose & Rose.....Each, $4.95
Complete Lamp and Shade $9.90

AO3016 – Bridge Lamp, ht. 58 in., Granada gold finish, solid brass arm and ornament, footed openwork base.
Each, $6.50
Silk Shades, 15x11 in., oval, georgette, Jap silk lined and interlined, art silk panels, silk ruching, 6-in. silk and bullion fringe and skirt.
AO3124 – Black & Rose.
AO3125 – Blue and Rose.
AO3126 – Rose & Rose.
Each, $7.75
Complete Lamp and Shade $14.25

AO3059 – Bridge Lamp, ht. 58 in., cherry & gold polychrome, fancy shape ornamental base and arm.
Each, $7.95
Parchment Shades, 12½ in. fancy shape beaded, hand decorated, 2-tone silk ruching, t-in ornamental glass bead pendant fringe to match.
AO3084 – Bird design on Gold background.
AO3083 – Bird and flower design, Gold background.
Each, $6.75
Complete Lamp and Shade $14.70

AO3065 – Bridge Lamp, ht. 58 in., polished brownstone ivory tinted, old gold finish ornaments, pink enamel decorated.
Each, $11.00
Silk Shades, 14x9½ in., georgette, Jap silk lined and interlined, wide gold braid and silk decoration with plaited silk ribbon, crochet basket & flower ornament in colors.
AO3121 – Taupe & Rose.
AO3122 – Blue & Rose.
AO3123 – Rose & Rose.
Each, $4.95
Complete Lamp and Shade $15.95

GRANADA GOLD FINISH LAMPS & TORCHERE

AO3021 – Bridge Lamp, ht. 58 in., polished Granada gold finish, 3 rods with ship design ornament and finial at top, openwork ornamental base and arm.
Each. $17.50
Parchment Shade, 13x10 in., oval beaded hand decorated, 2-tone silk ruching in panel effect.
AO3082 – Bird & flower design on pink background......Each. $5.00
Complete Lamp and Shade $22.50

AO3031 – Torchere, 2-ft. ht. 64 in., polished Granada gold finish, 3 rods with solid brass arms and ornaments, openwork ornamental base, 2 pull-chain sockets and twisted frosted bulbs......Each. $19.85
AO3029 – Floor Lamp, ht. 64 in., polished Granada gold finish, 3 rods with ship design ornament and finial at top, openwork ornamental base. Each. $17.50
Linen Shades, 20x15 in. beaded hand decorated, 2-tone silk ruching in panel effect, 6-in ornamental glass bead pendant fringe.
AO3089 – Peacock on Gold sunset background.
AO3090 – Humming bird and flowers on Rose background.
Each. $12.00
Complete Lamp and Shade $29.50

AO3020 – Bridge Lamp, ht. 58 in., polished Granada gold finish, solid brass, 10x7¼ in. genuine black and gold Italian marble base.
Each. $12.50
Silk Shades, 14x8 in., georgette, Jap silk lined and interlined, sunburst panels, heavy gold braid trimmed, 6-in. colored glass bead pendant fringe.
AO3127 – Black & Tangerine.
AO3128 – Taupe & Rose.
AO3129 – Blue & Rose.
Each, $9.75
Complete Lamp and Shade $22.25

AO3029   AO3031   AO3021

AO3055 – Floor Lamp, ht. 62 in., old gold stippled finish, octagon shape openwork foot and ornaments.
Each, $4.75
Silk Shades 20x14 in. oval georgette, Jap silk lined, gold tinsel braid and 2-tone silk ruching, braid & flower ornament in colors.
AO3130 – Black & Tangerine.
AO3131 – Blue & Rose.
AO3132 – Rose & Rose. . Each, $5.50
Complete Lamp and Shade $10.25

AO3025 – Floor Lamp, ht. 62 in. browntone & old ivory, ornamental base and ornament, highly polished, glass finial at top, 2 silk pull cords with gold tassels.......Each, $7.95
Silk Shades, 18 in. georgette, Jap silk lined and interlined, closely plaited closed top, gold braid and silk ruching in panel effect, 6-in silk and bullion fringe, colored silk ornaments.
AO3144 – Taupe & Rose.
AO3145 – Blue & Rose.
AO3146 – Rose & Rose . Each, $8.95
Complete Lamp and Shade $16.90
AO3055   AO3025

NOTICE

Lamps and Shades are Priced and Sold Separately or Complete (No Electric Bulbs).

AO3061 – Floor Lamp, ht. 62 in., polished brass and old gold finish, footed openwork base, embossed and ornamented.
Each, $9.75
Silk Shades, 22x15 in., georgette, Jap silk lined, heavy gold braid trimmed in panel effect, 2-tone silk ruching, large hand crochet flower ornament in colors to match.
AO3133 – Black & Tan erine.
AO3134 – Blue & Rose.
AO3135 – Taupe & Rose. Ea., $7.70
Complete Lamp and Shade $17.45

AO3026 – Floor Lamp, ht. 64 in. old gold finish, footed heavily embossed base and ornament, ship finial at top..............Each, $9.50
Silk Shades, 20x16 in. georgette, Jap silk lined and interlined, wide silk ruching, ornamental fringe, silk flowers in colors.
AO3136 – Black & Tangerine.
AO3137 – Blue & Rose
AO3138 – Champagne & Rose. Each, $8.95
Complete Lamp and Shade $18.45
AO3061   AO3026

WIRED READY FOR INSTALLATION —ELECTRIC FIXTURES— PRICES QUOTED INCLUDE BULBS AND GLASSWARE

VELVET BROWNTONE AND GOLD FINISH ELECTRIC FIXTURES

Spun Brass body and canopy. Cast Brass embossed arms and ornaments. Allover soft browntone finish, highly polished trimmings and Brush Brass heavy link chain. Crowfoot and hickies included. Prices quoted include bulbs and glassware.

VELVET BROWN-TONE AND GOLD WALL BRACKETS

Complete With Switch

A1457
A1457—1-lt., extends 5 in. Each. $1.95

A1458
A1458—2-lt., extends 5 in. Each. $2.85

A1408—1-lt., extends 5 in., key socket. Each. $1.65

Prices Include Electric Bulbs

Velvet Browntone Finish

Prices Include Electric Bulbs

BEDROOM~
A1450—2-lt., length 40 in., spread 14 in. ...... Each. $3.50
A1451—3-lt., length 40 in., spread 17 in. ...... Each. $5.25

LIVING ROOM~
A1452—4-lt., length 40 in., spread 19 in. ...... Each. $6.95
A1453—5-lt., length 40 in., spread 19 in. ...... Each. $8.75

DINING ROOM~ 10-Inch Opal Embossed Bowl With One Light Inside.
A1454—4-lt., length 40 in., spread 20 in. ...... Each. $8.75
A1455—5-lt., length 40 in., spread 21 in. ...... Each. $10.25

CEILING FIXTURE~
A1456—5-lt., spread 21 in. Each. $8.75

VELVET BROWNTONE AND GOLD FINISH ELECTRIC FIXTURES—With Glassware and Bulbs

A1400
KITCHEN PENDANT~
A1400—1-lt., length 45 in. Each. $1.45

A1432
HALL LANTERN~
A1432—1-lt., length 45 in. Each. $2.75

BEDROOM~
A1401—2-lt., length 40 in., spread 14 in. ...... Each. $3.95
A1402—3-lt., length 40 in., spread 17 in. ...... Each. $6.25

LIVING ROOM~
A1403—4-lt., length 40 in., spread 19 in. ...... Each. $8.25
A1404—5-lt., length 40 in., spread 19 in. ...... Each. $9.95

DINING ROOM~ 10-In. Opal Embossed Bowl With One Light Inside.
A1405—4-lt., length 40 in., spread 20 in. ...... Each. $9.50
A1406—5-lt., length 40 in., spread 21 in. ...... Each. $11.25

GENUINE SILVER FINISH ELECTRIC FIXTURES

Highest grade workmanship and material. Newest reeded design oval tubing. Allover polished silver finish, will not tarnish. Wired ready for installation.

Genuine silver finish embossed parts traced in light blue. Highest grade workmanship. Heavy oval tubing. Glass tear drop pendant in center. Wired ready for installation.

Prices Include Frosted Bulbs

Neat Blue Traced Decoration

Prices Include Frosted Bulbs

LIVING ROOM~
A1415—5-lt., length 40 in., spread 18 in. Each. $11.75

LIVING ROOM~
A1416—5-lt., length 40 in., spread 18 in. Each. $11.75

WALL BRACKETS~
A1417—1-lt., extends 5 in. Each. $2.10
A1418—2-lt., extends 5 in. Each. $2.95

LIVING ROOM~
A1419—5-lt., length 40 in., spread 16 in. Each. $13.25

LIVING ROOM~
A1420—5-lt., length 40 in., spread 16 in. Each. $13.25

SILVER AND GOLD POLYCHROME FINISH FIXTURES

Made of solid brass throughout, finished in gold or silver polychrome, blended in soft tone colors. Designed to harmonize with most any decorative scheme. Wired ready for installation. Prices include frosted bulbs.

Prices Include Frosted Bulbs

BEDROOM~
A12057—2-lt., gold polychrome, length 36 in., spread 13 in. ...... Each. $6.00
A12067—2-lt., silver polychrome, length 36 in., spread 13 in. ...... Each. $6.00
A12058—3-lt., gold polychrome, length 36 in., spread 13 in. ...... Each. $9.45
A12068—3-lt., silver polychrome, length 36 in., spread 13 in. ...... Each. $9.45

LIVING ROOM~
★A12061—5-lt., gold polychrome, length 36 in., spread 16 in. ...... Each. $11.50
★A12071—5-lt., silver polychrome, length 36 in., spread 16 in. ...... Each. $11.50

LIVING ROOM~
★A12062—5-lt., gold polychrome, length 42 in., spread 16 in. ...... Each. $11.50
★A12072—5-lt., silver polychrome, length 42 in., spread 16 in. ...... Each. $11.50

CEILING FIXTURE~
A12060—3-lt., gold polychrome, length 5 in., spread 9 in. ...... Each. $6.00
A12070—3-lt., silver polychrome, length 5 in., spread 9 in. ...... Each. $6.00
A12059—5-lt., gold polychrome, length 6 in., spread 14 in. ...... Each. $8.50
A12069—5-lt., silver polychrome, length 6 in., spread 14 in. ...... Each. $8.50

WALL BRACKETS COMPLETE WITH SWITCH
A12055—1-lt., gold polychrome, extends 5 in. Each. $3.85
A12065—1-lt., silver polychrome, extends 5 in. Each. $3.85
A12056—2-lt., gold polychrome, extends 5 in. Each. $5.85
A12066—2-lt., silver polychrome, extends 5 in. Each. $5.85

GENUINE WROUGHT STRAP IRON BALL LIGHT ELECTRIC FIXTURES

Strap iron with brass parts attractively designed and finished, deep russet color shaded and tinted. Embossed parts hand decorated in polychrome colors. ROUND FROSTED BULBS ILLUSTRATED ARE INCLUDED IN PRICES QUOTED.

A1470 DROP TYPE
A1469—Living Room, 4-lt. length 36 in., spread 17 in. Each. $9.00
A1470—Living Room, 5-lt. length 36 in., spread 18 in. Each. $10.50

A1472 CANDLE TYPE
A1471—Living Room, 4-lt. length 36 in., spread 17 in. Each. $9.00
A1472—Living Room, 5-lt. length 36 in., spread 18 in. Each. $10.50

CEILING TYPE
A1473—Living Room, 5-lt. length 18 in., spread 18 in. Each. $10.50

HALL LANTERN
A1476—1-lt. length 36 in. ornamental frame 12x8 in. Each. $5.50

A1475 CANDLE BRACKETS WITH SWITCH
A1474—1-lt., wall plate 10½x4½ in., extends 4½ in. from wall. Each. $2.75
A1475—2-lt., wall plate 10½x4½ in., extends 6½ in. from wall. Each. $3.95

SPANISH ANTIQUE GOLD AND POLYCHROME BALL LIGHT ELECTRIC FIXTURES

Cast aluminum, all parts embossed and finished in polychrome to resemble old gold, soft velvet finish (will not tarnish). Colors richly blended to harmonize with most any decorative or color schemes.

> ROUND FROSTED BULBS ILLUSTRATED ARE INCLUDED IN PRICES QUOTED

A1460 DROP TYPE
A1460—Bedroom, 2-lt. length 36 in., spread 14 in. Each. $5.80
A1461—Bedroom, 3-lt. length 36 in., spread 16 in. Each. $7.00

DROP TYPE
A1462—Living Room, 5-lt. length 36 in., spread 20 in. Each. $11.00

A1464 CANDLE TYPE
A1463—Bedroom, 3-lt. length 36 in., spread 16 in. Each. $7.00
A1464—Living Room, 5-lt. length 36 in., spread 20 in. Each. $11.00

A1466 CEILING TYPE
A1465—Bedroom, 3-lt. length 8 in., spread 18 in. Each. $7.00
A1466—Living Room, 5-lt. length 8 in., spread 20 in. Each. $11.00

A1468 CANDLE BRACKETS WITH SWITCH
A1467—1-lt., wall plate 10½x4½ in., extends 4½ in. from wall. Each. $3.50
A1468—2-lt., wall plate 10½x4½ in., extends 6½ in. from wall. Each. $4.25

ELECTRIC LANTERNS AND PORCH LIGHTS

GENUINE COPPER PORCH LANTERNS

Wired complete, ready for installation. (No bulbs) for bulbs see page 532. Extra heavy stock, strongly made, polished finish, weatherproof seams, will not rust or tarnish, amber glass panels. Each in carton.

AO1587—Wall Bracket, ht. 9½ in., extends 8½ in. from wall, 4 amber glass panels, 4½x3½ in. Each. $3.95

AO1589—Wall Bracket, ht. 9½ in., extends 9½ in. from wall, 4 amber glass panels 6x4½ in. Heavy copper glass protectors. Each. $4.95

AO1586—Ceiling Light, ht. 14 in., 4 amber glass panels, 4½x3½ in. Each. $3.95

AO1588—Ceiling Light, ht. 14 in., 4 amber glass panels, 6x4½ in., closed bottom. Heavy copper glass protectors. Ea. $4.95

ANTIQUE VERDE FINISH WROUGHT IRON LANTERNS
(Interior or Outside)
Wired ready for use. (No bulbs)

AO1590—Length 15 in., cast metal 11x5½ in., back plate 4x6 in., antique crystal cylinder, pull-chain socket. Each. $8.75

AO1592—Length 14 in., cast metal 11x6½ in., back plate 7x4½ in., lantern with 6 amber panels, pull-chain socket. Each. $9.25

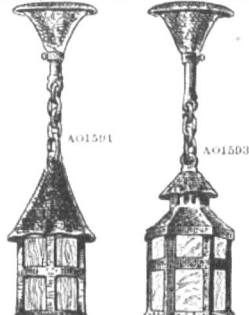

AO1591—Length 24 in., 12x4½ in., lantern 4x6 in., antique crystal glass cylinder, cast metal canopy and chain, pull-chain socket. Each. $8.75

AO1593—Length 24 in., 11x6½ in. lantern, 6 amber panels, cast metal canopy and chain, pull-chain socket. Each. $9.25

CAST METAL HALL LANTERNS
OLD GOLD FINISH
WIRED READY FOR USE

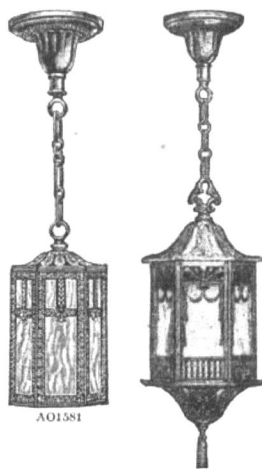

A1581—Lantern, 6½x10 in., hexagonal, 36-in. over all, open bottom, with 6 large amber art glass panels and 6 small insert sunset panels, ventilated top. Wired complete with chain and canopy and keyless socket ready to hang. Antique gold finish. Packed individually in a heavy shipping corrugated carton. Each. $6.25

AO3069—Length 36 in., lantern 8x13 in. Antique gold finish, six amber glass panels with ruby inserts, ventilated top and bottom, metal tassel, pull-chain sockets. Each in carton. Each. $7.85

SILVER AND GOLD POLYCHROME FINISH HALL LANTERNS

Solid cast brass throughout, gold or silver polychrome finish blended in soft color tones to harmonize with color schemes. Wired ready for installation (No bulbs).

A12063 — Gold and polychrome finish, length 45 in., amber cylinder shape globe 7x5 in., embossed finish. Each. $6.75

A12073 — Silver and polychrome finish, length 45 in., amber cylinder shape globe 7x5 in., embossed finish. Each. $6.75

ELEC. PORCH & CEILING LIGHTS

Frosted Inside Will Not Wear Off.

A1430—6¼-in. brush brass ring, porcelain socket, 3½-in. fitter, 7-in. white globe, frosted inside, complete. (Doz. $6.00); Each. 55c

A1431—5¼-in. spun brass fixtures, with porcelain socket, 3½-in. fitter, 7-in. white globe, frosted inside. (Doz. $8.50); Each. 75c

GLASS LAMPS—All numbers are packed in small quantities so you can get a large assortment for a small investment. Note our low prices. No Charge For Packing.

ONE-PIECE GLASS SEWING LAMPS WITH PATENTED GLASS COLLARS

Complete with burners and chimneys. No wicks.

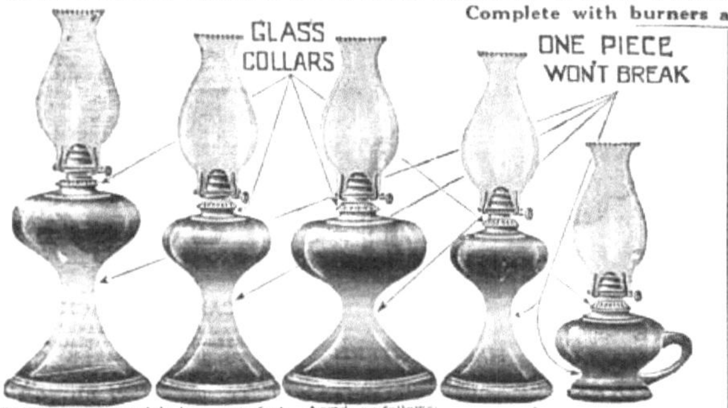

AO1172—Heavy crystal glass, wide foot. Asstd. as follows:
¼ doz. hand lamps, ht. 12 in. No. 1 burners and chimneys.......
¼ doz. stand lamps, ht. 15½ in. No. 1 burners and chimneys.....
¼ doz. stand lamps, ht. 17½ in. No. 2 burners and chimneys.....
¼ doz. stand lamps, ht. 18½ in. No. 2 burners and chimneys.....
¼ doz. sewing lamps, ht. 18 in. No. 2 burners and chimneys
Total, 1¼ doz. complete in barrel and carton, wt. 80 lbs.
Doz **$6.75**

AO1124—Heavy crystal glass, wide foot. Ht. 18 in., with No. 2 burners and chimneys. 1 doz. each style. Total, 24 lamps in bbl and carton. No less sold. Wt. 80 lbs. Each **55c**

JUMBO LAMP

Complete with Burner and Chimney

2-pc. construction

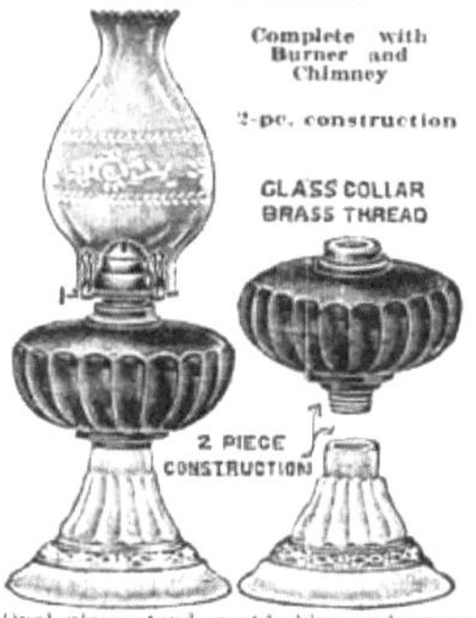

Opal glass stand, asstd. blue and green removable fount attached to base by brass threaded collar, making the weakest point strong and safe. Complete with No. 2 brass burner and large enameled globe chimney. 1 doz. in dustproof carton.

STAR VALUE ★
AO1125 — Ht. 17½ in. .... Doz. **$7.50**
AO1126—Ht. 18½ in. .... Doz. **$8.25**

No. 2 NICKEL "ROYAL" STORE LAMPS

For Kerosene Oil

AO1238 AO1239

AO1238—Length 28 in. No. 2 Royal center-draft burner with oil drip cup, 15-in. embossed tin shade, smoke bell, wick and chimney. Each in case. Wt. 19 lbs. .... Each. **$3.25**

AO1239—Length 28 in. 6-in. solid brass fount. No. 2 Royal center burner, oil drip cup, 10-in. opal shade, smoke bell, wick and chimney. Each in case. Wt. 20 lbs. .... Each. **$3.65**

ONE-PIECE GLASS LAMPS—(Without Burners and Chimneys)

Heavy crystal glass—will not break like the ordinary lamp. Brass collar clinched on so it will not come off. No plaster. **Packed in clean dustproof carton, no less sold.**

AO1117 AO1118 AO1119 AO1120 AO1121

AO1117—Ht. 6¾ in., cap. 10 oz. 1½ doz. in carton, wt. 32 lbs. Doz. **$2.25**
AO1118—Ht. 7¾ in., cap. 10 oz. 1½ doz. in carton, wt. 35 lbs. Doz. **$2.25**
AO1119—Ht. 9 in., cap. 16 oz. 1½ doz. in carton, wt. 40 lbs. Doz. **$2.50**
AO1120—Ht. 9½ in., cap. 20 oz., 1½ doz. in carton, wt. 52 lbs. Doz. **$3.25**
AO1121—Ht. 8¼ in., cap. 27 oz. 1 doz. in carton, wt. 37 lbs. Doz. **$3.25**

PLAIN GLASS STAND LAMPS

AO1372/2 AO1373

No. 2 Brass Shrunk-on Collars (No Plaster) Complete With No. 2 Sun Burner and Chimney.

AO1372/2—Ht. 18 in., heavy crystal glass "B" stand lamp, complete with No. 2 Sun burner and crimped chimney. Pkd. 1 doz. complete .... Doz. **$4.80**

AO1373—Ht. 18½ in., heavy crystal glass "C" sewing lamp, complete with No. 2 Sun burner and large globe enameled chimney. Pkd. 1 doz. complete .... Doz. **$5.85**

BRONZE BRACKET LAMPS COMPLETE

No Wicks

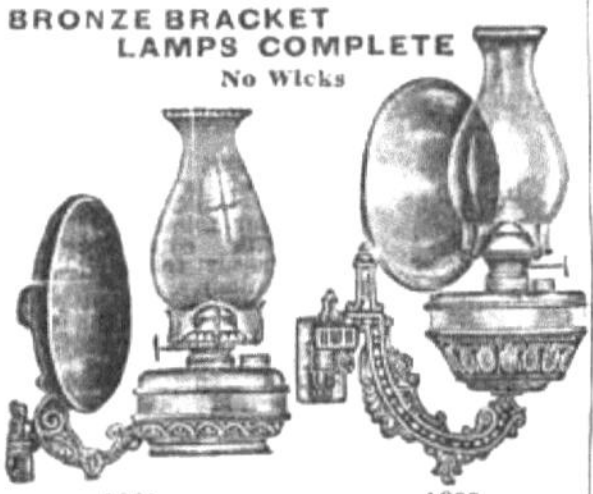

A891 A892

A891—Complete with No. 2 filler fount, No. 2 Sun Burner, No. 2 Sun chimney and 7-in. silvered glass reflector. ½ doz. in case. Doz. **$10.50**

A892—No. 2 filler fount, No. 2 Sun burner, No. 2 Sun chimney and 8-in. silvered glass reflector, adjustable reflector throws light up or down. ½ doz. in box. Doz. **$13.50**

MILK WHITE OPAL SHADE

A1535 — 10 in., best quality milk white opal glass, fits Rayo nickel lamp and our A1240. ½ doz. in carton .... Doz. **$6.50**

NO. 3 MAMMOTH BANNER STORE LAMP

For Kerosene Oil

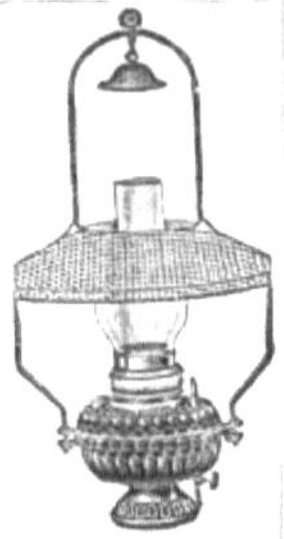

AO1235—No. 3 Banner, 1-gal. brass fount, burns 7½ hours, improved ratchet wick lift and oil indicator, complete with tin reflector, harp, smoke bell and chimney, each complete in case. Wt. 20 lbs. Each. **$4.95**

CRYSTAL GLASS SEWING LAMP

Shrunk-on collar, complete with No. 2 large globe chimney and brass burner. No wick.

AO272 — Ht. 19 in., heavy crystal glass base, globe shape chimney. 1 doz. in bbl. No less sold. Each. **65c**
(Total $6.96)

CRYSTAL GLASS HAND LAMP

Without Burner and Chimney

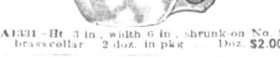

A1331—Ht. 3 in., width 6 in., shrunk-on No. 1 brass collar. 2 doz. in pkg. .... Doz. **$2.00**

GLASS BRACKET LAMP FOUNT

Fits any "B" ring or cup bracket

A1330—Flat filler fount with heavy No. 2 brass collar and side filler. 1 doz. in box. Doz. **$1.95**

DECORATED NIGHT LAMP

AO1379 — Ht. 8½ in. decorated crystal glass, Ruby, Pink and Canary, complete with nutmeg burner and chimney to match. 1 doz. asstd. in box .... Doz. **$2.15**

NICKEL-PLATED LAMPS

For Kerosene Oil

Ht. 20 in. Nickel-plated center draft burner, complete with tripod, 10-in. opal shade, wick and No. 2 Rochester chimney.

AO1240—1 doz. in case. Doz. **$27.00**

AO1240½ — ½ doz. in case. Doz. **$30.00**

No. 3 MAMMOTH BANNER LAMP

Brass finish. Can be lighted without removing chimney.

For Kerosene Oil

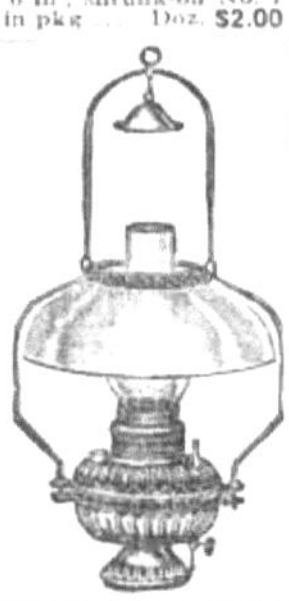

AO1236—No. 3 Banner, 1-gal. brass fount, burns 7½ hours, improved ratchet wick lift and oil indicator, complete with 14-in. dome shade, harp, smoke bell and chimney. Each in case. Wt. 21 lbs. Each. **$6.45**

DIETZ CRYSTAL CLASS PATENTED LANTERN GLOBES

(No Slipping—No Breaking)

AO539 — Sport (formerly Scout). Packed 1 doz. in carton .... Doz. **85c**

AO537 AO538

AO537—Little Wizard. Packed 1 doz. in carton. Doz. **$1.30**
AO538—Dietz Jr. Packed 1 doz. in carton. Doz. **$1.35**

AO535 AO536

AO535—Fitzall, Blizzard, Cold Blast or Tubular. Packed 1 doz. in carton. Doz. **$1.35**
AO536—"D-Lite." Packed 1 doz. in carton. Doz. **$1.35**

HAND-MADE FLINT GLASS LAMP CHIMNEYS

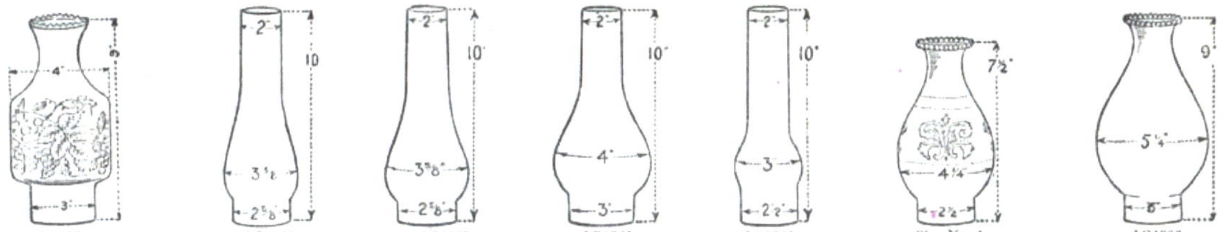

AO1075 | AO1064 | AO1057 | AO1061 | AO1065 | Size No. 1 | AO1066

Full size No. 2 Victor Etched— Fits No. 2 Sun or Climax burners, ht. 8½ in., diam. of bulb 3¾ in., each in corrugated tubes.
AO1075—6 doz. in case, 37 lbs. . . . . Doz. **OUT**
AO1076—3 doz. in case, 21 lbs. . . . . Doz. **OUT**

No. 2 B. & H. or Rayo—Packed in corrugated tubes.
AO1063—Size No. 2, B & H., fits our Rayo Lamp, 3 doz. in case (weight 30 lbs.). Doz. **$1.32**
AO1064—Same as AO1063, packed 6 doz in case; (wt. 55 lbs.) . . . Doz. **$1.25**

Rochester No. 2—Packed in corrugated tubes.
AO1057—No. 2 Rochester; fits No. 2 Royal, Rochester and Bristol Center draft burners. 3 doz. in case (wt. 27 lbs.) . . . . Doz. **$1.32**
AO1058—Same as AO1057, 6 doz. to case (Wt. 50 lbs.) Doz. **$1.25**

Electric No. 2—Packed in corrugated tubes.
AO1061—Size 2 Electric, fits any No. 3 flat wick burner and No. 2 Sun, 3 doz. in case (weight 34 lbs.) . . Doz. **$1.32**

Asstd. Large Bulb Enameled—
AO1071—Asst. 1 doz. fit size No. 1 Burner; 2 doz. fit size No. 2 Burner; total 3 doz. in case (wt. 42 lbs.) Doz. **$1.45**

Large Bulb Crystal Flint Chimneys—
AO1066—Fits size No. 2 Sun or No. 3 Climax Burner, ht 9 in., diam. of bulb 5 in.; 3 doz. in case (weight 45 lbs.) . . . . Doz. **$1.35**

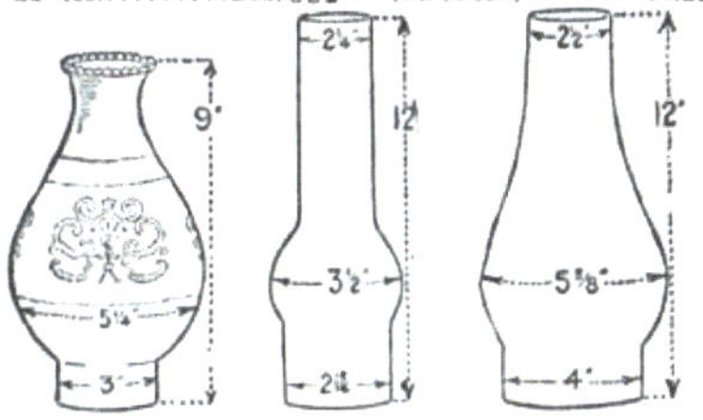

AO1069—Size No. 2 | AO1065½ | AO1060

Large Bulb Enameled—Wrapped in tissue paper, packed in straw.
AO1069—Fits size No. 2 Sun or Climax Burner, ht. 9 in., diam. of bulb 5 in.; 3 doz. in case (wt. 42 lbs.). Doz. **$1.35**

Belgian or Success—Packed in corrugated tubes.
AO1065—Size No. 1 Belgian, fits Belgian or Success center draft burner. 1 doz. in case (weight 12 lbs.) . . Doz. **$1.45**
AO1065½—Size 00 Belgian, fits No. 3 Plumwood or Success Store Lamp. 1 doz. in case (weight 16 lbs.) . . Doz. **$2.50**
AO1060—No. 3 Rochester, fits No. 3 Banner Rochester or Juno Store Lamps. 1 doz. in case (wt. 22 lbs.) Doz. **$2.65**

LIME BEAD TOP CHIMNEYS

Unselected: packed in corrugated tubes

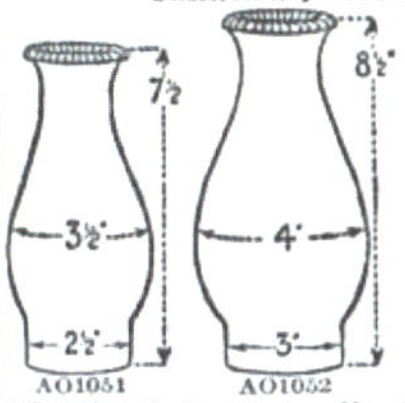

AO1051 | AO1052

AO1051— Fits size No. 1 Sun Burner, height 7½ in., 6 doz. in case (weight 22 lbs.). Doz. **69c**
AO1051½ — As AO1051, packed 3 doz. in carton (weight 12 lbs.) Doz. **82c**
AO1052— Fits size No. 2 Sun Burner, height 8½ in., 6 doz. in case (weight 30 lbs.) . . . . Doz. **79c**
AO1052½—As AO1052, pkd. 3 doz. in carton. Doz. **89c**
AO1053—2 doz. fit size No. 1 Sun Burner, height 7½ in; 4 doz. fit size No. 2 Sun Burner, height 8½ in.; Total 6 doz in case asstd. (weight 98 lbs.) . . . . Case, **$4.75**

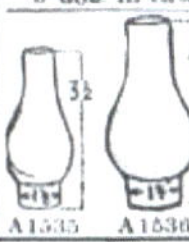

A1535 | A1536

NIGHT LAMP CHIMNEYS

A1535— Nutmeg chimney, fits Nutmeg burner, ht. 3½ in., diam. at bottom 1⅛ in. 1 doz. in pkg. Doz. **37c**
A1536—Gem chimney, fits Hornet or Gem burners, ht. 4¾ in., diam. at bottom 1½ in. 1 doz. in pkg. Doz. **45c**

FROSTED TIPLESS CARBON CLOW LAMPS

A18 | A25

Round incandescent 115 volt carbon lamps, extensively used in all styles of electric lighting fixtures. Each bulb in corrugated cardboard tube, 5 in display box.

	C. P.	Style	Voltage	5 or more Each	100 or more Each
A18	16	G-18½	115	17c	15c
A25	25	G-25	115	18c	16c

"Nulite-Matchlite" LAMPS, LANTERNS AND CHANDELIERS—

These guaranteed appliances are lighting thousands of homes, stores and public buildings. Each is a complete lighting unit in itself. All are equipped with patented "Nulite" generator. There is no lighting purpose that one of these fixtures will not serve. These nickel-plated gasoline fixtures all light instantly with common match. Gas generates from gasoline which produces a bright mellow light "Nulite" Fixtures all burn 12 to 15 hours on 3 pts. of gasoline. Each complete with mantle, shade, pump, wrench, tip cleaner, extra rubber washer and instruction sheet. Packed each complete in shipping carton.

GASOLINE LANTERN

Marvel for Outdoor Use

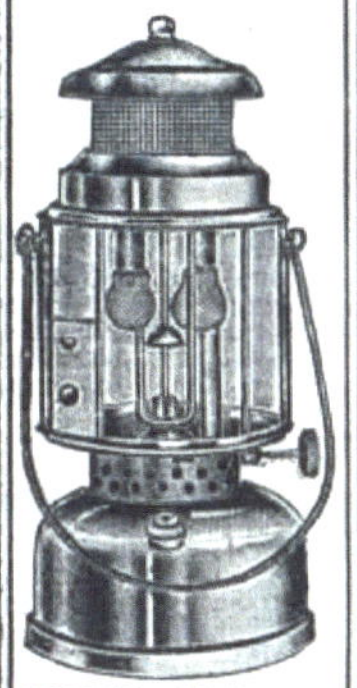

AO299—Ht. 13 in., cap. 1 qt., 2 mantles, mica chimney. Produces 400 candle-power. Each, **$5.25**
Lots of 6. Ea. **$5.00**

GASOLINE CHANDELIER

One Filling (3 pints) Burns from 12 to 15 hours.

Just the Fixture for Large Rooms, Stores, Halls, Churches

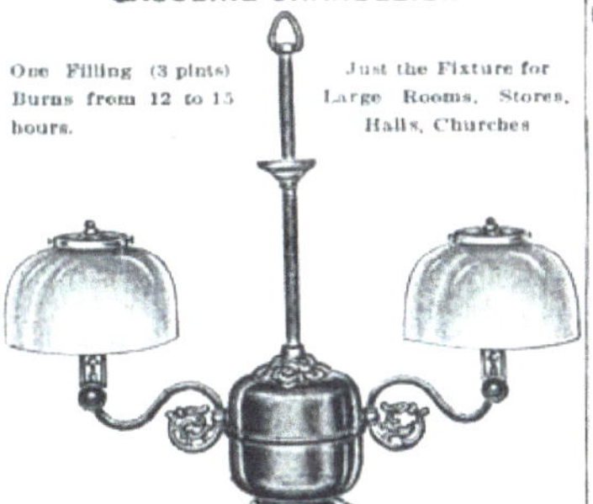

AO297—Length 30 in., spread 27 in., capacity 2 qts.; four mantles produce 800 candlepower, 10-in. white shades. Wt. 7½ lbs. Each, **$11.25**

"NULITE" BUG SCREEN

A302 — A protection to the burner and mantle against flying bugs and insects. . . . . Each, **75c**

GASOLINE HANGING LAMP

A Popular Number

Burns 12 to 14 hours.

AO296—Length 30 in., spread 11 in., capacity 1 qt., two mantles produce 400 candlepower, 10 in. white shade. Wt. 7 lbs. . . . Each, **$7.00**

GASOLINE PORTABLE WALL LAMP

Burns 12 to 14 hrs.

Specially adapted for very low or extremely high ceilings

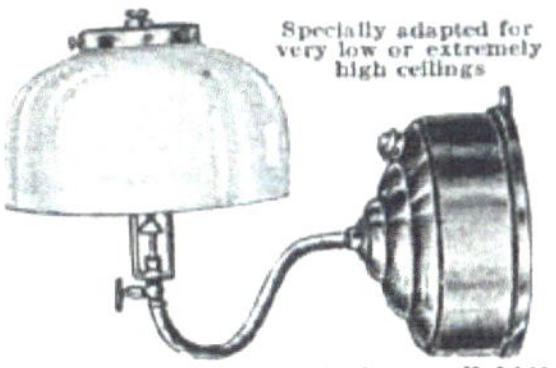

AO295—Ht. 10 in., extends from wall 14½ in., capacity 1 qt., two mantles produce 400 candlepower. 10-in. white shade, wt. 10 lbs. . . . . Each, **$6.00**

PATENTED GENERATOR FOR GASOLINE LAMPS

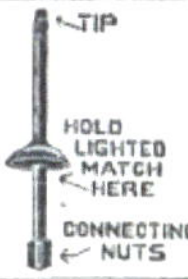

A300—Fits all styles of "Nulite-Matchlite" fixtures. . Doz. **$3.60**

Same Goods for Less Money—
More Goods for Same Money.

GASOLINE LAMP

A lighting marvel for home and office use.

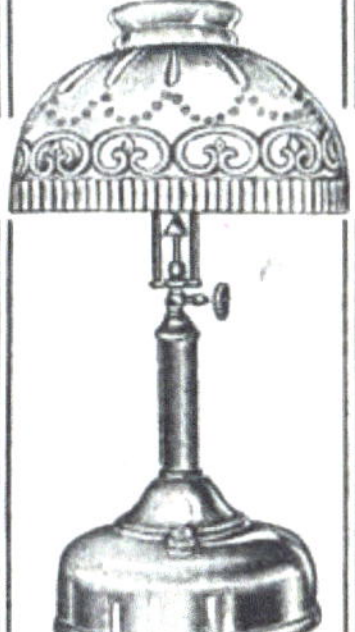

AO298—Ht. 22 in., cap. 3 pts., 2 mantles, 10-in. white porcelain shade. Produces 400 candlepower. Shipping weight 6 lbs. Each, **$5.50**

INVERTED GAS MANTLE

A1119 — Single weave, cotton covered, magnesia ring. Each in tube. 4 1/6 doz. in box. Doz. **80c**

IMITATION PARCHMENT ELECTRIC SHADE

Fitted over electric bulbs will increase the light diffusion with decorative effect.

A11—Size 4¾x4½ in., asstd. colors with silhouette decorations in colors all over, metal holder. 3 doz. asstd. in carton. No less sold (Gro. $7.50); Doz. **68c**

"NULITE" GASOLINE MANTLE

Best grade. No shirring, bunching or tying at bottom to obstruct flow of light.

A301—Fits any of the "Nulite" Gasoline Lamps or Lanterns. Long fiber cotton closely woven, best grade asbestos string, 2 mantles in oiled envelope (will not dry out). 1 doz. in carton, 12 doz. in display box.
Lots of 12 doz. Doz. **67c**
Lots of 6 doz. Doz. **75c**
Lots of 1 doz. Doz. **82c**

LINDSAY SOFT INVERTED GASOLINE MANTLE

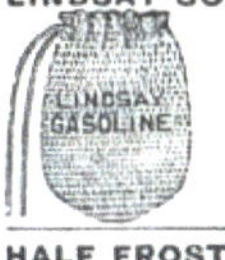

A1117— Lindsay Soft Inverted Mantle, for gasoline system, single weave, fits any standard burner. Each in envelope, full directions with each mantle, strong and powerful light. 1 doz. in pkg. Doz. **92c**

HALF FROSTED AND INVERTED GAS GLOBE

Fits Any Inverted Gas Lamp

AO1334—Ht. 3¼ in., fitter 3⅝ in., clear crystal glass, half frosted body, will fit on any inverted light. Packed 6 doz. in case. Doz. **82c**

STAPLE TABLE TUMBLERS — The best tumblers made to sell at these low prices. Machine made, clear crystal, free from air bubbles, smooth edges and bottoms, fire polished.

ASSTD. STYLES STAPLE TABLE TUMBLERS

AO2001–Cap. 9 oz., half fluted taper shape clear crystal, fire polished, smooth edge. Asstd. 7 doz. each horseshoe, plain and star bottom. Total 21 doz. in crate. No less sold. Wt. 155 lbs. .... Doz. 30c

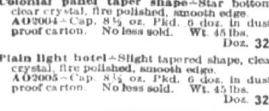

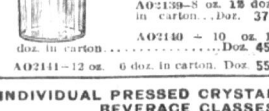

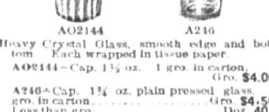

AO2000–Cap. 9 oz., plain taper shape, clear crystal, fire polished smooth edge. Asstd. 7 doz. each, horseshoe, plain and star bottom. Total, 21 doz. in crate. No less sold. Wt. 155 lbs. .... Doz. 30c

AO2003 AO2004 AO2005

Half fluted taper shape–Horseshoe bottom, clear crystal, fire polished, smooth edge. AO2003–Cap. 9 oz. Pkd. 6 doz. in dustproof carton. No less sold. Wt. 45 lbs. Doz. 32c

Colonial panel taper shape–Star bottom, clear crystal, fire polished, smooth edge. AO2004–Cap. 8½ oz. Pkd. 6 doz. in dustproof carton. No less sold. Wt. 45 lbs. Doz. 32c

Plain light hotel–Slight tapered shape, clear crystal, fire polished, smooth edge. AO2005–Cap. 8½ oz. Pkd. 6 doz. in dustproof carton. No less sold. Wt. 45 lbs. Doz. 32c

PLAIN HORSESHOE TABLE TUMBLER

AO2002–Cap. 9 oz., plain taper shape, horseshoe bottom, clear crystal, fire polished, smooth edge. Pkd. 6 doz. in dustproof carton. No less sold. Wt. 45 lbs. .... Doz. 32c

PLAIN BELL SHAPE TUMBLERS

Clear crystal glass, semi-blown, smooth melted edges, bell shape, slightly concave edge to prevent breaking.

AO2138–6 oz. 12 doz. in carton . . Doz. 30c

AO2139–8 oz. 12 doz. in carton. . . Doz. 37c

AO2140 – 10 oz. 12 doz. in carton .... Doz. 45c

AO2141 – 12 oz. 6 doz. in carton. Doz. 55c

9-OZ. BLOWN PLAIN TUMBLERS

Straight shape, ht. 3⅝ in., diam. top 2¾ in., smoothly finished.

AO2131—6 doz. in carton, 25 lbs. .... Doz. 37c

AO2132—12 doz. in carton, 40 lbs. .... Doz. 35c

HOTEL TUMBLERS

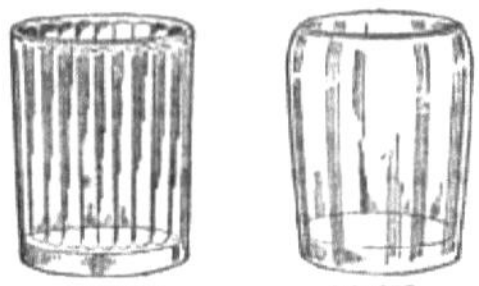

AO2006 AO2007

Optic Shaped Hotel Tumbler–Narrow optic straight shape, clear crystal, fire polished, smooth edge.

AO2006–Cap. 8½ oz. Pkd. 6 doz. in dustproof carton. No less sold. Wt. 45 lbs. Doz. 32c

Plain Cupped Edge Hotel Tumbler–Cupped plain light hotel non-nestable (prevents breakage) clear crystal, fire polished, smooth edge.

AO2007–Cap. 8½ oz. Pkd. 6 doz. in dustproof carton. No less sold. Wt. 45 lbs. Doz. 42c

AO2009 AO2008 AO2010

Plain heavy hotel–Heavy bottom, clear crystal, fire polished, smooth edge.

AO2008–Cap. 9 oz. Pkd. 6 doz. in dustproof carton. .... Doz. 48c

Fluted cupped hotel tumbler–Cupped, half fluted hotel non-nestable (prevents breakage) clear crystal, fire polished, smooth edge.

AO2009–Cap. 8½ oz. Pkd. 6 doz. in dustproof carton. No less sold. Wt. 45 lbs. Doz. 48c

Barrel shape hotel tumblers–Barrel shape hotel, finger fluted, clear crystal, fire polished smooth edge.

AO2010–Cap. 9 oz. Pkd. 6 doz. in dustproof carton. No less sold. Wt. 48 lbs. Doz. 48c

9-OZ. BLOWN BANDED TUMBLERS

AO2133 — Straight shape, ht. 3⅝ in. diam., top 2¾ in., 3 asstd. etched bands. 12 doz. in carton. 50 lbs. .... Doz. 40c

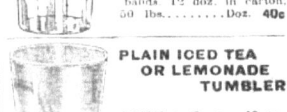

PLAIN ICED TEA OR LEMONADE TUMBLER

AO2011 – Cap. 12 oz., 5¼x3⅜ in., iced tea heavy plain taper shape, clear crystal, fire polished, smooth edge. Pkd. 6 doz. in dustproof carton. No less sold. Doz. 42c

THIN-BLOWN CRACKLED DESIGN TUMBLERS

AO2268 AO2269 AO2270

Full finish, light thin-blown crystal. Packed in shipping cartons.

AO2268—5 oz., beverage, 12 doz. in carton .... Doz. 35c

AO2269—9 oz., table, 12 doz. in carton .... Doz. 35c

AO2270—12 oz., iced tea, 6 doz. in carton .... Doz. 55c

THIN-BLOWN SPIRAL DESIGN TUMBLERS

AO1384 AO1385 AO1386

New and attractive spiral design, clear crystal, melted edge, plain bottom, fire polished.

AO1384—Cap. 4 oz., ht. 3⅜ in., diam. at top 2⅛ in., fruit juice sizes, 12 doz. in carton, no less sold .... Doz. 40c

AO1385—Cap. 8 oz., ht. 3¾ in. diam. at top 2⅝ in., table tumbler 12 doz. in carton, no less sold .... Doz. 40c

AO1386—Cap. 12 oz., ht. 5½ in., diam. at top 3 in., Iced Tea Tumbler. 6 doz. in carton, no less sold .... Doz. 55c

OPTIC BELL SHAPE TUMBLERS

Semi-blown clear crystal, fire polished, smooth plain bottoms, melded edges.

AO2100 AO2102 AO2103

AO2100– 6 oz., pkd. 12 dz. in carton. Doz. 35c

AO2101– 8 oz., pkd. 12 dz. in carton. Doz. 45c

AO2102–10 oz., pkd. 12 dz. in carton. Doz. 55c

OPTIC BLOWN CRYSTAL ICED TEA TUMBLERS

AO2134 — 13 oz., optic-blown, tall straight shape, 6 doz. in carton, 35 lbs. Doz. 55c

BELLED OPTIC ICED TEA TUMBLER

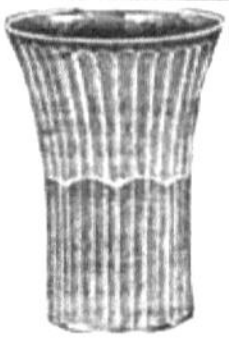

AO2014–Cap. 12 oz., iced tea heavy optic half fluted bell shape, clear crystal, fire polished, smooth edge. Pkd. 6 doz. in dustproof carton. No less sold. Wt. 50 lbs .... Doz. 65c

COLONIAL PANEL ICED TEA TUMBLER

AO2012–Cap. 12 oz., iced tea heavy straight panel shape, clear crystal, fire polished, smooth edge. Pkd. 6 doz. in dustproof carton. No less sold. Wt. 70 lbs. ..... Doz. 65c

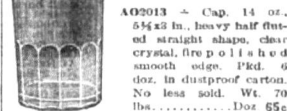

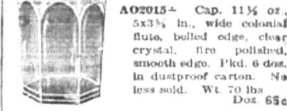

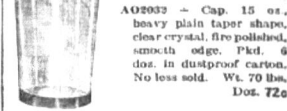

HALF FLUTED ICED TEA TUMBLER

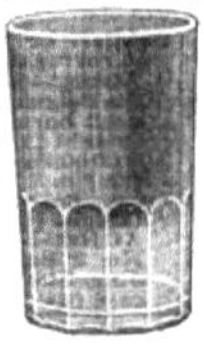

AO2013 – Cap. 14 oz., 5⅜x3 in., heavy half fluted straight shape, clear crystal, fire polished smooth edge. Pkd. 6 doz. in dustproof carton. No less sold. Wt. 70 lbs. .... Doz. 65c

HEAVY COLONIAL PANEL ICED TEA TUMBLER

AO2015– Cap. 11½ oz., 5x3⅛ in., wide colonial flute, belled edge, clear crystal, fire polished, smooth edge. Pkd. 6 doz. in dustproof carton. No less sold. Wt. 70 lbs. Doz. 65c

PLAIN TAPER SHAPE ICED TEA TUMBLER

AO2032 – Cap. 15 oz., heavy plain taper shape, clear crystal, fire polished, smooth edge. Pkd. 6 doz. in dustproof carton. No less sold. Wt. 70 lbs. Doz. 72c

INDIVIDUAL PRESSED CRYSTAL BEVERAGE GLASSES

AO2144 A246

Heavy Crystal Glass, smooth edge and bottom. Each wrapped in tissue paper.

AO2144–Cap. 1½ oz. 1 gro. in carton. Gro. $4.00

A246–Cap. 1½ oz. plain pressed glass. 1 gro. in carton .... Gro. $4.50
Less than gro. .... Doz. 40c

OPTIC BEVERAGE GLASSES

Semi-blown clear crystal, fire polished, smooth edges, plain bottoms, melded edges.

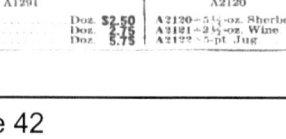

A2104 A2105 A2106 A2107

A2104–1½ oz., pkd. 12 doz. in carton. Doz. 32c
A2105–2½ oz., pkd. 12 doz. in carton. Doz. 35c
A2106–5 oz., pkd. 12 doz. in carton. Doz. 35c
A2107–5 oz., pkd. 12 doz. in carton. Doz. 35c

GENUINE GRAPE LIGHT CUT TABLEWARE

Thin-blown, smooth melded edges.

A1285 A1286 A1287 A1289

A1285– 5-oz. Tumbler .... Doz. $1.00
A1286–10-oz. Tumbler .... Doz. 1.00
A1287–12-oz. Iced Tea .... Doz. 1.55
A1289–5½-oz. Sherbet .... Doz. 2.75

A1290 A1288 A1291

A1290 – 2-oz. Wine .... Doz. $2.50
A1288–10-oz. Goblet .... Doz. 2.75
A1291– 3½-pt. Jug .... Doz. 5.75

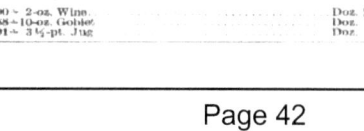

IRIDESCENT LUSTER OPTIC THIN-BLOWN TABLEWARE

Clear thin-blown, smooth melded edges, radiant iridescent luster.

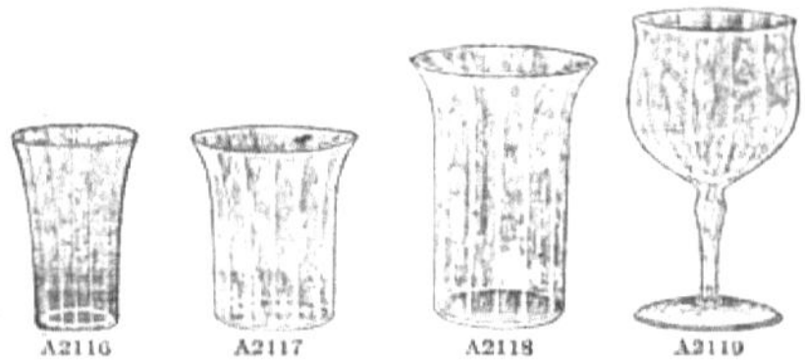

A2116 A2117 A2118 A2119

A2116– 5-oz. Tumbler .... Doz. $1.45
A2117–10-oz. Tumbler .... Doz. 2.10
A2118–12-oz. Iced Tea .... Doz. 2.25
A2119– 9-oz. Goblet .... Doz. 3.65

A2120 A2121 A2122

A2120–5½-oz. Sherbet .... Doz. $3.25
A2121–2½-oz. Wine .... Doz. 3.15
A2122–5-pt. Jug .... Each. 1.00

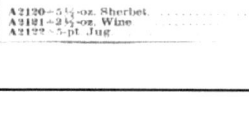

STAPLE SELLING GLASSWARE

CRYSTAL OR GOLDEN LUSTER LIGHT BLOWN SHERBETS

AO2336 AO2243 AO2242

CRYSTAL OPTIC

AO2236—Sherbet, ht. 3⅛ in., low style, plain finish, 6 doz. in carton... Doz. **75c**

AO2235—Sherbet, ht. 4½ in., high style plain finish, 6 doz. in carton... Doz. **$1.10**

AO2234—Goblet, ht. 7 in., tall shape, plain finish, 6 doz. in carton........Doz. **$1.10**

GOLDEN LUSTER

Same as shape above.

AO2244—Sherbet, ht. 3⅛ in., low style, golden luster finish, 6 doz. in carton. Doz. **$1.20**

AO2243—Sherbet, ht. 4½ in., high style, golden luster finish. 6 doz. in carton. Doz. **$1.65**

AO2242—Goblet, ht. 7 in., tall shape, golden luster finish. 6 doz. in carton. Doz. **$1.65**

GENUINE CUT LIGHT BLOWN GOBLETS AND SHERBETS

Floral, leaf and band cutting, clear crystal, plain polished finish.

AO2240 AO2239 AO2238

AO2240—Sherbet, ht. 3¼ in., low style 6 doz. in carton....................Doz. **89c**

AO2239—Sherbet, ht. 4½ in., high style 6 doz. in carton....................Doz. **$1.85**

AO2238—Goblet, ht. 7 in., tall shape, 6 doz. in carton....................Doz. **$1.85**

SHERBET PLATES

Clear Crystal, Golden Luster and Genuine Cut

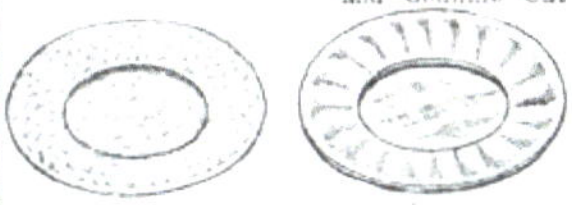

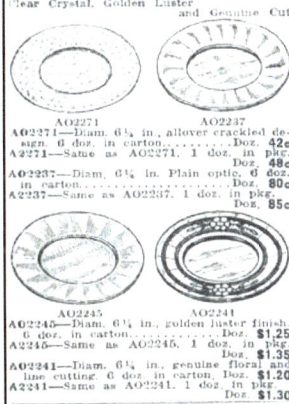

AO2271 AO2237

AO2271—Diam. 6¼ in., allover crackled design. 6 doz. in carton.........Doz. **42c**

A2271—Same as AO2271. 1 doz. in pkg. Doz. **48c**

AO2237—Diam. 6¼ in. Plain optic, 6 doz. in carton....................Doz. **80c**

A2237—Same as AO2237. 1 doz. in pkg. Doz. **85c**

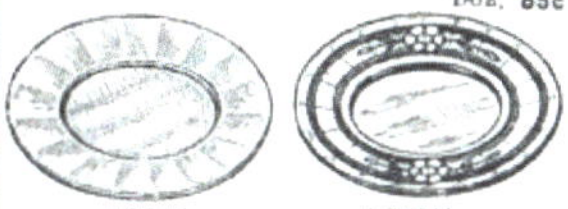

AO2245 AO2241

AO2245—Diam. 6¼ in., golden luster finish. 6 doz. in carton.............Doz. **$1.25**

A2245—Same as AO2245. 1 doz. in pkg. Doz. **$1.35**

AO2241—Diam. 6¼ in., genuine floral and line cutting. 6 doz. in carton, Doz. **$1.20**

A2241—Same as AO2241. 1 doz. in pkg. Doz. **$1.30**

CRYSTAL GLASS WINES IN OPEN STOCK

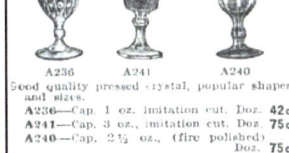

A236 A241 A240

Good quality pressed crystal, popular shapes and sizes.

A236—Cap. 1 oz. imitation cut. Doz. **42c**

A241—Cap. 3 oz., imitation cut. Doz. **75c**

A240—Cap. 2½ oz., (fire polished) Doz. **75c**

A237 A238 A430

A237—Cap. 1 oz............Doz. **42c**

A238—Cap. 2¼ oz............Doz. **44c**

A430—Cap. 1¾ oz............Doz. **35c**

CRYSTAL GLASS BERRY OR SALAD NAPPIES

A227 A228

A227—Size 4¼ in. colonial fire polished glass.......................Doz. **OUT**

A228—Size 4½ in., imitation cut sunburst star.......................Doz. **OUT**

BERRY NAPPIES AND BOWLS

AO2023 — Diam. 4 in. heavy crystal glass smooth edges. Pkd. 3 doz. each style. Total 6 doz. in carton........Doz. **35c**

AO2024 — 8-in. block design Berry Bowl. Pkd. 2 doz. in carton. Doz. **$1.75**

4-IN. COLONIAL STYLE BERRY NAPPIES

STAR VALUE

Diam. 4 in., clear crystal glass, smooth melted edges.

A2049—32 doz. in bbl. Doz. **15c**

A2049½—6 doz. in case. Doz. **20c**

7-IN. GLASS BOWL

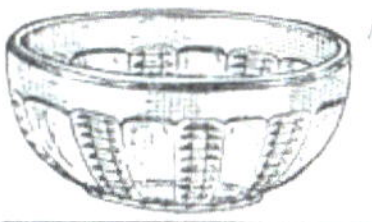

AO2050—Diam. 7-in. clear smoothly finished glass, fancy pattern. 3 doz. in carton. (Total $2.25); Doz. **OUT**

CRYSTAL BERRY SET

STAR VALUE **AO2060**— 8-in. Berry Bowl, six 4¼-in. nappies to match, block panel design, 15 sets in bbl.........(Total, $5.25); Set, **35c**

IMITATION CUT GLASS FOOTED BON BON

AO217 — Diam. 5¼ in., clear crystal glass, smooth edges. 2 doz. in carton, no less sold. Doz. **87c**

COLONIAL CRYSTAL GLASS HANDLE BON BON

AO218 — Diam. 5¼ in., clear crystal glass, smooth edge. 2 doz. in carton, no less sold. Doz. **87c**

FRUIT JUICE EXTRACTORS

Clear heavy crystal glass, fire polished, smoothly finished edges, corrugated cones, perfectly shaped to extract the juice completely with one turn of the hand.

A247 A2142

A247—Diam. 4 in., fits over top of tumbler, patent seed retainer, wide opening in bottom for juice to drain through. Doz. **65c**

A2142—Diam 5½ in. extra heavy handled and lipped,improved extra high cone. Doz. **56c**

AO1371 AO2143

AO1371—Diam. 5¾ in., newly improved retainer, separates pulp and seeds from juice, handled and lipped. 2 doz. in carton, no less sold. ....Doz. **77c**

AO2143—Orange Reamer, diam. 6¼ in., extra heavy glass, large rounded cone, deep body, handled and lipped. 3 doz. in carton.......................Doz. **$1.00**

COLONIAL STYLE CRYSTAL GLASS SUNDAES

Heavy crystal glass, smooth edges.

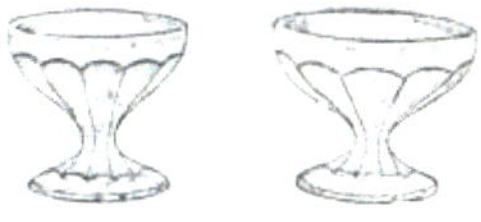

AO2058 AO2059

Clear crystal, colonial pattern, plain foot.

AO2058—3⅛x3 in. 3 doz. in carton. Doz. **40c**

AO2059—3x3¾ in. 3 doz. in carton. Doz. **45c**

A429 AO428

A429—Size 3x3¼ in. fire polished. Doz. **82c**

STAR VALUE **A428**—Size 3¼x3 in. cap. 5 oz. fire polished, optic, plain foot.......................Doz. **60c**

AO428—Packed 25 doz. in bbl. Wt. 150 lbs.......................Doz. **54c**

CRYSTAL GLASS TABLEWARE

AO2055 AO2056

Bright clear glassware, smoothly finished edges, colonial designs.

AO2055—Creamer, ht. 4 in., diam. 3½ in. 3 doz. in carton. 45 lbs.......Doz. **85c**

AO2056—Spooner, ht. 3¾ in., diam. 3¾-in., double handled, 3 doz. in carton. 45 lbs.......................Doz. **87c**

AO2053 AO2054

AO2053—Covered Butter, diam. 6¾ in., flanged style, handled cover, 3 doz. in carton, 60 lbs...............Doz. **$1.25**

AO2054—Covered Sugar, ht. 5½ in., diam. 3¾ in., double handled, 3 doz. in carton. 50 lbs.......................Doz. **$1.25**

TABLEWARE

AO214—Heavy crystal glass, fire-polished.

1½ doz. covered Butters.
1½ doz. covered Sugars.
1½ doz. Creams.
1½ doz. Spoon Holders.

Total, 6 doz. asstd. in bbl. (Wt. 135 lbs.). No less sold.................Doz. **$1.75**

METAL TOP SUGAR SHAKER

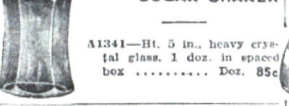

A1341—Ht. 5 in., heavy crystal glass. 1 doz. in spaced box .... Doz. **85c**

TOOTHPICK HOLDER

AO2020—Colonial style, heavy crystal glass, smooth edge. Pkd. 3 doz. in carton. No less sold.................Doz. **35c**

INDIVIDUAL SALTS

Clear Crystal Glass

AO2022—Size 1x1¾ in. 1 doz. in spaced box.................(Gro. $2.75); Doz. **25c**

ALUMINUM TOP SALTS AND PEPPERS

Heavy Crystal Glass. 6 salts and 6 peppers in box.

A2031 A2029 A2030 A2028

A2031—Ht. 3 in., heavy blue glass. (Gro. $3.25); Doz. **30c**

A2029—Ht. 3 in. (Gro. lots. $4.50)...Doz. **40c**

A2030—Ht. 3 in. (Gro. lots. $4.50)...Doz. **40c**

A2028—Ht. 3 in (Gro. lots $4.50)...Doz. **40c**

COASTER

Used as plates for Iced Tea Tumblers and Sundae Glasses.

AO2021—Heavy glass. Diam. 3¼ in., Star bottom, (Gro. $3.60); Doz. **35c**

OIL OR VINEGAR BOTTLES

Fire polished, clear crystal glass, smooth edges, attractive shapes.

AO2025 A244

AO2025—8 oz., ht. 6 in., squat shape. 3 doz. in carton, no less sold. ..Doz. **84c**

A244—7 oz., ht. 7 in., colonial style, full finished. ....Doz. **$2.25**

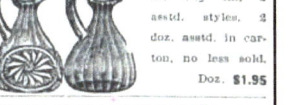

AO1348— 12 oz., ht. 7½ in., 3 asstd. styles, 2 doz. asstd. in carton, no less sold. Doz. **$1.95**

SYRUP OR MOLASSES PITCHERS

Removable sanitary tops. Heavy clear crystal glass.

AO1323 AO2026

STAR VALUE **AO1323**—13 oz., brilliant fluted design, patent nickeled top. 1 doz. in carton. Doz. **$3.25**

AO2026—12 oz., heavy removable polished top. 2 doz. in carton, no less sold. Doz. **$1.35**

AO1317 AO1322

AO1317—15 oz., 2 styles asstd., removable polished tops. 2 doz. in carton. Doz. **$1.75**

AO1322—25 oz., plain swell shape, extra heavy, easily removable heavy metal top. 1 doz. in carton. ....Doz. **$3.65**

STAPLE SELLING GLASSWARE

HEAVY CRYSTAL GLASS MIXING BOWL SET

Each set in carton

AO2034—5 sizes, 1 each 5, 6, 7, 8 and 9 in. nested in carton. Clear heavy crystal glass, deep shape, smooth edges. ½ doz. sets in shipping carton, 60 lbs., no less sold. Doz. sets. **$6.25**

BIG VALUE IRIDESCENT GLASS ASSORTMENT

Popular inexpensive gifts, extensively used for premiums, souvenirs, etc. Golden iridescent finish, embossed fruit and floral designs in radiant golden iridescent effect, fancy shapes.

AO615—Asst. contains ½ doz. each of the following pieces:

- ½ doz. 5x4 in., footed tulip Bonbon.
- ½ doz. 5½x4 in., footed tulip Bonbon, fruit embossed.
- ½ doz. 10½ in., Vases.
- ½ doz. 5½ in., scalloped Nappy.
- ½ doz. 4¾ in., three-footed crimped Nappy.
- ½ doz. 6½ in., footed flared Nappy.
- ½ doz. 6¼ in., violet Vase.
- ½ doz. crimped edge Nappy.
- ½ doz. 5½ in., scalloped edge Bonbon.
- ½ doz. 7 in., double handled Tray.
- ½ doz. 5¾ in., Nappy, openwork Bonbon.
- ½ doz. 6 in., three-footed Bonbon.

Total 6 doz. asstd. in bbl. (No less sold) Wt. 70 lbs. (Total, **$5.10**);

Big Value To Sell From 10c Up To 25c — Doz. **85c**

PERCOLATOR TOP, CRYSTAL GLASS

STAR VALUE AO2035 – Diam. 2¼ in., crystal glass, smooth finish. Fits all standard percolators. 1 gro. in carton. Gro. **$1.89**

SANITARY DIPPER

AO222–Graduated 4 and 8 ozs., heavy enameled crystal glass, patent attachment for wood handle, 2 doz. in case. (Wt. 16 lbs.) No less sold .... Doz. **$1.65**

CRYSTAL GLASS COVERED BUTTER TUB

AO215 — Size 5½x3½ in., heavy crystal glass, smooth edge. 2 doz. in carton. Doz. **$1.95**

REFRIGERATOR SET

AO2052 — 3 pcs., 5x4½ in., takes up space 6x6x4½ in., oblong shape, clear smooth finish glass, each set (3 pcs.) in carton. ⅛ doz. sets in carton, no less sold. Doz. sets. **$3.75**

OPAL GLASS NEST EGGS

A5015–Opal nest eggs. Average size 6 in. circum. Packed 1 gro. in spaced shipping carton, wt. 9 lbs. Gro. **$1.75**

HEAVY CRYSTAL GLASS MEASURING CUP

Graduated ¼, ½, ¾ and 1 cup.

A1345–Side lip, smooth edges........ Doz. **82c**

GLASS CANDY TRAYS

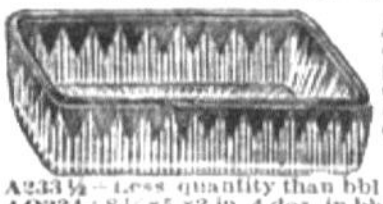

AO233 – 7¾x4¾ x 1¾ in., plain pressed clear crystal, star bottom, 6 doz. in bbl. Doz. **$1.50**

A233½–Less quantity than bbl. .... Doz. 1.75
AO234–8¼x5 x2 in. 4 doz. in bbl. .... Doz. 1.90
AO234½–Less quantity than bbl. .... Doz. 2.15

GLASS SALT AND PEPPER SHAKERS

6 Salts and 6 Peppers in Spaced Box.

AO2031 — Ht. 3 in., smooth edges, blue glass, aluminum tops, attractive shape...... Doz. **30c** (Gro. $3.25

FRUIT JAR CAP

A7007 – Mason, genuine Boyd patent top of heavy zinc and porcelain lined, fits standard size jars; without rubbers. Gro. **$2.95**

HEAVY CRYSTAL GLASS, FIRE-POLISHED, FULL-FINISH CANDLESTICKS

A678

A678–Ht. 5½ in..... Doz. **$2.25**
A679–Ht. 8½ in..... Doz. **4.25**

ROUND COVERED DISPLAY JARS

Heavy clear crystal glass close fitting cover.

AO1325 — 1 gal., ht. 9 in., diam. 8 in. 1 doz. in crate. Doz **$6.00**

AO1326—2 gal., ht. 11¼ in., diam. 10 in. Each in carton. .... Each. **90c**

AO1327—3 gal., ht. 12 in., diam. 12 in. Each in carton. .... Each. **$1.45**

OCTAGON COVERED DISPLAY JAR

AO1326½—2 gal., ht. 11¼ in., diam. 9½ in. Each in carton. Each. **95c**

DECORATED OPAL CUSPIDORS

AO1329 – Size 7½x5½ in., crystal and opal glass, tinted and decorated with roses and gold bands. 1 doz. in crate. Wt. 50 lbs...... Doz. **$4.25**

GOLDEN LUSTER CUSPIDOR

AO2267–7x4 in., allover luster finish **(will not wash off)** embossed full finish iridescent effect, wide mouth, octagon shape. 3 doz. in carton. Doz. **$2.25**

NOVELTY COLORED GLASS CANDLESTICKS

AO2258 AO2259

AO2258—Ht. 3½ in., diam. of foot 4½ in., solid Orange color with Black band. Doz. **$2.25**

AO2259—Ht. 3½ in., diam. of foot 5 in., Green luster finish, wide Black band on foot, edged with gold lines and hand decorated with natural color floral sprays. Doz. **$6.00**

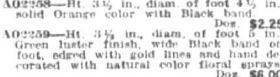

CRYSTAL GLASS ASH TRAYS

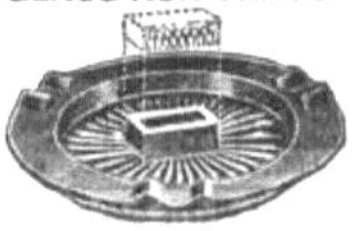

AO95 — Diam. 5¾ in., clear crystal, smoothly finished, 3 cigar rests and matchbox holder, 3 doz. in carton. Doz. **78c**

A93—Diam. 4½ in., 3 cigar rests and match-box holder. Doz. **87c**

PATENT CHO-KR MODEL

A94 — Instantly extinguishes cigarette when inserted in Cho-kr-hole. Made of high grade clear glass, diam. 4 in., either box or book matches may be used. Doz **$2.05**

FISH BOWLS WITH WROUGHT IRON STANDS

A2—Wrought Iron Stand, ht. 32 in., complete with heavy crystal glass 2-gallon fish bowl. (Doz. $16.20); Each. **$1.50**

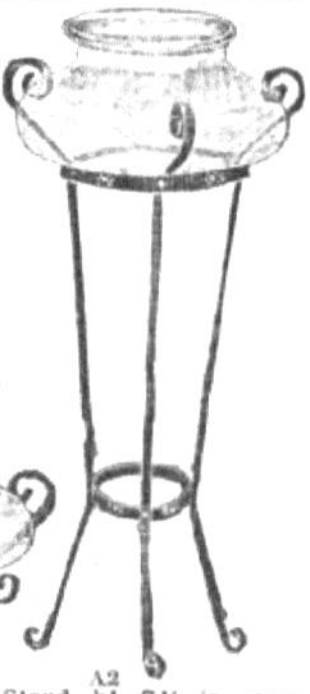

A1

A2

A1—Wrought Iron Stand, ht. 7¼ in., complete with heavy crystal glass 2-gallon fish bowl.....(Doz. $9.00); Each. **85c**

GLASS FLOWER VASES

High-grade crystal glass, fire-polished, full finished vases.

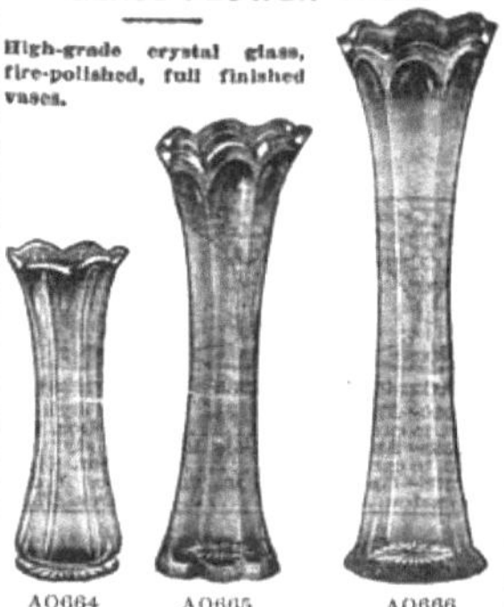

AO664 AO665 AO666

AO664—Ht. 8 in. 4 doz. in bbl. No less sold. Wt. 55 lbs.............. Doz. **$1.50**
AO665—Ht. 11¼ in. 4 doz. in bbl. No less sold. Wt. 90 lbs.......... Doz. **$1.95**
AO666—Ht. 16 in., suitable for long-stem flowers. 3 doz. in bbl. No less sold. Wt. 90 lbs.................. Doz. **$3.00**

GLASS DISPLAY VASES

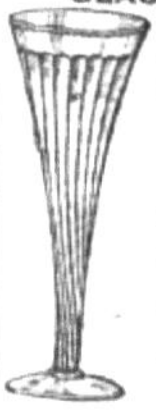

Extensively used to support glass shelves in window displays.

SPIRAL FLUTED DESIGN

Tapered Shape

A680—Ht. 6 in. Doz. **$2.40**
A681—Ht. 9 in. Doz. **$3.25**
A682—Ht. 13 in. Doz. **$4.25**

COLONIAL DESIGN

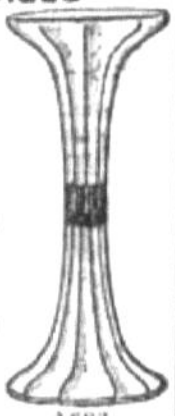

A680 A683

2-pc. patented construction, joined in center with brass ferrule, nickeled, ground and polished to set perfectly level.

A683—Ht. 8 in .... Doz. **$3.50**
A684—Ht. 10 in .... Doz. **4.50**
A685—Ht. 12 in .... Doz. **4.75**
A686—Ht. 14 in .... Doz. **4.95**

GLASS CASTERS

Will save the wear and tear of carpets, rugs and polished floors. Heavy Crystal Glass, smooth edges.

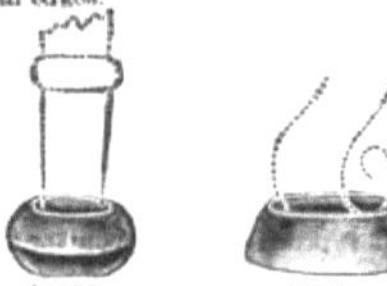

A2036 A1344

A2036–Diam. 2 in., for tables........ Doz. **45c**
A1344–Diam. 3 in., for beds........ Doz. **78c**

SQUAT SHAPE FISH GLOBES

AO1316—Heavy Crystal Glass, cap. 2-gal. fits standard size aquarium stands. Pkd ½ doz. in crate, no less sold... Doz. **$6.95**

CRYSTAL GLASS BEVERAGE SETS—EACH SET COMPOSED OF 1 JUG AND 6 TUMBLERS TO MATCH

A variety of the most popular styles, shapes and sizes in the best staple sellers. Priced to give you a GOOD PROFIT and a QUICK TURN. Good quality clear sparkling glass, durably made, neatly finished. Each set in strong carton and 4 sets in reshipping carton.

COLONIAL WATER SET

AO2065—Water Set, colonial style, 1½-qt. jug, six 9-oz. tumblers, 1 doz. sets in bbl, weight 100 lbs.
(Total $4.80); Set, 40c

CRACKLED DESIGN WATER SET

AO2246—Water Set, ½ gal. tankard shape jug, optic effect inside, six 9 oz. tumblers to match. Each set in carton, 4 in reshipping carton, no less sold. (Total $2.10); Set 55c

PANEL EFFECT WATER SET

AO2200—Water Set, optic, panel effect ½-gal. jug, ht. 8½ in., six 9-oz. tumblers, 4 sets in reshipping carton, no less sold. (Total $2.28); Set, 57c

OPTIC EFFECT WATER SET

AO1314—Water Set, optic, tankard ½-gal. jug, stuck handle, six 9-oz. tumblers, 4 sets in reshipping carton, no less sold. (Total $2.60); Set, 65c

GRAPE CUT WATER SET

AO2247—Water Set, ½ gal. tankard shape jug, genuine clear crystal glass, genuine grape cutting with 2 wide bands, six 9-oz. tumblers to match. Each set in carton, 4 in reshipping carton. Set, 85c

POPULAR CRACKLED DESIGN WATER & ICED TEA SETS

AO2201—Water Set, 70 oz. Colonial jug, optic effect, ht. 8 in., six 9-oz. tumblers. 4 sets in reshipping carton, no less sold. (Total, $2.88); Set, 72c

AO2202—Iced Tea Set, 70 oz., Colonial covered jug, optic effect, ht. 8 in., six 12 oz. tumblers, 4 sets in reshipping carton, no less sold. (Total, $3.80); Set, 95c

DECORATED SOLID COLOR ICED TEA SET

AO2250—Iced Tea Set, 70 oz. covered Colonial shape jug, crackled design, decorated in solid Orange color, Black band edges, six 12-oz. tumblers to match. Each in carton, 4 in reshipping carton. Set, $1.45

DECORATED SOLID COLOR WATER SET

AO2248—Water Set, ½ gal. tankard shape jug, solid orange decoration with hand painted flowers and foliage in Yellow and Green, gold edges, six 9-oz. tumblers to match. Each set in carton, 4 in reshipping carton. Set, 95c

COLD BAND WATER SETS

AO1420—Water Set, gold decorated, ½-gal. optic jug, stuck handle, ht. 8¼ in., six 9-oz. tumblers, 4 sets in reshipping carton. Set, $1.10

AO1421—Water Set, gold decorated, ½-gal. optic tankard jug, stuck handle, six 9-oz. tumblers, 4 sets in reshipping carton. Set, $1.20

GOLDEN LUSTER ICED TEA SET

AO2251—Iced Tea Set, 70 oz., covered Colonial shape jug, bright golden luster finish, Topaz handle, attractive spiral design, six 12 oz. tumblers to match. Each set in carton 4 in reshipping carton. Set, $1.82

CRYSTAL GLASS ICED TEA SET

AO1315—Iced Tea Set, panel shape, ½-gal covered jug, six 12-oz. tumblers. 4 sets in reshipping carton, no less sold. (Total, $3.00); Set, 75c

NEEDLE ETCHED ICED TEA SET

AO1368—½-gal. covered jug, six 12-oz. tumblers, needle etched scroll design decoration. 4 sets in reshipping carton. Set, $1.35
Less than carton. Set, $1.50

GOLD BAND ICED TEA SET

AO1369—½-gal. optic covered jug, six 12-oz. blown tumblers, fired gold band decoration, 4 sets in reshipping carton. Set, $1.50
Less than carton. Set, $1.65

COLOR BAND ICED TEA SETS

AO1377—½-gal optic covered jug, six 12-oz. blown tumblers, fired wide orange color band decoration. 4 sets in reshipping carton. Set, $1.75
Less than carton. Set, $1.95

CRYSTAL GLASS TUMBLERS, JUGS, ETC.

COLD BAND GENUINE BLOWN OPTIC TABLEWARE

Light, thin-blown clear crystal, smooth melded edges, bright polished finish. 3/16 in. notched matt gold band edge and pencil line.

A1275
A1276
A1277
A1278
A1279
A1280

A1275—5-oz. fruit juice tumbler. Doz. $4.75
A1276—9-oz. table tumbler. Doz. 4.75
A1277—12-oz. iced tea tumbler. Doz. 4.75
A1279—5-oz. sherbet. Doz. 5.75
A1278—9-oz. goblet. Doz. 5.75
A1280—2½-oz. wine. Doz. 5.75

IMITATION CUT JUGS

AO204—Two-style, ½ gal. heavy crystal glass; ht. 8½ in.; fire polished glass. 1/12 doz. Each style pkd. 2 1/6 doz. in bbl., wt. 120 lbs. No less sold. Doz. $4.15

PANEL-SHAPED CLEAR CRYSTAL GLASS JUGS

AO1313—7¼ in. high, cap. 60 oz. Wide Mouth, Star Bottom, stuck-on handle, fire polished, smooth edge. 1 doz. in carton. Doz. $4.10

STAR-BOTTOM JUGS

AO205—2 styles, ½ gal. capacity, ht. 8½ in. fire polished glass, star bottom, 1 1/12 doz. each style, 2 1/6 doz. in bbl. (Wt. 120 lbs) No less sold. Doz. $4.15

JUMBO JUG

AO206—Jumbo, capacity 5 pints, Colonial shape, clear crystal glass, fine finish, fire-polished. 2 doz. in bbl. (Wt. 130 lbs.) No less sold. Doz. $5.25

ICE WATER JUG

Bent-In Lip, Holds Ice While Pouring.

AO202—Capacity ½ gal., heavy clear crystal glass. 2 doz. in bbl. Weight 100 lbs. Doz. $3.95

DECANTERS OR WATER BOTTLES

Brilliant full finished crystal, colonial panel pattern, fancy stopper.

AO2661—1 qt., ht. 8 in. 2 doz. in carton. Doz. 86c

AO2662—1 qt., ht. 9½ in. 1 doz. in carton. Doz. $1.50

TABLE GLASSWARE ASSORTMENTS

CRYSTAL GLASS FLORAL BAND TABLEWARE ASSORTMENT

A0200—Brilliant full finish clear crystal glass, bright attractive floral band. Standard pcs used daily. Asst. as follows.

- 1/2 doz. Covered Butters.
- 1/4 doz. Covered Sugars.
- 1/4 doz. Creams.
- 1/4 doz. Spoon Holders.
- 1/4 doz. 1/2 Gal. Pitchers.
- 1 1/2 doz. Tumblers.
- 1 doz. Goblets.
- 1/2 doz. 5 1/2-in. Bon Bons.
- 1/2 doz. 8 1/2-in. Pickle Dishes.
- 1/4 doz. 8 1/2-in. deep Berry Bowls.
- 1 1/2 doz. 4 1/4-in. Nappies.
- 1/4 doz. 9-in. Berry Bowls.
- 1 1/2 doz. 4 1/2-in. Berry Nappies.
- 1/4 doz. Covered Honey Dishes.
- 1/2 doz. 4 3/4-in. Covered Bowls.
- 1/2 doz. 5 1/2-in. Covered Bowls.
- 1/4 doz. 6 1/2-in. Belled Berries.
- 1/4 doz. 6 1/2-in. Crimped Berries.
- 1/4 doz. 6-in. Deep Berries.

Total 120 pieces asstd. in bbl., no less sold.
Total for asst. **$12.60** ...Each. **10½c**

COLONIAL STYLE TABLEWARE ASSORTMENT

A0286—Heavy crystal glass, smooth finished edges, fire polished. Staple standard size pieces that are used daily. Asstd. as follows:

- 1/4 doz. Covered Butters.
- 1/4 doz. Covered Sugars.
- 1/4 doz. Creams.
- 1/4 doz. Spoon Holders.
- 1/4 doz. 55-oz. Jugs.
- 1 1/2 doz. Tumblers.
- 1/4 doz. Berry Bowls, 7 1/2 in.
- 1 doz. Berry Nappies, 4 1/2 in.
- 1/4 doz. Berry Bowls, 8 1/2 in.
- 1 doz. Berry Nappies, 4 3/4 in.
- 1/2 doz. Celery Trays.
- 1/2 doz. Pickles.
- 1/2 doz. Handled Olives, 5 1/2 in.
- 3/4 doz. Footed Jellies.
- 1 doz. Goblets.
- 1 doz. Iced Teas.

Asstd. 100 pcs. in bbl. No less sold. About 150 lbs. Total for bbl. **$11.00** Each. **11c**

The quality of A.W.C. goods is not a matter of anybody's opinion but of material facts, easy to ascertain by examination, test and comparison—

UTILITY GLASSWARE ASST.

A02048—Clear crystal, colonial styles, smoothly finished. Asstd. 3 doz. 4-in. nappies, 1/2 doz. 8-in. bowls, 1 doz. 3 1/2-in. sherbets, 1/2 doz. sugars 5 1/2x3 3/4 in., 1/2 doz. creamers 3 3/4x3 1/4 in., 1/2 doz. spooners 3 3/4x3 3/4 in., 1/2 doz. butters, diam. 6 3/4 in., 1/2 doz. 3-pt. water pitchers, 3 doz. 9-oz. tumblers. Popular numbers which may be sold singly or in sets. Total 10 doz. pcs. asstd. in bbl. 150 lbs., no less sold.

(Total $7.50): Doz. **75c**

"DAISY" ASSORTMENT DECORATED GLASS TABLEWARE

Standard sizes, effectively decorated in Ruby, Green and Gold Bronze.

A0287—Asst. comprises 10 doz. pcs. as follows:

- 1/3 doz. Cov. Butters, 1/3 doz. Cov. Sugar Bowls, 1/3 doz. Cream Pitchers, 1/3 doz. Spoon Holders — 4 Tea Sets.
- 1/4 doz. Large Pitchers, 1 1/2 doz. Tumblers — 3 Water Sets.
- 1/4 doz. 8 1/2-in. Deep Berry Bowls, 1 1/2 doz. 4 3/4-in. Berry Dishes — 3 Berry Sets.
- 1/6 doz. 9-in. Berry Dishes, 1 doz. 4 1/4-in. Dessert Dishes — 2 Berry Sets.
- 1/2 doz. ftd. Jelly Bowls.
- 1/2 doz. Tall Celeries.
- 1/2 doz. 8 1/2-in. Pickles.
- 1/2 doz. 5 1/2-in. Handled Olives.
- 1/2 doz. 10 1/2-in. Celery Trays.
- 1/2 doz. 6 1/2-in. Deep Berries.
- 1 doz. Goblets.

10 doz. in bbl. Wt. 140 lbs. ... Doz. **$1.50**

CRYSTAL GLASS TABLEWARE ASST.

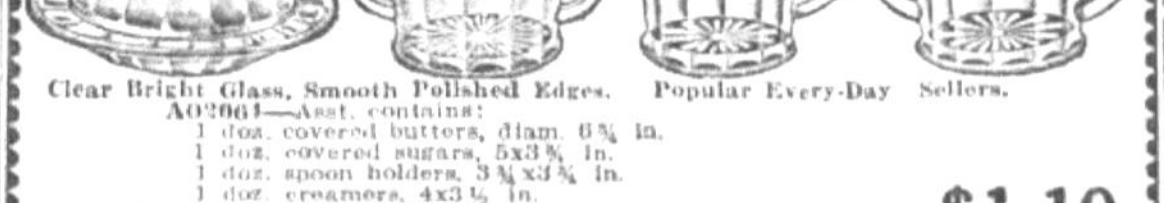

Clear Bright Glass, Smooth Polished Edges. Popular Every-Day Sellers.

A02061—Asst. contains:

- 1 doz. covered butters, diam. 6 3/4 in.
- 1 doz. covered sugars, 5x3 3/4 in.
- 1 doz. spoon holders, 3 3/4x3 3/4 in.
- 1 doz. creamers, 4x3 1/2 in.

Total, 4 doz. asstd. in bbl., 90 lbs., no less sold.
(Total $4.40): Doz. **$1.10**

"PYREX" OVEN GLASSWARE—THE NEW STYLE "PYREX" WITH HANDLES IS EASIER TO HANDLE AND MUCH MORE ATTRACTIVE.

The best, durable and most efficient glassware made for baking and serving directly from the dish. "PYREX" is easily cleaned— it bakes quicker and browns foods evenly, is sanitary and will not chip. Any piece of "PYREX" which breaks from heat while in the oven will be replaced.

Round Casseroles. Each in carton.
A1700—(Mfrs. 622) cap. 1 qt., 6⅝x2¾ in. Each, 98c
A1701—(Mfrs. 623) cap. 1½ qt., 7⅝x3 in. Each, $1.13
A1702—(Mfrs. 624) cap. 2 qts. 8⅞x3¼ in. Each, $1.30

Oval Shallow Casseroles. Each in carton.
A1703—(Mfrs. 643) cap. 1½ qt., 10x7½ in. Each, $1.13
A1704—(Mfrs. 644) cap. 2 qts. 11¼x8⅛ in. Each, $1.30

Oval Deep Casseroles. Each in carton.
A1705—(Mfrs. 633) cap. 1½ qt., 9⅛x6¾ in. Each, $1.13
A1706—(Mfrs. 634) cap. 2 qt., 10¼x7½ in. Each, $1.30

Square Casserole. Each in carton.
A1707—(Mfrs. 653) cap. 1½ qt., 7¼x2¾ in. Each, $1.13

Round Pie Plates. Each in carton.
A1709—(Mfrs. 208) 8⅞x1⅛ in. Each, 49c
A1710—(Mfrs. 209) 9⅞x1⅛ in. Each, 58c
A1711—(Mfrs. 210) 10⅞x1⅛ in. Each, 65c

Hexagonal Pie Plate. Each in carton.
A1718—(Mfrs. 200) 9¾x1⅛ in. Each, 65c

Square Cake Baker. Each in carton.
A1719—(Mfrs. 809) 9⅛x1⅞ in. Each, 70c

Oblong Biscuit Baker. Each in carton.
A1720—(Mfrs. 235) 11⅞x8⅛ in. Each, 80c

Teapots. Each in carton.
A1730—(Mfrs. 22) cap. 2 cups. Each, $1.65
A1731—(Mfrs. 24) cap. 4 cups. Each, $1.95
A1732—(Mfrs. 26) cap. 6 cups. Each, $2.28

Round Pudding Dishes. Each in carton.
A1721—(Mfrs. 022) cap. 1 qt. 6¾x2¾ in. Each, 55c
A1722—(Mfrs. 023) cap. 1½ qt. 7⅞x3 in. Each, 65c
A1723—(Mfrs. 024) cap. 2 qts. 8¾x3¼ in. Each, 78c

Round Cake Baker. Each in carton.
A1712—(Mfrs. 221) 9¾x1¼ in. Each, 49c

2-pc. Baking Dish. Each in carton.
A1708—(Mfrs. 110) cap. 10x7⅛ in. Each, $1.30

Oblong Bread or Loaf Bakers. Each in carton.
A1715—(Mfrs. 212) 9⅞x5⅛ in. Each, 58c
A1716—(Mfrs. 214) 10⅞x5⅝ in. Each, 98c

Oval Platter. Each in carton.
A1717—(Mfrs. 316) 15⅝x11⅛ in. Each, $1.30

Round Custard Cups. ½ doz. in carton.
A1726—(Mfrs. 424) cap. 4 oz. 3⅛x2⅛ in. Doz. $1.56
A1727—(Mfrs. 426) cap. 6 oz. 3⅝x2⅛ in. Doz. $2.04

Individual Baker (Ramekin) Round. ½ doz. in carton.
A1725—(Mfrs. 442) cap. 4 oz. 3¾x1½ in. Doz. $1.56

Individual Pie Baker. ½ doz. in carton.
A1729—(Mfrs. 452) cap. 6 oz. 4½x1⅛ in. Doz. $2.04

Oblong Utility Dish. Each in carton.
A1713—(Mfrs. 231) 10½x6⅛ in. Each, 65c
A1714—(Mfrs. 232) 12⅝x8⅛ in. Each, $1.13

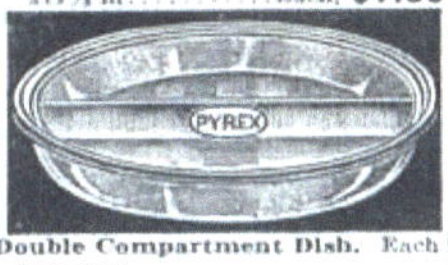

Double Compartment Dish. Each in carton.
A1724—(Mfrs. 130) 9¾x1⅞ in. Each, 98c

Percolator Top. ½ doz. in carton.
A1728—(Mfrs. 053) diam. 2⅛ in., ht. 1-13/16 in. Doz. 84c

"PYREX" MOUNTED CASSEROLES, PIE BAKERS AND STEAK DISHES

Heavy gauge solid brass mountings. Nickel-plated perforations are all etched, giving a refined touch. Cast metal feet and handles. Fitted with "PYREX" Oven Glass.

Heavy gauge solid brass mountings. Bulged shapes, perforated and finely etched, cast metal feet and handles. Fitted with Genuine Cut "PYREX" oven Glassware.

ROUND MOUNTED CASSEROLES.
A9875—Round, 7 in., cap. 2 pints. Each, $2.15
A9876—Round, 8 in., cap. 3 pints. Each, 2.75

OVAL MOUNTED CASSEROLES.
A9877—Oval, 8 in., cap. 2 pints. Each, $2.75
A9878—Oval, 9 in., cap. 3 pints. Each, 3.25

ROUND BULGED MOUNTED CASSEROLES
A9881—Round, 7 in., cap. 2 pints. Each, $3.50
A9882—Round, 8 in., cap. 3 pints. Each, 4.20

OVAL BULGED MOUNTED CASSEROLES.
A9883—Oval, 7 in., cap. 3 pts. Each, $4.20
A9884—Oval, 8 in., cap. 2 qts. Each, 5.00

ROUND MOUNTED PIE BAKER.
A9879—Round, 9 in. Each, $1.75

OVAL MOUNTED STEAK DISH.
A9880—Oval, 10½ in., cap. 3 pts. Each, $3.50

ROUND BULGED MOUNTED PIE BAKER.
A9885—Round, 9 in. Each, $2.95

OVAL MOUNTED STEAK CASSEROLES.
A9886—Oval, 9 in., cap. 1 qt. Each, $3.95
A9887—Oval, 10½ in., cap. 3 pints. Each, 5.00

9-PC. PYREX HOLIDAY GIFT ASST.

Nine of the most popular pieces in the Pyrex line, neatly packed in Holiday display box. Attractive and useful Holiday gifts.

AO1733—Asst. consists of 1 only 1½-qt. Casserole. 1 only 10½ x 6½-in. Utility Dish. 1 only 9-in. Pie Plate. 6 only 6-oz. Custard Cups.

Total 9 pcs. in attractive box. SET (9 pcs.), $3.25

PYREX MOUNTED CASSEROLES & PIE BAKERS

Heavy gauge solid brass mountings, nickel plated, highly polished, perforated carved design, metal feet and handles, fitted with **PYREX OVEN GLASS.**

ROUND CASSEROLES.
A9894—Diam. 7 in., cap. _ qt. (Doz. $21.00); Each, $1.85
A9895—Diam. 8 in., cap. 1½ qts. (Doz. $27.00); Each, $2.40

ROUND PIE BAKERS.
A9892—Diam. 8 in. (Doz. $13.50); Each, $1.20
A9893—Diam. 9 in. (Doz. $16.50); Each, $1.45

BEVERAGE SETS FOR HOLIDAY SELLING

IMPORTED NOVELTY GLASS LIQUOR SETS

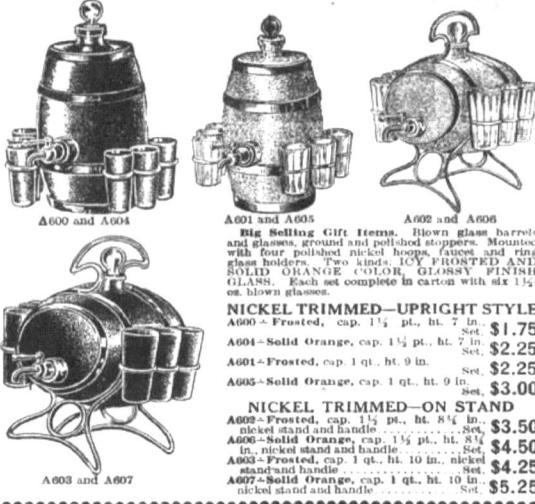

A600 and A604

A601 and A605

A602 and A606

Big Selling Gift Items. Blown glass barrels and glasses, ground and polished stoppers. Mounted with four polished nickel hoops, faucets and ring glass holders. Two kinds. ICY FROSTED AND SOLID ORANGE COLOR, GLOSSY FINISH GLASS. Each set complete in carton with six 1½-oz. blown glasses.

NICKEL TRIMMED—UPRIGHT STYLE

A600—Frosted, cap. 1½ pt., ht. 7 in. Set. $1.75
A604—Solid Orange, cap. 1½ pt., ht. 7 in. Set. $2.25
A601—Frosted, cap. 1 qt., ht. 9 in. Set. $2.25
A605—Solid Orange, cap. 1 qt., ht. 9 in. Set. $3.00

NICKEL TRIMMED—ON STAND

A602—Frosted, cap. 1½ pt., ht. 8¾ in., nickel stand and handle. Set. $3.50
A606—Solid Orange, cap. 1½ pt., ht. 8¾ in., nickel stand and handle. Set. $4.50
A603—Frosted, cap. 1 qt., ht. 10 in., nickel stand and handle. Set. $4.25
A607—Solid Orange, cap. 1 qt., ht. 10 in. nickel stand and handle. Set. $5.25

A603 and A607

FANCY DECORATED IMPORTED WATER SETS

Set consists of fancy shape decorated blown glass Jug and six 9-oz. glasses to match. Clear blown glass in a variety of shapes and colored. Each set in carton.

A631—Tall jug, cap. 48 oz., wide green band edged with deep red and gold, white enamel flowers and fresco border, gold edge and bottom......SET (8 pcs.). $1.50

A632—Tall jug, cap. 44 oz., solid light green with enameled fresco designs tinted with red and edged with gold, white enamel flowers.............SET (8 pcs.) $2.10

A633—Tapered jug, cap. 42 oz., gold band and connecting lines, edge and bottom, white and tan enameled fancy designs. SET (8 pcs.) $2.10

BEVERAGE SETS

Mounted On Gilt Finish Stands

A634—Ht. 10½ in., cap. 12 oz., violet colored, decorated with gold band and white enamel fresco border and design, handled glasses.

SET (8 pcs.), $1.85

A636—Ht. 12 in., cap. 12 oz., solid blue, embossed finished, gold band decorated tapered handled glasses and bottle, fancy stand.

SET (8 pcs.), $2.75

EFFICIENT LIGHTING UNITS FOR STORES, SCHOOLS, CHURCHES, ETC.—See Page 91

FANCY DECORATED WINE AND BEVERAGE SETS

Clear sparkling blown glass, colored and decorated in a variety of bright attractive colors, fancy shapes, ground glass stoppers. Each complete in carton with tray and 6 glasses to match.

A621—Tray 7 in., bottle 9 in., cap. 13 oz., decorated with gold bands and flowers in green and white enamel with red centers. SET (8 pcs.) 95c

A622—Tray 8½ in., bottle 11 in., cap. 17 oz., light blue and crystal, gold band and edges, fresco enameled designs in blue and tan, fancy shape glasses. SET (8 pcs.), $1.45

A624—Tray 8 in., bottle 10½ in., cap. 12 oz., wide solid blue band edged with gold, decorated with red, tan and white enamel, fancy shape footed glasses. $1.95

A625—Tray 8½ in., bottle 12 in., handled, cap. 12 oz., green and crystal, embossed with gold, white enamel decorations. SET (8 pcs.). $2.50

A626—Tray 8½ in., bottle 11½ in., handled, cap. 12 oz., ruby and icy frosted, wide gold band and enameled flowers and foliage in green and white. SET (8 pcs.). $2.95

A627—Tray 8½ in., bottle 12 in., handled, cap. 20 oz., corduroy spiral shape in two-tone iridescent light and dark amber. SET (8 pcs.). $4.50

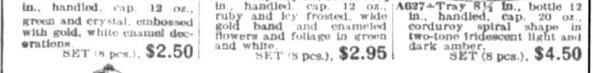

A628—Tray 9 in., bottle 12 in., cap. 20 oz., gold band decoration, frosted and white enameled designs dotted with green. SET (8 pcs.) $1.95

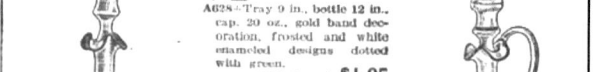

A630—Tray 9 in., bottle 12 in., handled, cap. 20 oz., one-half solid green, large gold flowers and gold bands, white enameled centers and designs, tall shape fancy glasses. SET (8 pcs.) $2.95

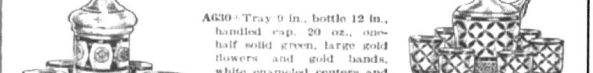

IMP. SOLID COLORED GLASS SMOKING TRAYS

Blown glass, squat shape, solid tango red color, mounted with heavy nickel rim and cigar or cigarette rests.

A608—Diam. 3½ in., 1 rest. Each. 45c
A610—Diam. 4¼ in., 2 rests. Each. 65c
A609—Diam. 5½ in., 3 rests. Each. 75c

BLOWN CRYSTAL GLASS WINE SETS

A02201—Decanter, ht. 11 in., cap. 33 oz., plain blown panel design, six 3-oz. glasses to match. Tray, diam. 10¼ in. Each set in carton. 6 sets in reshipping carton, no less sold. SET (8 pcs.). 80c
Total (6 sets), $4.80

A02205—Decanter, ht. 11 in., cap. 33 oz., wide gold band decoration, six 3-oz. glasses to match. Tray, diam. 10¼ in., solid orange with black edge. Each set in carton, 6 sets in reshipping carton, no less sold. SET (8 pcs.), $1.35
Total (6 sets), 8.10

A02206—Decanter, ht. 11 in., cap. 33 oz., cut grape design, six 3-oz. glasses to match. Tray, diam. 10¼ in., solid orange with black edge. Each set in carton, 6 sets in reshipping carton........SET (8 pcs.) $1
Total (6 sets)

HOLIDAY GLASSWARE—FANCY DECORATED AND SOLID COLORS

COLORED GLASS CONSOLE SETS

Newest shapes and solid color combinations, attractively decorated. Fired colors, will not wear off.

ORANGE GLASS WITH JET BLACK BASE

AO1184—9-in. bowl with detachable foot, two 7-in. candlesticks. 1 doz. in bbl.

Doz. sets, **$9.50**

ORANGE GLASS WITH JET BLACK BASE

AO2261—9¼-in. bowl with detachable foot, two 8¾-in. candlesticks. 1 set in carton.............SET (4 pcs.), **$1.20**

SOLID AMBER COLOR

AO291—9-in. footed and handled spiral bowl, two 8½-in. candlesticks. 1 set in carton..............SET (3 pcs.), **$1.10**

ASSTD. COLORS WITH JET BLACK BASE AND BORDER

A288—4 sets in carton, 1 blue, 1 canary, 2 orange, 10-in. bowls, 8¾-in. candlesticks jet black base, jet black border.

(Total, $4.40); SET (4 pcs.), **$1.10**

AO288½—10-in. orange color bowl only with jet black base and border, two 8¾-in. candlesticks. 1 set in carton.

SET (4 pcs.), **$1.25**

ORANGE GLASS WITH JET BLACK BASE AND BORDER

AO2262—9½-in. orange color bowl with jet black detachable base, wide black border, two 8½-in. candlesticks. 1 set in carton....................SET (4 pcs.), **$1.85**

ORANGE GLASS WITH JET BLACK BASE AND BORDER

AO2273—9-in. orange color bowl, satin finish, black detachable base and border, four 3½-in., Colonial candlesticks. 1 set in carton.......................SET (6 pcs.), **$1.25**

SOLID GREEN WITH JET BLACK BASE

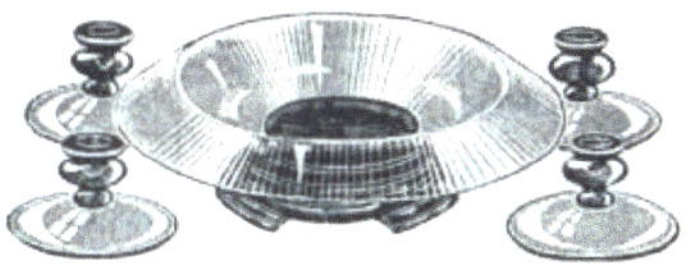

AO2263—12-in. solid color bowl, jet black detachable base, four 3½-in. Colonial candlesticks. 1 set in carton.

SET (6 pcs.), **$1.95**

DECORATED ORANGE AND BLACK GLASS ASSTS.

Orange color glassware, decorated with wide black band and enameled floral sprays and foliage in colors, fired decorations, full polished finish.

AO2266—Asst. consists of:
1 only 9-in. Footed Fruit Bowl.
1 only 5-in. Low Footed Bonbon.
1 only 1-lb. Candy Jar.
1 only 8-in. rolled edge Vase.
1 only 8½-in. Footed Comport.
1 only 9½-in. Footed Nappy.
Total 6 pcs. in asst. in bbl., no less sold.

ASST. (6 pcs.), **$5.70**

RIBBED ORANGE AND BLACK GLASS ASST.

Ribbed design, orange color glassware, fired black band decoration. Full polished finish.

AO267—Asst. consists of:
5 only footed Mayonnaise Sets.
5 only ½-lb. Candy Jars and Covers.
5 only 6½-in. high Footed Comports.
5 only 8½-in. Footed Salad Bowls.
5 only 6½-in. Covered Bonbon Dishes.
5 only 8-in. tall shape Vases.
Total 2½ doz. pcs. in bbl., no less sold.

(Total, $10.62); Doz. **$4.25**

SOLID GREEN GENUINE CUT GLASS

AO2264—12-in. solid color bowl, jet black detachable base, four 3½-in. Colonial candlesticks, genuine deep floral cutting. 1 set in carton......SET (6 pcs.), **$2.95**

DECORATED ORANGE AND BLACK GLASS ASST.

Orange color glassware, decorated with wide black band and enameled floral sprays and foliage in colors, fired decorations, full polished finish.

AO2265—Asst. consists of:
1 only 6¼-in. Vases.
1 only 10-in. Fruit Bowls & Base.
1 only 9-in. Nappies and Base.
1 only 9-in. Flared Nappies and Base.
1 only 10½-in. Sandwich Tray.
1 only 8½-in. Flared Comport.
1 only 8¾-in. rolled edge Comport.
1 only 6½-in. Mayonnaise Bowl.
1 only High Footed Bonbon & Cover.
1 only Low Footed Bonbon & Cover.
1 only ½-lb. Candy Jar and Cover.
1 only 1-lb. Candy Jar.
Total 12 pcs. asstd. in bbl., no less sold.

ASST. (12 pcs.), **$10.50**

SPIRAL AMBER COLOR GLASS ASST.

Big $1.00 to $1.50 Retailers

Genuine amber color glassware, full polished finish. All popular sellers that retail quickly from $1.00 to $1.50.

AO266—Asst. consists of:
⅙ doz. 11-in. Footed Cabarettes.
⅙ doz. 11½-in. Handled Sandwich Trays.
⅙ doz. 7½-in. blown Vases.
⅙ doz. 3-pc. Mayonnaise Sets.
⅙ doz. Handled 9-in. Console Bowls.
⅓ doz. 9-in. Candlesticks.
Total 14 pcs. in bbl., no less sold. ASST. (14 pcs.), **$6.25**

ORANGE AND BLACK ASST.

Orange color glassware, full polished finish, fired decorations.

AO265—Asst. consists of:
⅙ doz. 11-in. Footed Cabarettes.
⅙ doz. 11½-in. Handled Sandwich Trays.
⅙ doz. 7½-in. blown Vases.
⅙ doz. handled 9-in. Console Bowls.
⅓ doz. 9-in. Candlesticks.
⅙ doz. 3-pc. Mayonnaise Sets.
Total 14 pcs. in bbl., no less sold. ASST. (14 pcs.), **$7.50**

BLOWN GLASSWARE—In Holiday Gift Boxes

Thin-Blown Table Glassware, put up in strong spaced cardboard Holiday gift boxes, covered with matt finished paper, lithographed Xmas scenes in bright colors on shaded green background. Exceptionally big selling Holiday gift line.

THIN-BLOWN OPTIC RICH GOLDEN LUSTER FINISH TABLE GLASSWARE

A2215—Fruit Juice Tumbler, 5 oz. ½ doz. in set...........Set, **60c**
A2216—Table Tumbler, 9 oz. ½ doz. in set...............Set. **60c**

A2217 — Beverage Tumbler, 8 oz. ½ doz. in set..........Set, **60c**
A2218—Iced Tea Tumbler, 12 oz. ½ doz in set............Set. **75c**

A2219—Sherbet, ht. 3 in. low shape. ½ doz. in set...........Set, **75c**
A2220—Sherbet, ht. 4½ in. tall shape. ½ doz. in set.........Set, **90c**

A2221—Goblet, ht. 7 in. high foot. ½ doz. in set.............Set, **90c**

THIN-BLOWN OPTIC CLEAR LIGHT CRYSTAL GENUINE FLORAL CUT GLASSWARE

A2223—Fruit Juice Tumbler, 5 oz. ½ doz. in set.............Set, **60c**
A2224—Table Tumbler, 9 oz. ½ doz. in set.................Set. **60c**

A2225—Beverage Tumbler, 8 oz. ½ doz. in set.............Set, **60c**
A2226—Iced Tea Tumbler, 12 oz. ½ doz. in set............Set. **75c**

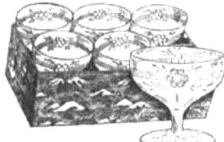

A2227—Sherbet, ht. 3 in. low shape. ½ doz. in set..........Set. **$1.25**
A2228—Sherbet, ht. 4½ in. tall shape. ½ doz. in set.......Set, **$1.25**

A2229—Goblet, ht. 7 in. high foot. ½ doz. in set............Set, **$1.25**

GENUINE CUT GLASS CONDIMENT SET

A2232—Consists of 6½-in. oil bottle, 6½-in. vinegar bottle, 4-in. covered syrup pitcher, two 2½-in. salts and peppers with silver finish tops. 5 pcs. in set.
SET (5 pcs.) **$1.00**

OPTIC CLEAR SPARKLING CRYSTAL LIGHT CUT PLATE

A2230—Diam. 7½ in. 6 in set. Each set in carton.
SET of 6. **$1.50**

GENUINE CUT GLASS SUGAR & CREAM SET

A2233—Sugar 3¼x3 in., cream 3¼x3 in., fine quality crystal glass, floral cutting, star bottom.
SET (2 pcs.). **55c**

GENUINE CUT GLASS BUD VASE

A2231—Ht. 10 in. fine quality crystal glass, genuine cut, 2 pieces in set.
SET of 2. **60c**

CLEAR CRYSTAL SPIRAL SHAPE TABLE TUMBLER SET

A1385/1—9 oz. spiral shape, clear crystal, smooth edges. 6 in set.
SET of 6 **32c**

OPTIC RICH GOLDEN LUSTER FINISH PLATE

A2272—Diam. 6½ in. 6 in set. Each set in carton.
SET of 6. **75c**

SOLID COLOR VANITY SETS

Fine quality glass ware allover solid color. Set consists of fancy shape Jar 4x4 in., two 6-in. perfume bottles with long ground grip stoppers.

A2255—Green. 1 set (3 pcs.) in box. Set, **95c**
A2256—Pink. 1 set (3 pcs.) in box. Set, **95c**

A2257—Orange and Black. 1 set (3 pcs.) in box.
Set. **$1.00**

GENUINE CUT GLASS WATER SET

A2249—60-oz. tall shape jug, six 9-oz. tumblers, deep cutting. Each set in box.
SET (7 pcs.) **$1.25**

GENUINE CUT GLASS ICED TEA SET

A2252—76-oz. tall shape covered jug, six 12-oz. tumblers, clear crystal, deep cutting. Each set in box.
SET (7 pcs.) **$1.50**

Page 50

HOLIDAY GIFT GOODS

HAVILAND FRENCH CHINA DINNER SETS
(Haviland-Abott, Limoges, France)

Rose decoration, bright pink bursting rosebuds in clusters with green foliage enlivened with tan, purple and green sprays. Pure white china body, pompadour shape, embossed basket weave panel effect, MATT GOLD HANDLES. See Composition Page 172.
AO17537 = 100-pc. trade marked Chas. Field Haviland, Limoges, France. ....Set, **$35.00**

FLOWER AND FRUIT ELECTROLIER
6-ft. silk cord and 2-pc. plug.

AO3529 = Ht. 20 in., cast aluminum base, spun brass bowl diam. 11 in., finished in bronze and gold, 4 ornamental lights with 6 amber tear drops on each, 6 in., flared top crystal cut vase filled with asstd. artificial flowers, complete with 4 frosted twisted bulbs. Socket in base. ..... Each complete, **$10.50**

JAPANESE CHINA DINNER SETS
Fine Japanese china body, pure white, light wt. Granada pattern effectively decorated in attractive colors on wide ivory band.

Granada pattern, wide ivory band edged with gold lines, openwork blue block border, natural color fruit and floral medallions on bright blue background, matt gold covered handles, extra gold line on all covered pieces. See Composition on Page 172.
AO6014 = 100-pc. trade marked NORITAKE. ....Set, **$52.00**
AO6009 = A2-pc. trade marked NORITAKE ....Set, **$28.50**

ELECTRIC FRUIT CONSOLE
6-ft. silk cord and 2-pc. plug.

AO3530 = Ht. 14 in., width 9 in., cast aluminum base and frame, bronze and gold polychrome finish, 4 hand-painted ribbed glass panels, artificial molded glass fruit, removable top, frosted inside, colored to show natural tints when lighted. Socket in base. .... Each, **$9.00**

Our Shades and Stands are Carefully Selected to Give Utmost Value for a Low Price.

METAL BRIDGE AND JUNIOR LAMPS
High grade materials and finishes. 8-ft. silk cord and 2-pc. connection plug. Standard adjustable sockets.

AO3081

AO3019 = **BRIDGE LAMP**, ht. 58 in., spiral brass standard, large openwork base, ship finial, artistically finished in black and gold. ..... Each, **$13.50**

AO3081 = **LINEN SHADE**, 13x13 in., fancy shape beaded and hand decorated with ship scene on gold background, 2-tone silk ruching in panel effect. ..... Each, **$5.00**

Complete Lamp and Shade **$18.50**

AO3019

AO3142

AO3063

AO3066 = **BRIDGE LAMP**, ht. 58 in., half spiral brass standard, browntone finish, fancy openwork base, embossed highly polished ornaments and arm, gold and polychrome finish. ....Each, **$15.00**

SILK SHADE, 15x8 in., fine georgette silk, lined and interlined, gold lace cover, vari-colored silk ruching, gold and silk floral ornament.
AO3986 4 = Taupe and Rose. .... Each, **$9.50**

AO3986 5 = Taupe and Orange. .... Each, **$9.50**

Complete Lamp and Shade **$24.50**

AO39864

AO3066

AO3063 = **JUNIOR LAMP**, ht. 60 in., half spiral brass standard, browntone finish, octagon shape openwork base, embossed highly polished ornaments, polished gold and polychrome finish. ....Each, **$15.00**
SILK SHADE, 22x15 in., georgette silk, Jap silk lined and interlined, sunburst and plaited panels, heavy gold braid and silk ruching, 6-in. colored glass bead pendant fringe.
AO3142 = Black and Tangerine. ....Each, **$13.50**
AO3143 = Blue and Rose. ....Each, **$13.50**
Complete Lamp and Shade, $28.50

HAND-DECORATED JAPANESE ART POTTERY VASE

A404 = Ht. 12¼ in., semi-porcelain body, artistically decorated in a variety of shades and designs, tan and brown background, embossed and enameled Oriental figures and landscape scenes, wide gold bands on shoulder, top and bottom. Unusually attractive and decorative. ....Each, **$4.25**

Our Shades and Stands are Carefully Selected to Give Utmost Value for a Low Price.

JET BLACK CHINA BASE TABLE LAMP

Fine quality china base, jet black, artistic design, round beaded parchment shade 15x8½ in., hand-painted flower and butterfly designs on vari-colored background, silk ruching edge, 2 pull-chain sockets, 6-ft. silk cord and 2-pc. plug, ready for use.
AO3102/2 = Ht. 20 in., 2-lt. Jet Black Base, yellow and black butterfly design shade. ....Complete, **$7.75**
AO3102 = Ht. 20 in., 2-lt. Blue base, blue and rose flower design shade. ....Complete, **$7.75**

23-PC. EUROPEAN CHINA LUSTER TEA SETS
Set contains 1 Teapot, 1 Sugar, 1 Creamer, 6 Cups, 6 Saucers and 6 Plates.

Fine quality light wt. china, allover luster finish. Cups decorated inside and out. All standard size pcs. Each set in carton.
A6611 = 23-pc., solid tan luster, blue band edged with narrow black lines. ....Set, **$5.50**
A6612 = 23-pc., solid iris luster, mother-of-pearl band edged with narrow black lines. ....Set, **$5.50**

Our Catalog is Known as the Best Merchandise Reference Book and Buyer's Guide in Existence.

SILVER AND POLYCHROME TABLE LAMP

AO3643 = Ht. 24 in., shade 18 in., silver and blue finish base, 6 amber dome panels and 6 blue skirt panels, 2 pull-chain sockets. ....Each, **$12.50**

DECORATED VASES, TABLE GLASSWARE, ETC.

DECORATED GLASS VASES—
Richly decorated in a variety of bright colors, attractive shapes and designs. Packed in small original packages and shipped direct from our warehouse. No charge for package.

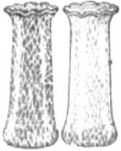

AO1401—Ht. 6 in., crackled design, solid orange and blue colors. 6 doz. asstd. in carton, no less sold.
Doz. 82c
(Total. $4.92)

STAR VALUE ★ AO1402—Ht. 6 in., thin blown glass, satin etched fresco designs on solid tinted colored body, blue, canary and orange. 6 doz. asstd. in carton, no less sold.... Doz. 77c
(Total. $4.62)

STAR VALUE ★ AO1403—Ht. 7½ in., tinted allover in colors, embossed fruit and flowers, ruby, green and gold bronze decorated. 3 doz. asstd. in carton, no less sold........Doz. $1.75
(Total. $5.25)

AO781—Ht. 8½ in., 2 styles, embossed florals and foliage, illuminated with gold bronze on two-tone blended background. 3 doz. asstd. in carton, no less sold. Doz. $1.85
(Total. $5.55)

AO1404—Ht. 9½ in. tinted allover in colors, large flowers and foliage on bright colors, enriched with gold bronze. 2 doz. asstd. in carton, no less sold. Doz. $2.15
(Total. $4.30)

AO282—Ht. 9½ in., 2 styles, embossed flowers and foliage on solid color tinted background, bright colors. 2 doz. asstd. in carton, no less sold. Doz. $2.15
(Total. $4.30)

AO283—Ht. 10 in., 3 styles, embossed bird and flower backgrounds, tinted and decorated in bright blue, red and green. 1 doz. asstd. in carton, no less sold. Doz. $3.75

AO1406—Ht. 12 in., 2 styles, hand painted with large showy flowers and foliage in natural colors on pink, blue or canary background. 1 doz. asstd. in carton, no less sold. Doz. $4.25

AO284—Ht. 15 in., 2 asstd. styles, embossed tropical and bird scenes, 2-tone green background, enriched with red and gold luster. 1 doz. asstd. in carton, no less sold. Doz. $5.50

LARGE SIZE UTILITY GLASS VASES

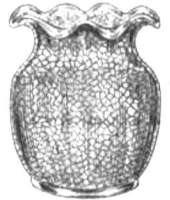

Ht. 7½ in., diam. 6 in., fine polished clear crystal glass, attractive designs, smooth molded edges. 1 doz. in shipping carton, 43 lbs.
AO2213—Popular crackled design. Doz. $2.25

DECORATIVE HANGING BASKETS
Strong, durable porcelain body, neatly molded. Expertly decorated, tinted and embossed, bright, attractively blended colors. Each suspended on strong twisted red cord hangers.

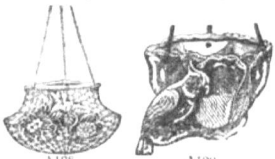

A108   A109
A108—Basket 7x5 in., tinted in green, raised flowers and foliage decorated in bright colors. 2-ft. red silk cord hanger. Each, 90c
A109—Basket 4½x5 in., decorated in red and green, parrot green, red and yellow, resting on green twig. Each $1.15

DECORATIVE FLOWER HOLDER
Light wt. porcelain body, highly embossed and decorated with bright colors. Perforations in base hold flowers.

A101—Ht. 7 in., plumage in bright colors, green, red, yellow and blue rustic pedestal in green. Each, 85c

SEMI-PORCELAIN FLOWER HOLDERS

A501   A502
A501—Ht. 8 in., semi-porcelain body, embossed plumage and flowers in bright green, blue and red colors. ⅓ doz. in pkg. Doz. $7.20
A502—Ht. 9½ in., semi-porcelain body, embossed and decorated in bright green and tan luster, 2-tone effect. ⅓ doz. in pkg. Each, 95c

LUSTER DECORATED WALL FLOWER VASES

A6147—Ht. 7½ in., 2 styles, china body, green luster branch red, tan and green birds, embossed and tinted plumage. ¼ doz. in pkg. Doz. $7.50

SEMI-PORCELAIN FLOWER HOLDER

A107—Pheasant, size 7½x13 in., decorated in bright colors, red, blue, brown and yellow, pedestal green. Each $2.50

LUSTER DECORATED WALL FLOWER VASES

A6145—Ht. 7 in., diam. 4 in., china body, half oval conical shape, asstd. blue and tan allover luster finish with hand-painted flowers, foliage and birds in natural bright colors. ¼ doz. asstd. in pkg. Each, 78c

LUSTER WALL FLOWER VASES

A6146—3 Styles, aver. ht. 5 in., china body, bright asstd. luster colors, red, tan, green and blue, embossed plumage and flowers. ⅓ doz. in pkg. Doz. $4.25

A6148—Ht. 9 in., 2 styles, china body, brown and tan luster vases, birds with embossed bright color luster plumage and flower decorations. ¼ doz. in pkg. Doz. $13.50

DECORATED GLASS CAKE PLATES AND BERRY BOWLS
Decorated Under Surface

AO283—Crystal glass, diam. 10 in., decorated with floral designs, bright colors, red and green, gold bronze background. 3 doz. in bbl. Wt. 100 lbs.
Doz. $3.15
AO283½—Same as above, 6 doz. asst. in bbl . Doz. $2.85

NICKEL-PLATED NUT SETS

A9857—Diam. 7½ in., polished nickel finish, beaded edge, picks and cracker. ...... Set. $1.85

MOUNTED RELISH OR SWEETMEAT DISHES
Heavily nickel plated solid brass frames with handles, footed. Removable colored glass spaced insets.

A9897-8
A9897—Diam. 8¼ in., 1¼-in. deep amber tray, spaced in three parts. Each, $1.35
A9898—Diam. 6¾ in., 1¼-in. deep green tray, spaced in three parts. Each, $1.35

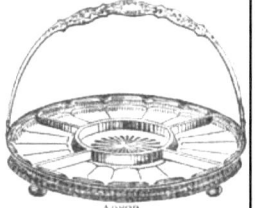

A9899
A9899—Diam. 10½ in., heavily nickel-plated and embossed footed tray, fancy shape perforated and embossed handle, scalloped edge, light green glass inset, spaced in four parts, deep round center. Each, $2.15

Page 52

STATUARY

Classic copies from expensive works of art. Made of Composition Plaster of Paris, artistically painted in colors and bronze. Sell with rapidity and allow you a good margin of profit.

FIGURES

A2/300G
A2/609
A2/704
A2/224

A2/300G—Cherry girl, ht. 20 in., painted features, costume in bright colors.....Each, 95c
A2/609—Water Carrier, ht. 17 in., painted in natural colors......Each, 95c
A2/704—"Rebecca at the Well," ht. 18½ in., painted in bronze.....Each, 95c
A2/224—"Venus," ht 19 in., old ivory finish.....Each, 95c

A2/160
A2/161
A2/183
A2/1376

A2/160—Female, ht. 24 in......Each, $1.75
A2/161—Male, ht. 24 in......Each, 1.75
A2/183—Female Figure, ht. 24½ in., painted in bronze.....Each, $1.75
A2/1376—Female figure with mirror, ht. 26 in., painted in bronze.....Each, $1.65

VASE / BUST

A2/713
A2/53

A2/713—Vase, ht. 16½ in., pearls in colors, vase in ivory.....Each, 90c
A2/53—Female bust, ht. 16 in., painted in bronze and oriental colors.....Each, 95c

BABY FIGURES

A2/819½
A2/817¼

A2/819½—Reading boy, size 14x6 in., costume and pedestal in ivory. Each, 85c
A2/817¼—Sitting boy, 10½x6 in., old ivory finish.....Each, 90c

LION
Old Ivory Finish

A2/79—Size 9x15.....Each, 95c

AMERICAN CHINA DECORATED BABY PLATE

A6864—Diam. 7¾ in., decorated in center with juvenile scenes and rhymes, "Hey Diddle, Diddle, The cat and the Fiddle, The Cow Jumped Over The Moon," etc., in colors, bright luster tinted edge.....Doz $3.00

DECORATED ORANGE COLOR GLASS CONSOLE SET
Burnt-in Colors— Will Not Wash Off

Comprises 9-in. orange color bowl, black detachable foot, two orange color candlesticks with red candles and 12 pcs. asstd. artificial fruit.
AO1184/1 — Decorated all-over orange color, complete with candles and asstd. fruits in natural colors, 1 doz. in bbl and case.....Doz. sets, $19.25
Less than doz sets.....Set, 1.87

AMERICAN CUT GLASSWARE
Sparkling Glassware, Genuine Cuttings in a Variety of Patterns.

A4673—Bonbon—9x5-in. diamond cutting on bottom floral sides, scalloped edge.....Each, 65c
A4363—Sugar And Cream Set. Sugar 6x3 in., cream 5x3 in., cut whirling star with diamond center, notched top, star bottom.....Set, $1.35
A4346—Butter Plate—Diam. 8-in. diamond cutting, scalloped edge, large three-spray cut daisy center. Each, $1.50

A4329—Celery Tray—12x4½ in., diamond and daisy cutting, scalloped edge, fancy shape.....Each, $1.50
A4347—Footed Comport—9¾ in. high, 5 in. wide, floral and leaf cutting, notched edge and stem.....Each, $1.50
A4666—Fruit Bowl—Diam. 8-in large floral and leaf cutting, scalloped edge.....Each, $1.50
A4656—Flower Vase—Ht. 10 in. round large tulip and floral cutting, band at top and bottom.....Each, $1.50
A4658—Ht. 10 in., square, large daisy with band at top and bottom.....Each, $1.50

A4656
A4658

CUT CLASS BASKET
Tall Crystal Handle

STAR VALUE
AO2199—Size 16x10 in., jewel and floral cutting, polished leaves and scalloped edge.
Six in carton.....Each, $1.75
Less than carton.....Each, $1.95

IVORY BODY EUROPEAN SEMI-PORCELAIN DINNER SETS
2 of the Newest Under-Glazed Border Decorations

The new and popular ivory body with its soft even color tone, blends more readily with the decorations than plain white gloss finish. It provides an ideal background for these 2 original decorations especially designed for this shape. For composition of sets see page 121.

Border decoration in blue, maroon and green, flowers in alternating colors with bright centers, green foliage and dotted border line.
AO6649—32-pc. set.....Set, $3.95   AO6651—51-pc. set.....Set, $9.50
AO6650—42-pc. set.....Set, 5.95   AO6652—100-pc. set.....Set, 16.50

Border decoration in scroll effect, flower center with blue and green shaded foliage, brown dotted border line.
AO6653—32-pc. set.....Set, $3.95   AO6655—51-pc. set.....Set, $9.50
AO6654—42-pc. set.....Set, 5.95   AO6656—100-pc. set.....Set, 16.50

IMPORTED CHINA—

Japanese china, allover luster decorations. The greatest values brought out of the Orient this year. Extra fine grade thin china, attractive shapes and decorations. Each set in carton. See composition below.

17 PCS. ALLOVER SOLID LUSTER COLOR

Beautifully decorated with bright luster colors inside and outside. Each set securely packed in strong carton. **17 pc. set service for four.**

A6102—17 pcs., Blue luster outside, tan luster inside..........
A6103—17 pcs., Tan luster outside, mother-of-pearl inside.......... } Set. **$2.95**

23 PCS. ALLOVER SOLID LUSTER COLOR

Beautifully decorated with bright luster colors inside and outside. Each set securely packed in strong carton. 23 pc. set service for six.

A2618—23 pcs., Orange luster outside, mother-of-pearl inside..........
A6100—23 pcs., Blue luster outside, tan luster inside..........
A6101—23 pcs., Tan luster outside, mother-of-pearl inside.......... } Set **$4.45**

ALLOVER LUSTER AND PLUM BLOSSOM DECORATION

A6106—23 pcs., blue luster outside, tan luster inside, decorated with white plum blossoms on natural color branches..........Set. **$5.95**

ALLOVER LUSTER AND FLORAL DECORATION

A6108—23-pc. allover blue luster outside, tan inside, wide tan border and handles, enameled floral decoration outlined with black..........Set. **$7.95**

ALLOVER LUSTER AND DAISY DECORATION

A6107—23 pcs., blue luster outside, tan luster inside, attractive ⅝-in., tan luster band edged with black lines, neat Daisy decoration in White, Black and Tan. Set. **$7.20**

ALLOVER LUSTER AND GOLD DECORATION

A6109—23-pc. set. Tan luster outside, Mother-of-pearl luster inside. Blue luster band with embossed gold decoration, gold covered handles, heavily gold traced edges. Set. **$11.50**

BRIDGE SETS

A6110—7¼ in., fancy shape tray, 2-tone Blue and Tan luster with cup to match..........Doz. sets. **$7.20**

A6111—Tray 7½x5½ in., solid blue luster band, tan luster center with black and green floral decoration, cup to match..........Doz. sets. **$10.50**

A6112—Fancy shape tray 10x8 in., blue and tan luster, hand-painted daisy and bird design, cup to match..........Doz. sets. **$13.50**

LUSTER MAYONNAISE AND WHIPPED CREAM SETS

A6115—Whipped Cream Set, footed bowl 4x2½ in., plate 6 in. diam., 5 in. ladle..........SET (3 pcs.). **85c**

A6116—Mayonnaise Set, bowl 5x2½ in., plate 6 in. diam., 5-in. ladle. SET (3 pcs.). **85c**

ASSORTED SHAPE SALTS AND PEPPERS

Cork stopper bottoms. 6 salts and 6 peppers in doz. in spaced box. 4 asstd. shapes and colors, Blue, Tan, Orange and Canary luster.

A6119—Aver. ht. 2 in..........Doz. **77c**

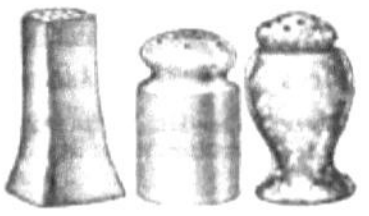

A6120—Average ht. 2¾ in. Doz. **85c**

A6121—3 asstd. shapes, average ht. 2¾ in. Plum Blossom Decoration..........Doz. **$1.75**

LUSTER SYRUP SET

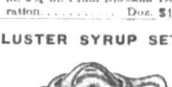

A6123—Blue luster, syrup pitcher 4½x3¼ in., 6-in. plate to match. SET (2 pcs.). **95c**

SUGAR AND CREAM SET

A6113—Set comprises 5x3½-in. sugar and 4x2¾-in. cream, Blue luster outside, Tan luster inside. SET (2 pcs.). **65c**

LUSTER CONDIMENT SETS

A6122—Handled tray 3¾x2¼ in., 2-in. salt and pepper, 2½-in. covered mustard, 3-in. spoon, allover blue luster finish..........Set. **55c**

A6124—Handled tray 7x2¼ in., 2-in. salt and pepper, 2½-in. covered mustard, 3-in. spoon, allover blue luster finish..........Set. **75c**

CHINA FLOWER BOWL CENTERPIECES

Large bowl and removable perforated flower holder, bird design. Used extensively for centerpiece decorations, also for bulb bowls by removing flower holder.

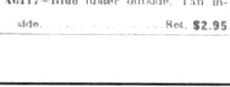

Luster, solid blue luster outside, tan inside, blue and white flower holder.

A6151—Diam. 4 in..........Doz. **$4.25**
A6152—Diam. 4½ in..........Doz. **7.20**
A6153—Diam. 5½ in..........Each. **.85**

COMPOSITION OF TEA SETS

23-pc. Sets comprise Service for Six.

6 only Cups 3¾x2 in.	6 pcs.
6 only Saucers 5½ in.	6 pcs.
6 only Plates 7¾ in.	6 pcs.
1 only Cov. Sugar	2 pcs.
1 only Teapot (6-Cup)	2 pcs.
1 only Creamer	1 pc.
Total,	23 pcs.

17-pc. Sets comprise Service for Four.

4 only Cups 3¾x2 in.	4 pcs.
4 only Saucers 5½ in.	4 pcs.
4 only Plates 7¾ in.	4 pcs.
1 only Cov. Sugar	2 pcs.
1 only Teapot (6-Cup)	2 pcs.
1 only Creamer	1-pc.
Total,	17 pcs.

FLOWER BOWL CENTERPIECES

Large bowl and removable perforated flower holder, bird design. Used extensively for centerpiece decorations, also for bulb bowls by removing flower holder.

Blue and Orange luster bowl, bird design with green plumage and long yellow beak, blue luster centerpiece with yellow and green bird.

A6139—Diam. 7½ in...Each. **$2.75**
A6140—Diam. 9 in...Each. **3.75**

Luster Openwork Flower Bowls

Blended lustrous tones of Turquoise and Ruby colors, molded Orange cluster and openwork leaf design shaded with gold, deep pink luster inside.

A6141—Diam. 6 in.....Each. **$1.45**
A6142—Diam. 7½ in...Each. **2.25**
A6143—Diam. 8½ in...Each. **3.50**

LUSTER CHOCOLATE SETS

Solid luster & hand decorated, fine body.

Set Comprises 9-in. Chocolate Pot, Six 2¾x2¾-in. Cups And 5-in. Saucers To Match.

A6117—Blue luster outside, Tan inside..........Set. **$2.95**

A6118—Blue luster outside, Tan inside, decorated with White plum blossoms and branches in natural colors..........Set. **$3.75**

BLUE LUSTER CUP AND SAUCER

Fine quality light wt. semi-porcelain body. Made by Japan's leading pottery.

STAR VALUE A6138—Cup 3⅝x2 in., saucer 5½ in. solid Blue luster outside, plain White inside. 12 doz. in case.

Doz. (24 pcs.) **$1.87**
2 doz. in pkg., Doz. (24 pcs.) **1.95**

DECORATED JAPANESE CHINA

23-PC. TEA SETS

Set comprises teapot 7½x5 in., sugar 6x4 in., cream 4½x3 in., 6 cups 3½x3 in., 6 saucers 6½ in., 6 plates 7 in.

A6125—Hand-painted landscape and water scenes in sunset effect, gold traced edges and handles, gold clouded knobs........Set, (23 pcs.) **$2.95**
A6126—Hand-painted pink roses and foliage (same design as A6127) in natural color on tinted background, gold traced edges, spout and handles, gold clouded knobs. Set, (23 pcs.) **$2.95**

14-PC. CHOCOLATE SETS

Set consists of chocolate pot, ht. 9½ in.: 6 cups 2¾x2½ in.: 6 saucers 5 in., to match.

A6133—Hand-painted with large pink roses and foliage in natural colors on delicate background, gold traced edge, spout and handles......Set, **$2.25**

A6134—Hand-painted lake and landscape scene with setting sun effect, gold traced edge, spout and handles.........Set, **$2.75**

...and-painted flowers in delicate colors on assd. color band edge, background traced in black, gold traced knob, gold stippled handles.
A113/1—Blue band ....Set, $1.85
A112/3—Blue band ....Set, 1.85
A113/5—Green band ....Set, 1.85

A131/1—Hand-painted floral medallions and panels in border effect, traced with gold, gold traced edges, bottom and spout, gold stippled knob and handles.......Set, **$2.85**

7-PC. HAND-PAINTED CELERY SET

Set comprises tray 11x5 in., six 4x2½ in., individual celery dips.

A2653—Hand-painted landscape and water scenes in sunset effect, gold traced edge. Set, **$1.25**

MARMALADE JAR AND PLATE

A2655—Jar 4½x5 in., plate 5½ in., hand-painted roses and foliage in natural colors, heavy gold clouded edge, gold traced handles. Jar and plate complete, **75c**

7-PC. NUT SET

Set comprises nut bowl 6x2½ in. and six individuals 2½x1½ in.

A2661—Hand-painted flowers, panel and fresco designs in border effect, gold traced edge and feet......Set, **65c**

7-PC. JELLY SET

Set comprises 7-in. jelly plate and six individuals 3½ in.

A2662—Delicate pink roses and foliage in panel effect on delicate ivory band, traced in colors, bright luster band......Set, **65c**

HONEY JAR & COVER

A156—Ht. 5½ in., white ivory body, decorated with bees and clover in natural colors......Set, **50c**

SALT AND PEPPER

Six salts and six peppers in doz.

A6135—Ht. 2½ in., decorated allover with landscape and sunset scenes, bright natural colors, gold decorated tops, cork stopper bottoms. 1 doz in spaced box......Doz, **85c**

BLUE AND TAN LUSTER CRACKER AND CHEESE DISH

A2664—Diam 9½ in.......Each, **$1.50**

SUGAR AND CREAM SETS

A6128—Sugar 4½x6½ in., cream 3½x4½ in., hand-painted with landscape and lake scenes in sunrise effect, gold traced edges and handles, gold clouded knob. 2 sets in pkg......Set, **75c**

A6127—Sugar 4½x5 in., cream 3x4 in., hand-painted berry foliage and blossoms in natural color and green tinted background, gold traced edge and handles, gold clouded knob. 2 sets in pkg......Set, **85c**

SALAD BOWLS

A6130—Diam. 9-in. hand-painted large pink roses and green foliage on delicate background, gold tinted edge......Each, **72c**

A6129—Diam. 9-in. hand-painted landscape and sunset scenes, gold traced edge......Each, **75c**

7-PC. BERRY SETS

Set comprises one large berry bowl and six nappies to match.

A6132—Bowl 9 in., nappies 5 in., hand-painted with large pink roses and foliage in natural colors on delicate tan background, gold tinted edge......Set, **$1.50**

A6131—Bowl 9 in., nappies 5 in., hand-painted landscape and lake scenes in sunset effect, gold traced edge......Set, **$1.50**

7-PC. BERRY SETS

Set comprises one 7½ in. berry bowl and six nappies to match.

Hand-painted flowers in delicate colors on assd. color band edge, background traced in black.
A113/1—Blue band ....Set, 95c
A113/3—Yellow panel ....Set, 95c
A113/5—Green band ....Set, 95c

Hand-painted floral border decorations in panel and fresco designs, gold covered cut-out openwork handles, gold traced edge.
A133/1—Lavender border............Set, $1.50
A133/3—Black floral panel............Set, 1.50
A133/5—Canary border............Set, 1.50

Hand-painted landscape and lake scene in colors on blended background.
A123/1—Sunrise scene............Set, $1.35
A123/3—Noontide scene............Set, 1.35
A133/5—Sunset scene............Set, 1.35

HAND-PAINTED CRACKER AND CHEESE DISH

A2663—Diam. 9 in., hand-painted pink roses, black and gold foliage on tan bar border, striped in gold, gold traced edge......Each, **$1.25**

WICKER HANDLE CAKE PLATE

A503—Diam. 10 in., fine grade china plate, decoration in black, red and gold with hand-painted flower clusters and landscape center, wicker frame and handle. Ea., **$1.50**

7-PC. HAND-PAINTED CAKE SETS

Set comprises cake plate 10 in., and six 6-in. plates to match.

A2645—Hand-painted pink roses, black and gold foliage illuminated on tan bar border, gold striped, gold traced edge......Set, **$2.25**

A2643—Hand-painted landscape and water scene in sunset effect, gold traced edge. Set, **$1.95**

DECORATED EUROPEAN CHINA

Pure white, light wt. European China, bright attractive decorations. All quick selling popular Holiday numbers.

DECORATED CUPS AND SAUCERS

A19030—Cup 3x3 in., saucer 5¾ in. asstd. luster tints and small rose clusters in border effect...Doz. **$1.95**

A19027—Cup 3¼x3 in., saucer 5¾ in. wide gold band decorated......Doz. **$2.05**

A19031—Cup 3¼x3¼ in., saucer 6 in. asstd. luster tint edges, rose clusters and foliage on border effect............Doz. **$2.05**

A19032—Cup 3¼x3¼ in., saucer 6 in. gold traced edges, natural color flowers and foliage....Doz. **$2.05**

A19033—Cup 3¼x3¼ in., saucer 6 in., gold traced edges and handles, asstd. luster stamp border, birds and flowers in natural colors............Doz. **$2.05**

A6697—Cup 3¼x3½ in. saucer 6 in., natural color flowers, heavy gold motto, gold traced edges Doz. **$2.10**

A6691—Cup 3¼x3¼ in., saucer 6 in., asstd FATHER, MOTHER, SISTER, BROTHER in gold letters, gold traced edges.........Doz **$2.25**

A19034—Cup 3½x3¼ in., saucer 6½ in., gold traced edges, natural color flowers and fancy border edge. Doz **$3.95**

A19035—Cup 3½x3½ in., saucer 6½ in., asstd. solid color tinted edges, natural color roses and foliage. Doz. **$4.10**

A19028—Cup 3¾x3¾ in., saucer 6⅝ in. asstd. FATHER, MOTHER, SISTER BROTHER in gold letters, gold edges. Doz. **$3.75**

A19029—**Jumbo,** cup 3⅞x3⅞ in., saucer 7 in., FATHER, MOTHER, SISTER, BROTHER in large gold letters, gold edges. Doz **$3.85**

A6694—**Jumbo,** cup 3⅞x3⅞ in., saucer 7 in., asstd. blue, green and brown Fat Man with inscription (I am not greedy but I like a lot.) gold traced edges.........Doz **$3.95**

DECORATED SALADS AND SALAD SETS

STAR VALUE ★ **A6667**—Diam. 9 in., asstd. blue, green and tan shadow tint border, fruit centers in natural color..............Doz. **$3.95**

3 UNUSUALLY BIG VALUES FOR $4.25 DOZ.

A6668—Diam. 9 in., asstd. 2-tone shadow tint borders, large flower, bird and bouquet centers in bright attractive colors.......................... Doz. **$4.25**

A6666—Diam. 9 in., asstd. blue, tan and green shadow foliage borders, 3 asstd., large rose centers, bright colors....Doz. **$4.05**

A6673—Salad 9 in., six 5¼ in. fruits, blue, tan and green shadow tint border, asstd. fruit centers. Set, (7 pcs.) **95c**

A6672—Salad 9 in., six 5¼ in. fruits, blue, tan and green shadow foliage border, asstd. rose centers.........Set, (7 pcs.) **$1.10**

A6676—Salad 9¼ in., six 5¼ in. fruits, 2-tone border, large basket or flowers in center. Set, (7 pcs.) **$1.35**

A19000—Diam. 9 in., **3 asstd. decorations,** tan, green and blue border, large bird and floral decorations in natural colors Doz. **$4.25**

A19001—Diam. 9 in., **3 asstd. decorations,** green, blue and tan luster border, gold stamp edge, large bird and floral centers in natural colors .... Doz. **$6.50**

DECORATED CAKE PLATES AND CAKE SETS

A6678—Cake plate diam. 9¼ in., 2 decorations, tan and green shadow border, asstd. natural color fruit centers, cut out handles.................Doz **$4.15**

A19006—Diam. 9½ in., fancy shape, asstd. tan, blue and green borders, bird and floral centers in natural colors, cutout handles Doz **$4.25**

A6680—Cake plate diam. 9½ in. wide, gold band edge and scroll design, large natural color rose and foliage center....Doz. **$7.50**

A6681—Cake plate 9½ in., six 6 in. individual plates, blue, tan and green shadow tints, floral centers, cut out handles Set, (7 pcs.) **$1.45**

A6682—Cake plate 10 in., six 6¾ in. individual plates, orange luster border, green shadow foliage and large roses, natural colors.........Set, (7 pcs.) **$2.45**

7-PC. CHOCOLATE SETS

Light weight European china, attractively decorated. Set consists of 10-in. chocolate pot and six cups and saucers to match.

A19013—7 pcs., bordered with light green tints and gold florals, large peacock and natural color pink and blue flowers, green foliage................Set. **$2.35**

A19014—7 pcs., allover mother-of-pearl luster effect, gold stamp border, large pink peony and green foliage ....Set. **$2.95**

SUGAR AND CREAM SETS

A6684—4½x3 in. sugar, 4x3 in. cream, blue, green and tan shadow tint and floral decoration, ¼ doz. sets in pkg. Doz. sets, (24 pcs.) **$4.15**

A6686—4½x3 in. sugar, 4x3 in. cream, Mother-of-Pearl luster, gold stamp border, rose decoration, ¼ doz. sets in pkg. Doz. sets, (24 pcs.) **$7.20**

SEE OUR NEW FRENCH HAVILAND CHINA DINNER SETS ON PAGE 116

2-PC. SYRUP SET

A19020—Light weight china body, blue tint and gold stamp border, bird and flowers in natural colors. Set consists of 4½-in. covered syrup and 6-in. plate to match. Doz. sets, **$6.00**

DECORATED AMERICAN SEMI-PORCELAIN

SALAD BOWLS, CAKE AND BERRY SETS—Cream white American semi-porcelain body, attractively decorated in a variety of designs and colors. GREAT FOR HOLIDAY SELLING.

A5002–Diam. 7½ in., embossed gold stippled edges, bright asstd. color flower and foliage center. (Gro. $18.00); Doz. **$1.60**

A5003–Diam. 7½ in., asstd. tan, pink and green tinted edges, black and tan bird and flower center. (Gro. $21.00); Doz. **$1.85**

A5004–Diam. 8½ in., embossed gold stippled edges, natural asstd. color rose and foliage center. (Gro. $22.50); Doz. **$1.95**

T5005–Diam. 8½ in., asstd. tan, pink and green tinted edges, bird and flower center in black and tan colors....(Gro. $24.00); Doz. **$2.15**

A5006–Diam. 9½ in., asstd. orange pink and green tinted edges, asstd color rose and foliage center. Doz. **$2.25**

A5007–Diam. 9½ in., asstd. gold band and embossed design border with large natural color (rose and foliage center .... Doz. **$2.25**

A5008–Diam. 9½ in., embossed gold stippled edges, shaded pink rose cluster and natural color foliage center. .... Doz. **$3.15**

A5009–Diam. 9¼ in., 2-tone blended pink and blue edge with large flower and landscape center in colors............... Doz. **$3.50**

A5010–Diam. 9½ in., shadow foliage on asstd. tinted backgrounds with large rose and foliage center in colors................ Doz. **$3.50**

A5011–Diam. 9½ in., asstd. canary, pink and blue 3-in. color bands, large parrot center decoration in bright colors.......... Doz. **$3.85**

A5012–Orange, tan and pink tinted edges, black and yellow bird and foliage design centers, deep shape bowl 8½ in. diam., six 5-in nappies. SET (7 pcs.), **65c**

A5013–Embossed gold stippled edges large rose cluster in natural colors in centers, bowl 9¼ in. diam., six 5¼ in. nappies. SET (7 pcs.), **75c**

A5014–Edges tinted in orange, pink and tan, black and yellow bird and foliage design centers, bowl 9¼ in. diam., six 5¼-in. nappies. SET (7 pcs.), **85c**

A5015–2-tone double tint blended in pink and blue with large rose centers in bright colors, bowl 9¼ in. diam., six 5¼-in. nappies. SET (7 pcs.), **95c**

A5016–Asstd. pink, green and blue wide solid color band edge with parrot centers in bright natural colors, bowl 9¼ in. diam., six 5¼ in. nappies.....SET (7 pcs.), **$1.10**

CAKE PLATES

★**A6710**–Fresco shadow tints in blue orange and pink on edge with gold stamp medallion and rose cluster center, diam. 9¼ in. Doz. **$1.75**

A5032–Decorated with gold band edge and inscription **GIVE US THIS DAY OUR DAILY BREAD** in gold, diam. 9¼ in.... Doz. **$2.25**

7-PC. CAKE SETS

A5017–Green, orange and pink asstd. tinted edges with bird and foliage centers in black and yellow. Cake plate 10 in. diam. Six 6¼-in. small plates........ Set. **85c**

A5018–2-tone double tint in pink and blue with bright colored rose cluster centers. Cake plate 10 in. diam. Six 6¼-in. small plates. Set. **95c**

8-PC. SALAD AND CAKE SET

A5019–Combination cake and salad set, consists of one 9¾x9¾-in. cake plate, one 8x8-in. salad bowl and six 8¼-in. plates, octagon shape, decorated in blue panel effect with bird and floral sprays in bright colors.......... Set. **$3.50**

SEMI-PORCELAIN GRILL PLATES

Pure white American semi-porcelain, extra heavy body, molded in 3 sections, glossy finish.

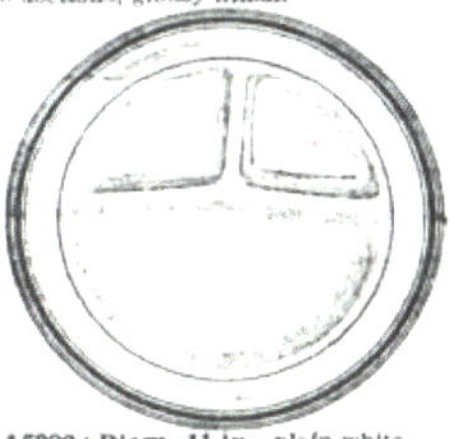

A5000–Diam. 11 in., plain white. Doz. **$6.00**

A5001–Diam. 11 in., decorated with green and brown shoulder lines. Doz. **$7.00**

SEMI-PORCELAIN GOLD MOTTO CUPS AND SAUCERS

Pure white, decorated with Mottoes in gold, ⅛-in. gold band, traced gold handles.

A6865–Cup 3¼x3¼ in. Saucer 6 in. **FATHER** Doz. (24 pcs.), **$2.25**

A6866–Cup 3¼x3¼ in. Saucer 6 in. **BROTHER** Doz. (24 pcs.), **$2.25**

Jumbo pure white, decorated with Mottoes in gold, ⅛-in. gold band, traced gold handles.

A6867–Cup 3¾x4 in., Saucer 6¾ in. **FATHER** Doz. (24 pcs.), **$3.25**

A6868–Cup 3¾x4 in., Saucer 6¾ in. **BROTHER** Doz. (24 pcs.), **$3.25**

SEMI-PORCELAIN LUSTER TINTED CUPS AND SAUCERS

Decorated with asstd. luster tints on edge, pink, green and blue, asstd. bird and flower decalcomanias.

A5022–Cup 3¼x3½ in., Saucer 6 in. Doz. (24 pcs.), **$2.25**

Jumbo decorated with asstd. luster tints on edge, pink, green and blue, asstd. bird and flower decalcomanias.

A5023–Cup 3¾x4 in., Saucer 5¾ in. Doz. (24 pcs.), **$3.25**

SEMI-PORCELAIN GOLD BAND MUG

A6871–3½x3½ in., decorated 3 16 in. gold band edge, gold striped handles.. Doz. **$2.15**

SEMI-PORCELAIN BRIDGE SET

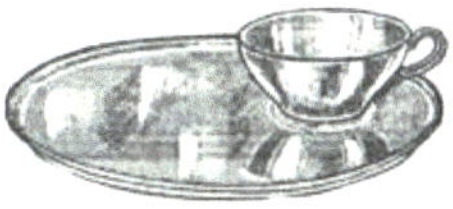

Decorated allover canary luster, high gloss finish. Set consists of 1 only 2¾x2½-in. cup and one 8¼-in. Bridge plate.

A5021–Pink .... Doz. sets. **$4.25**

A5021/1–Canary............ Doz. sets. **4.25**

AMERICAN SEMI-PORCELAIN 13-PC. LUSTER BRIDGE SET

Decorated allover luster, high gloss finish, white inside. Set consists of 4 Cups 2¾x2½ in., 4 Bridge Plates, 8¼ in. diam., 1 Teapot cap. 4 cups, 1 Sugar, ht. 4 in., 1 Creamer ht. 2¾ in.

A5021–Pink .... Set. **$2.95**

A5021/1–Canary.............. Set. **2.95**

REBECCA LUSTER TEAPOTS

Best fire-proof clay, glazed inside and outside. Old style Rebecca teapots with a new dress. Allover luster finish, raised designs decorated in colors, edges are all traced in black. Very effective and will prove big sellers for the Holidays.

A5025–Canary 42's.	Cap. 32 oz.	Doz.	**$7.50**
A5026–Rose 42's.	Cap. 32 oz.	Doz.	**7.50**
A5027–Ivory 42's.	Cap. 32 oz.	Doz.	**7.50**
A5028–Canary 30's.	Cap. 58 oz.	Doz.	**9.00**
A5029–Rose 30's.	Cap. 58 oz.	Doz.	**9.00**
A5030–Ivory 30's.	Cap. 58 oz.	Doz.	**9.00**

SEMI-PORCELAIN LUSTER COVERED JUG

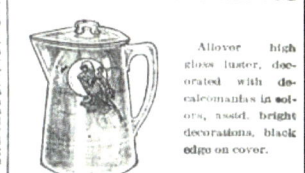

Allover high gloss luster, decorated with decalcomanias in colors, asstd. bright decorations, black edge on cover.

A5031–Green, ht. 8 in., cap. 1½ qt. Doz. **$9.00**

A5031/1–Rose, ht. 8 in., cap. 1½ qt. Doz. **$9.00**

A5031/2–Canary, ht. 8 in., cap. 1½ qt. Doz. **$9.00**

AMERICAN SEMI-PORCELAIN DINNER SETS

Floral and border patterns. Cream white ware with a soft color tone that blends very readily with these decorations. All pieces are full standard size and are guaranteed to be the best values on the market. See composition on page 121

Staple Bluebird decoration. Large sprays of bluebirds and small pink blossoms, and foliage all in natural colors, neat blue color line on edge, blue traced handles.

A05074—31-pc. Set...........................Set,	$3.15
A05075—42-pc. Set...........................Set,	4.50
A05076—51-pc. Set...........................Set,	7.25
A05077—100-pc. Set..........................Set,	14.25

Panel spray border entwined with flowers and foliage in delicate pink, blue and green, gold edge on all pieces and extra gold lines on all covered ware, gold traced handles and knobs.

A05054—42-pc. Set...........................Set,	$5.50
A05055—51-pc. Set...........................Set,	8.60
A05056—100-pc. Set..........................Set,	16.85

Dresden border, cream background, delicate green tracing, small sprays of June roses, black dotted edge, gold traced handles and knobs.

A05058—51-pc. Set...........................Set,	$9.25
A05059—100-pc. Set..........................Set,	18.25

Pheasant, basket and floral designs all in bright natural colors, blue line edge and hairline on flange, blue traced handles and knobs.

A05061—51-pc. Set...........................Set,	$10.35
A05062—100-pc. Set..........................Set,	20.50

Pansy decoration, 5 sprays of yellow, blue and red Pansies and clusters of green leaves, orange color edge and hairline on flange, orange traced handles and knobs. A very pleasing decoration.

A05063—51-pc. Set...........................Set,	$10.35
A05064—100-pc. Set..........................Set,	20.50

Blue & yellow combination border with medallion roses and forget-me-nots in natural colors, gold edge and hairline on flange, gold traced handles and knobs.

A05065—51-pc. Set...........................Set,	$11.50
A05066—100-pc. Set..........................Set,	22.50

Floral medallion with roses and festoons of forget-me-nots and foliage in natural colors, neat blue line on all pieces, blue traced handles.

A05050—31-pc. Set.......Set,	$2.35	A05052—51-pc. Set......Set,	$5.50
A05051—42-pc. Set.......Set,	3.50	A05053—100-pc. Set.....Set,	10.75

Decorated ⅝-in. gold band with extra band on all covered pieces, gold traced handles.

A05067—31-pc. Set.......Set,	$2.95	A05069—51-pc. Set......Set,	$7.15
A05068—42-pc. Set.......Set,	4.50	A05070—100-pc. Set.....Set,	14.00

Neat wide gold band edge; gold line on flange with extra gold line on handles and covered ware. Initial in gold on each piece. Specify initial desired.

A05071—42-pc. Set. (Specify initial)...................Set,	$6.25
A05072—51-pc. Set. (Specify initial)...................Set,	9.75
A05073—100-pc. Set. (Specify initial)..................Set,	18.95

Large floral spray of birds and flowers in a combination of black and tan, neat black color line on edge and tan line on flange, black traced line on handles.

A01635—42-pc. Set...........................Set	$5.25
A01636—51-pc. Set...........................Set	8.25
A01637—100-pc. Set..........................Set	16.25

JAPANESE CHINA DINNER SETS

Light wt., pure white strong, translucent china body. Popular shapes attractively decorated by skilled artists in the newest designs and color combinations. Each set securely packed in case. No packing charge. See composition on page 122.

Delicate Yellow and Black fresco border linked with small Pink rose clusters in Black border frame, Ivory band flange, edges gold traced, gold covered handles.
AO6003—100-pc., Dinner Set ....Set, $33.75
AO6000—52-pc., Dinner Set ....Set, $17.50

Narrow lace design border on black background, natural color fruit medallions, ⅝-in. delicate ivory band, coin gold covered handles, gold edges and hairlines.
AO6004—100-pc., Dinner Set..........Set, $37.25
AO6001—52-pc., Dinner Set............Set, $19.50

Neat ivory band beautifully enriched with natural bright colored flower and fruit medallions, Black border edge, coin gold handles, gold traced edges and hairlines.
AO6005—100-pc., trade marked "NORITAKE." Set, $41.75
AO6002—52-pc., trade marked "NORITAKE." Set, $21.50

Bright colored flowers and foliage with large center decoration, light brown edge and shoulder band, gold shoulder hairline, gold covered handles and traced edges.
AO6012—100-pc., trademarked "NORITAKE." Set, $47.50
AO6007—52-pc., trade-marked "NORITAKE." Set, $24.00

Wide ivory band with lace effect border linked with small pink rosebuds, dark background, gold shoulder hairline, gold covered handles and traced edges.
AO6011—100-pc., trade-marked "NORITAKE." Set, $47.50
AO6006—52-pc., trade-marked "NORITAKE." Set, $24.00

Dark brown openwork border, black edged, Royal blue scroll designs with natural color pink roses, ivory band, coin gold covered handles, gold traced edges and hairlines.
AO6013—100-pc., trade marked "NORITAKE." Set, $49.50
AO6008—52-pc., trade marked "NORITAKE." Set, $26.50

BAVARIAN CHINA DINNER SETS

Best quality, pure white translucent European china. Artistically decorated with neat designs and color combinations. Each set securely packed in case. No packing charge. For composition see page 122.

Decorated with clusters of Pink floral sprays and foliage in natural colors, gold striped edge, coin gold covered handles.
AO19036—100-pc. Set...............Set, $29.50
AO19044—51-pc. Set................Set, $16.75

Neat border, panel effect, joined with Pink roses and small black leaflets on Ivory background edged with Tan color line, gold striped edge, coin gold covered handles.
AO9040—100-pc. Set...............Set, $42.50

Tan fresco band on edge enriched with stencil and Pink rose clusters with natural color foliage, gold striped edge, coin gold covered handle.
AO9041—100-pc. Set...............Set, $42.50

Empire rose decoration, Tan border with small Pink roses and foliage in empire wreath effect, bouquet and basket in scroll frame, gold traced edge, coin gold covered handles.
AO19039—100-pc. Set..............Set, $45.00

Blue and Tan border, rose and orange blossoms in Blue scroll effect frame, gold striped, coin gold covered handles.
AO9043—100-pc. Set...............Set, $45.00

Matt gold ½-in. band with neat black Laurel wreath decoration. Matt gold covered handles, all covered pieces have gold lines.
AO19042—100-pc. Set..............Set, $82.50

HAVILAND FRENCH CHINA DINNER SETS— FOR COMPOSITION OF DINNER SETS SEE PAGE 122

(Haviland–Abott., Limoges, France)

Pure white, light weight translucent body, high glossy finish, Pompadour shape, embossed basket weave panel effect, attractively decorated. MATT GOLD HANDLES. 100-pc. Sets service for twelve. Each piece trade marked Haviland, Limoges.

Popular basket of flowers decoration. Tan color wicker design basket filled with large pink roses and trailing arbutus with natural foliage, all in their natural colors, large roses and dainty rosebud sprays.
AO12346—100-pc. Set......................Set. $35.00

Rose decoration. Bright pink bursting rosebuds in clusters with green foliage, made more attractive with black, tan and purple sprays.
AO12337—100-pc. Set......................Set. $35.00

Decorated with vine and blossom clusters and large Bird of Paradise center, green and black color scheme, enlivened with blue, tan and pink.
AO12170—100-pc. Set......................Set. $35.00

SEMI-PORCELAIN DINNER SETS

ATTRACTIVE INDIAN TREE DECORATION
American Semi-Porcelain

Pure white, strong semi-porcelain body, lightweight. Beautifully decorated with large clusters of crimson blossoms and small bright flowers with yellow centers, natural color dark brown branches and bright green foliage, neat brown band on edge, green color line. See composition on page 121.

AO5838—51-pc. Set.................................Set. $11.63
AO5839—100-pc. Set...............................Set. 23.50

FAMOUS BLUE WILLOW DECORATION
American Semi-Porcelain

Lightweight, pure white, semi-porcelain body, attractive shape, decorated with famous old blue willow landscape and water scenes, birds and flowers, blue color line on edges, handles and covered ware. See composition on page 121.

AO5835—42-pc. Set...............................Set. $ 5.47
AO5836—51-pc. Set...............................Set. 8.4
AO5837—100-pc. Set..............................Set. 17.47

DECORATED SEMI-PORCELAIN TABLEWARE

Homer Laughlin SECOND SELECTION. Good salable merchandise at a very low price. All staple pieces, used every day. We give actual and trade size.

Decorated with Gold Floral Stamp

STAR VALUE A2300—Cups and Saucers (24 pcs)	Doz. $1.25

	Act.				Doz.
A2301—Plates	4 in.	6 in.			.60
A2302—Plates	5 in.	7 in.			.68
A2303—Plates	6 in.	8½ in.			.82
A2304—Plates	7 in.	9½ in.			.95
A2305—Plates	8 in.	10½ in.			1.20
A2306—Coupes	7 in.	8½ in.			1.20
A2307—Bakers	5 in.	7 in.			1.20
A2308—Bakers	6 in.	8 in.			1.50
A2309—Bakers	7 in.	9 in.			1.80
A2310—Bakers	8 in.	10 in.			2.70
A2311—Dishes	6 in.	8 in.			1.05
A2312—Dishes	8 in.	10 in.			1.50
A2313—Dishes	10 in.	13 in.			2.70
A2314—Fruits	4 in.	5¼ in.			.45
A2315—Nappies	5 in.	6¾ in.			1.20
A2316—Nappies	6 in.	7 in.			1.50
A2317—Nappies	7 in.	8½ in.			1.80
A2318—Nappies	8 in.	9½ in.			2.70
A2319—Oatmeals	36's	6 in.			.95

Bluebird Decoration

STAR VALUE A2400—Cups and Saucers (24 pc.)	Doz. $1.35

	Act.				Doz.
A2401—Plates	4 in.	6 in.			.67
A2402—Plates	5 in.	7 in.			.67
A2403—Plates	6 in.	8½ in.			.90
A2404—Plates	7 in.	9½ in.			1.15
A2405—Plates	8 in.	10½ in.			1.55
A2406—Coupes	7 in.	8½ in.			1.25
A2407—Bakers	5 in.	7 in.			1.25
A2408—Bakers	6 in.	8 in.			1.58
A2409—Bakers	7 in.	9 in.			1.90
A2410—Bakers	8 in.	10 in.			2.80
A2411—Dishes	6 in.	8 in.			1.10
A2412—Dishes	8 in.	10 in.			1.58
A2413—Dishes	10 in.	13 in.			2.80
A2414—Fruits	4 in.	5¼ in.			.50
A2415—Nappies	5 in.	6¾ in.			1.25
A2416—Nappies	6 in.	7 in.			1.58
A2417—Nappies	7 in.	8½ in.			1.90
A2418—Nappies	8 in.	9½ in.			2.80
A2419—Oatmeals	36's	6 in.			1.05

DECORATED JAPANESE SEMI-PORCELAIN TEAPOTS

White semi-porcelain highly glazed inside and outside, perforated strainer, Oriental and floral decorations in bright colors.

A6154—3-cup size ....Doz. $2.25
A6155—4-cup size ....Doz. 3.95
A6156—6-cup size ....Doz. 6.50

BROWN JAPANESE CHINA TEAPOTS

Light wt. China body, brown glossy finish inside and outside, perforated strainer, notched lid which prevents it from falling off, popular square shape.

A509—3-cup size ....Doz. $2.10
A510—4-cup size ....Doz. 3.75
A511—5-cup size ....Doz. $4.25
A512—6-cup size ....Doz. 6.00

SEMI-PORCELAIN WARE

15-PC. IMPORTED DECORATED SEMI-PORCELAIN CEREAL SETS

Pure white glossy finish, light weight semi-porcelain, decorated in neat attractive colors, 15-pc. sets, all have tight fitting covers and easy to grasp handles, clear black lettered names on each piece.

Composition: 1 VINEGAR BOTTLE, ht. 9½ in.; 1 OIL BOTTLE, ht. 9½ in.; 6 CEREAL JARS, ht. 8½ in.; 6 SPICE JARS, ht. 4 in.; 1 SALT BOX (wooden cover), ht. 6¾ in.

A641—Clear white highly glazed semi-porcelain body, blue and white block border on 3 sides blue lined panels .... Set (15 pcs.) **$3.45**

A642—Clear white highly glazed semi-porcelain body, Delft blue Dutch landscape decoration, blue block and dotted lined border on 3 sides ..... Set (15 pcs.) **$3.25**

A643 — Clear white highly glazed semi-porcelain, with famous Delft blue old Dutch windmill scene; Set (15 pcs.) **$3.75**

A645—Clear white highly glazed semi-porcelain body, old Dutch landscape and water scene, blue, yellow and a light shade of green .... Set (15 pcs.) **$4.50**

JAPANESE CHINA DINNER SET
Coin Gold Handles and Band
Trademark "NORITAKE"—(Service for Six.)

AO26—Pure white transparent china, coin gold edge, coin gold covered handles. Set comprises the following:

6 only Cups, 3 5/12x2 in.	6 only Fruits, 5¼ in.
6 only Saucers, 5½ in.	1 only Cream Pitcher, 4½x3¼ in.
6 only B. & B. Plates, 6½ in.	1 only Meat Platter, 11¾x8¾ in.
6 only Dinner Plates, 9½ in.	1 only Baker, 10½x7¾.
6 only Coupe Soups, 7¾ in.	1 only Cov. Sugar, 4x6 in.

41-pc. set in case **$9.50**

8 sets in case. (Total $53.50) **8.75**

IMPORTED ENGLISH BLUE WILLOW DINNERWARE

Genuine imported lightweight English semi-porcelain, famous underglazed dark blue "Pekin" allover decoration, absolutely will not craze. Each pc. trade marked. For composition of Dinner Sets see page 131.

AO6115—51-pc. Dinner Set .... Set.	$	9.50
AO6150—100-pc. Dinner Set .... Set,		19.75
AO6160—Cups and Saucers only .... Doz. (24 pcs.)		2.40
AO6161—Plates 7 in., actually 9½ in. only .... Doz.		2.25

LIGHTWEIGHT SEMI-PORCELAIN DINNER SETS

Pure white, no better quality ware made. The neatest dinner patterns ever put on the market at such low prices. See composition on page 121.

Narrow gold band edge with hairline on flange, full traced handles. All hollow pieces have extra hairlines in gold.

A4/42—42-pc. DINNER SET.	Shipping wt. 42 lbs.	Set of 42 pcs.	**$3.97**
A4/51—51-pc. DINNER SET.	Shipping wt. 51 lbs.	Set of 51 pcs.	6.44
A4/100—100-pc. DINNER SET.	Shipping wt. 100 lbs.	Set of 100 pcs.	12.64

Medium blue band with gold hairline, full color traced handles. All hollow pieces have extra hairlines in gold.

A5/42—42-pc. DINNER SET.	Shipping wt. 42 lbs.	Set of 42 pcs.	**$3.97**
A5/51—51-pc. DINNER SET.	Shipping wt. 51 lbs.	Set of 51 pcs.	6.44

CHINAWARE — LIGHTING GOODS

23-PC. TEA SETS

Light weight European china, decorated in a variety of bright colors in the latest designs. All standard size pieces. For composition see page 120

A19022—23-pc. fancy shape, wide green shadow tint border in panel effect, birds and flowers in natural colors..........................Set, $3.50

A4914—23-pc. solid green color outside, plain white inside, neat black line edges........ Set, $5.25
A4911—23-pc. Ox-blood color outside, plain white inside, neat black line edges........ Set, $5.25

A19024—23-pc. fancy shape, allover mother-of-pearl luster, gold floral border, attractive birds and flowers in natural colors.......Set, $6.00

A19023—23-pc. fancy shape, allover flower and foliage decoration in green, pink and yellow, edged with black, gold traced edges.........Set, $6.25

7-PC. CAKE SETS

Light weight china body, decorated in a variety of colors and designs. Set consists of one 10-in. cake plate and six 7-in. individuals to match.

A19010—Wide green luster border, gold stamp edge, large peacock and floral centers in natural colors, shadow foliage, cutout handles.......Set, $2.35

A19011—Allover mother-of-pearl luster, gold stamp border, large flower and foliage centers in natural colors.......Set, $2.95

HAND-PAINTED PARCHMENT PAPER CANDLE SHADES

A10—5¼ x3½ in., tinted and decorated in asstd colors and designs, fruit, flowers and birds, black edges, heavy cardboard holder fits over top of bulb.

1 doz. asstd. in pkg.

(Gro. $10.00); Doz. 85c

HAND-PAINTED JAPANESE SILK CANDLE OR BOUDOIR SHADE

A11—4½ x4½ in., octagon shape, canary and rose asstd. solid color silk tightly stretched on wire frame, hand-painted floral decorations. Snap spring fits over bulb. 1 doz. asstd. colors in pkg. ....Doz. $2.25

CARVED TEAKWOOD TABOURETTE

Made of hard light weight wood, hand carved turned wood top, highly polished, jet black finish.

AO1289—Ht. 18 in., width 12 in. ....Each, $7.50
AO1290—Ht. 24 in., width 13 in. ....Each, $9.50

DECORATED CRYSTAL GLASS PARLOR LAMP

AO271—Ht 26 in., crystal glass, raised grape, rose and vintage decoration in bright colors on gold bronze background. No.2 brass shrunk-on collar. No. 2 burner; large decorated globe chimney to match. 6 complete in bbl., wt. 65 lbs.

Each 95c

CRYSTAL GLASS LAMPS DECORATED WITH WIDE GOLD BAND

Shrunk-on collars, complete with No. 2 burners and decorated chimneys. No wicks.

AO270—Two styles. Asstd. as follows: ¼ doz. stand lamps, ht. 18 in. ¼ doz. sewing lamps, ht. 17½ in. Total, 12 in bbl., wt. 85 lbs. ....Each, 85c

DECORATED LAMP ASST.

AO1422—Asstd. rose and blue decoration with large red roses, complete with No. 2 burners and chimneys to match. 1 doz. ht. 18½ in. and 1 doz. ht. 17 in., total, 24 in bbl., no less sold.

Doz. $9.00

HIGH GRADE SOLID BRASS CANDELABRUM

Genuine Cut Glass Prisms

AO3032 – 2-lt. Candelabrum, ht. 18 in., spread 12 in., solid brass shaft and arms, 6½x5-in. metal base, finished in Spanish brass, ornamented with cut glass amber prisms. Complete with switch and frosted bulbs.

Each complete, $10.50

PORTABLE BRONZE DESK LAMP

AO594 — Ht. 18 in., felt base 6 in., bronze finish, flexible arm. Complete with 6-ft. silk cord and 2-pc. connection plug, turn knob socket. Each in carton. (Less electric bulbs). 1 doz. in case.

Doz. $24.00
(Less than case.)
Each, $2.15

ART DECORATED GLASS SHADE BOUDOIR LAMPS

Wired ready for use. Prices do not include bulbs. Well designed metal stand, ivory and antique gold finish, ht. 13½ in., solid brass key socket, cord and 2-pc. connection plug.

A8118   A8114

A8118—Antique gold stand, 7½ in., floral and embossed, salmon tinted shade. Each, $1.95
A8114—Ivory stand, 7¼ in., hand-painted shade, landscape and lake scene in colors on light pink background.......Each, $2.35
A8114/1—Antique gold stand, 7¼ in., hand-painted shade, landscape and lake scenes in colors on blue background..Each, $2.35

DE-LUXE DESK OR READING LAMPS

Green Cased Glass Shades 8½x4½ in.

6-ft. silk cord and 2-pc. connection plugs, pull-chain sockets, heavy metal ornamental base, adjustable shade holder. Each in carton.

AO795—Ht. 8 in., base 6½x6½ in., pompeian bronze finish, adjustable arm.

Each, $5.25

AO796 — Ht 18 in., base 6½x6½ in., verde green finish, adjustable arm.

Each, $6.50

EARTHENWARE and STONEWARE

RED CLAY FLOWER POTS AND SAUCERS

A0778 — Embossed porous body, mold made, hand-finished. Asstd. as follows:

2 doz. 4-in. flower pots and saucers.
2 doz. 5-in. flower pots and saucers.
2 doz. 6-in. flower pots and saucers.
1 doz. 7-in. flower pots and saucers.
1 doz. 8-in. flower pots and saucers.
Total, 96 pots and saucers in crate, no less sold. ....Crate. **$9.25**

A0779½—Embossed porous clay body, mold made, hand finished. Asst. as follows:

2½ doz. 5-in. flower pots and saucers.
2½ doz. 6-in. flower pots and saucers.
2½ doz. 7-in. flower pots and saucers.
Total, 90 pots and saucers in crate, no less sold..............Crate, **$10.25**

A0779 — Embossed porous body, mold made, hand-finished. Asstd. as follows:

1 doz. 8-in. flower pots and saucers.
½ doz. 9-in. flower pots and saucers.
½ doz. 10-in. flower pots and saucers.
½ doz. 12-in. flower pots and saucers.

Total, 30 pots and saucers in crate, no less sold. ....Crate, **$11.25**

RUSTIC JARDINIERES

Suitable for 7-in. flower pot

A0783— Diam. 8 in. hard fired clay body, decorated in gray brown bisque, large stock colors. Pkd 1 doz. each. Total 3 doz. asstd. in crate. Doz. **$2.67**

JAPANESE KOCHI JARDINIERES

Light weight hard semi-porcelain body, beautifully raised flowers and fancy designs, high luster glazed, asstd. blends: orange, green and dark brown. Asst. contains
1 only 3¾x2½ in.
1 only 5¼x4 in.
1 only 9x7½ in.
1 only 7x5½ in.
Total 4 asstd. sizes in nest,
A106—Per nest of 4. Nest, **$2.95**
A0106—Same as A400 12 nests in case...Nest, **$2.75**

DECORATED POTTERY ASST.

A0788—Hard earthenware body, allover marbleized finish in yellow and dark backgrounds, highly glazed inside and outside. Asstd. contains
4 only 8½-in. jardinieres.
4 only 6½-in. jardinieres.
4 only 7½-in. vases.
4 only 8½-in. vases.
4 only 6-in. candlesticks.
4 only 4-in. candlesticks.

Total 2 doz. pcs. asstd. in bbl. ......(Total $9.60); Doz. **$4.80**

WHITE GRANITE FLUTED CHAMBERS
Covered

A208—9s........Doz. **$8.50**
A209—6s........Doz. **9.65**

FLUTED CHAMBERS
Uncovered

A1875—9s......Doz. **$5.50**
A1876—6s......Doz. **6.65**

HANGING FLOWER HOLDER

A4002—Largely used for decoration of porches, lawns, etc. Hard porous red clay body, molded design, 3 wire hangers, 9x4 in. Doz. **$1.85**

JAPANESE EARTHENWARE WALL FLOWER VASE ASST.
Embossed and Hand Decorated

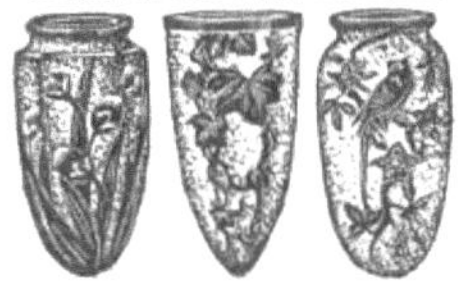

A500—Ht. 7½ in., 3 asstd. shapes, light wt. earthenware body, rustic finish in red, blue and yellow with bright hand painted and embossed birds, flowers and foliage.
½ doz. in pkg..................Doz. **$3.75**

STONEWARE BAKING PANS

A0787 — Diam. 9¼ in., extra hard embossed body, dark brown glazed inside and outside, 4 doz. pkd. in crate. Doz. **$1.50**

ART DECORATED JARDINIERE ASST.

A0789—Hard earthenware body, allover marbleized finish in shaded tones of yellow and dark green, highly glazed inside and outside. Asst. contains:

4 only 6½-in. jardinieres.
4 only 8½-in. jardinieres.
4 only 10½-in. jardinieres.

Total 1 doz. asstd. sizes in bbl. Doz. **$9.00**

DECORATED TOKONOBE GIFT SHOP ASSORTMENTS
Embossed and Hand Decorated

Light weight earthenware body, asstd. colored rustic finishes, raised and embossed flowers, birds and foliage in bright showy colors outlined with gold. Staple numbers to sell at popular prices.

All good selling items on which you can make a good profit.

A0400—Light weight earthenware, asstd. color rustic finishes, raised and embossed flowers and birds in bright, showy colors, outlined in gold. Asst. contains 36 all-the-year-round good selling pieces.

	Sell For	Total
4 only Jardinieres, 5 in.	$ .50 Each	$ 2.00
4 only Jardinieres, 7½ in.	1.00 Each	4.00
4 only Jardinieres 10 in.	3.00 Each	12.00
2 only Vases 5 in.	.35 Each	.70
2 only Vases 6 in.	.50 Each	1.00
2 only Vases 7½ in.	.75 Each	1.50
2 only Vases 8 in.	1.00 Each	2.00
2 only Vases 10 in.	1.25 Each	2.50
2 only Vases 12 in.	2.00 Each	4.00
3 only Bulb Bowls 6 in.	.50 Each	1.50
3 only Bulb Bowls 7½ in.	.75 Each	2.25
3 only Bulb Bowls 8½ in.	1.00 Each	3.00
3 only Bulb Bowls 9½ in.	1.50 Each	4.50

Total 36 pcs. in case............Total Resale Value **$40.95**

Cost to you.....**$19.50**
Your profit.......**$21.45**

10-IN. TOKONOBE VASE ASST.

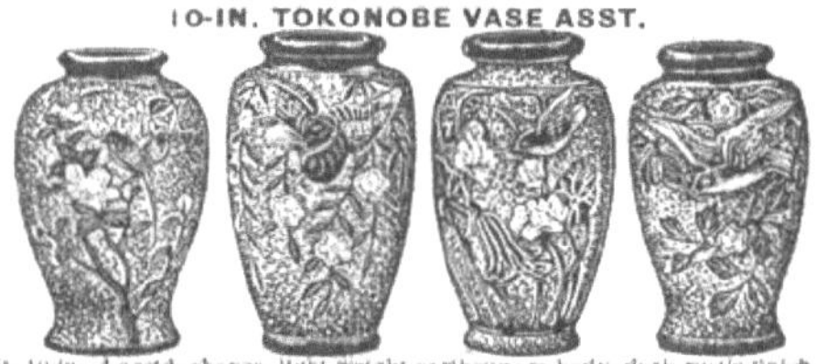

A0403—Ht. 10 in., 4 asstd. shapes, light weight earthenware body, dark rustic finish, embossed flowers, foliage and birds, bright hand-painted colors, outlined with gold. 2 doz. asstd. in case. Doz. **$7.20**
A403/1—1 doz. in case.............................Doz. **7.80**

12¾-IN. TOKONOBE VASE ASST.

Ht. 12¾ in., 4 asstd. shapes, light weight earthenware body, asstd. color rustic finish embossed flowers, birds and foliage, bright hand-painted colors, outlined with gold asstd. in case.
A0401—2 doz. in case..........................Doz. **$12.00**
A401/1—1 doz. in case..........................Doz. **13.50**
A401/2—............................Each, **1.25**

TOKONOBE JARDINIERES

Tan finish outside, brown inside, embossed and hand decorated in bright colors, traced with gold panel effect. Asst. contains
1 only 7½-in. Jardiniere }
1 only 10-in. Jardiniere } Nested.

A402—Single nest (2 pcs.) ...... Nest, **$1.95**

A402½—Three nests (6 pcs.) .... Nest, **1.75**

WHITE AMERICAN SEMI-PORCELAIN TABLEWARE

SHIPPED FROM BALTIMORE — Pure white semi-porcelain body, extra hard fired glaze, all standard sizes and shapes. We give both actual and trade sizes. Every piece warranted not to craze. Cups and saucers are counted 24 pcs. to the doz. — NO PACKAGE CHARGE ON ANY GOODS

FANCY TEA CUP AND SAUCER

12 Cups and 12 Saucers to doz.

A1800–Cups 2½x3½ in., saucers 5½ in. .... Doz. $1.35

ST. DENIS TEA CUPS AND SAUCERS

12 Cups and 12 Saucers to doz.

A1803–Cups 3½x3¼ in., saucers 6½ in .... Doz. $1.35
A1804–Cups only .... Doz. 95c
A1805–Saucers only .... Doz. 50c

ST. DENIS COFFEE CUPS AND SAUCERS

12 Cups and 12 Saucers to doz.

A1806–Cups 3½x3¼ in., saucers 6¾ in .... Doz. $1.90
A1807–Cups only .... Doz. 1.30
A1808–Saucers only .... Doz. 55c

PLATES

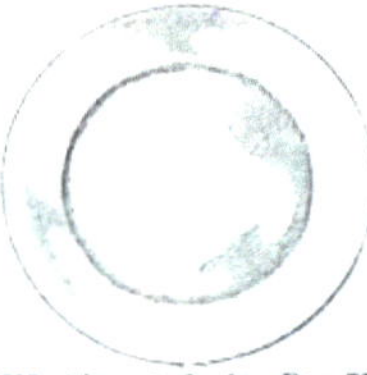

A1809–4-in., act. 6 in. .Doz. $0.70
A1810–5-in., act. 7⅛ in. .Doz. .77
A1811–6-in., act. 8⅜ in. .Doz. .95
A1812–7-in., act. 9⅜ in. .Doz. 1.15
A1813–8-in., act. 10½ in. .Doz. 1.45

SOUP PLATES

A1814–7-in., act. 9½ in. .Doz. $1.40
A1815–8-in., act. 10⅜ in. .Doz. 1.65

INDIVIDUAL MEAT PLATTERS—Hotel Thick

A1816–2½-in. act. 5¼ in. Doz. $1.05
A1817–3 -in. act. 6¼ in. Doz. 1.05
A1818–4 -in. act. 7¼ in. Doz. 1.05
A1819–5 -in. act. 8¼ in. Doz. 1.15

MEAT PLATTERS

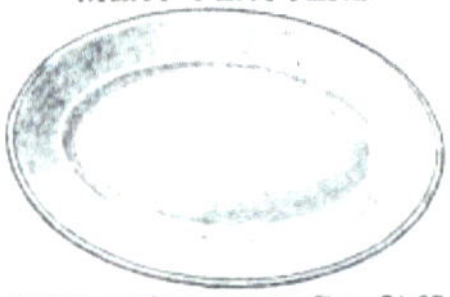

A1820– 6-in. act. 9¼ in. .Doz. $1.25
A1821– 8-in. act. 11⅜ in. Doz. 1.75
A1822–10-in. act. 13¼ in. Doz. 3.15
A1823–12-in. act. 15 in. Doz. 5.25

SHELL NAPPIES

A1852–5-in. act. 6¼ in. ... Doz. $1.40
A1853–6-in. act. 7½ in. ... Doz. 1.75
A1854–7-in. act. 8½ in. ... Doz. 2.10
A1855–8-in. act. 9⅜ in. ... Doz. 3.15
A1856–9-in. act. 10 in. ... Doz. 4.20

VEGETABLE DISHES OR BAKERS

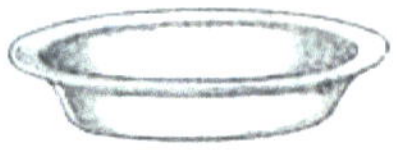

A1832–5 in. act. 7¼ in. .Doz. $1.40
A1833–6-in. act. 8¼ in. .Doz. 1.75
A1834–7-in. act. 9½ in. .Doz. 2.10
A1835–8-in. act. 10 in. .Doz. 3.15
A1836–9-in. act. 11 in. .Doz. 4.20

HALL BOY JUG

A1850–24s, ht. 6¼ in. ... Doz. $3.55

MIXING BOWLS

A1837–42s, act. 5¼ in. Doz. $1.05
A1838–36s, act. 6 in. Doz. 1.25
A1839–30s, act. 6¾ in. Doz. 1.50
A1840–24s, act. 7¼ in. Doz. 1.75
A1841–18s, act. 8¼ in. Doz. 2.65
A1842–12s, act. 9¼ in. Doz. 3.50
A1843– 9s, act. 11 in. Doz. 5.05
A1844– 6s, act. 11¾ in. Doz. 6.60

BOWLS

OYSTER

A1848–30s, cap. 1½ pts. .Doz. $1.75

ST. DENIS

A1845–36s, cap. 1 pt. .Doz. $1.40
A1846–30s, cap. 1½ pts. .Doz. 1.75
A1847–24s, cap. 2 pts. .Doz. 2.10

DAIRY MUG

A1851–Handled .... Doz. $1.55

JUGS AND PITCHERS

A1824–36s, cap. 1 pt .Doz. $2.45
A1825–30s, cap. 2 pts .Doz. 2.80
A1826–24s, cap. 3 pts .Doz. 3.50
A1827–12s, cap. 4 pts .Doz. 4.75
A1828– 6s, cap. 6 pts .Doz. 7.00

INDIVIDUAL VEGETABLE DISHES OR BAKERS—Hotel Thick

A1829–2½-in. act. 4½ in. .Doz. $1.25
A1830–3 -in. act. 5¼ in. .Doz. 1.25
A1831–4 -in. act. 6¾ in. .Doz. 1.25

FRUIT SAUCER

A1849–4-in. act. 5¼ in. .... Doz. 53c

FANCY OATMEAL

A1858–Diam. 5 in. .... Doz. $1.10

SOAP DISH

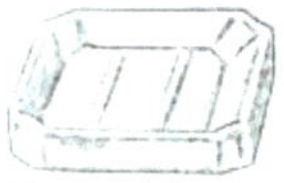

A1859–Size 4½x3¾ in. .Doz. $1.05

DOUBLE EGG CUP

A1857–4½x2½ in. .... Doz. $1.25

SEMI-PORCELAIN DINNERWARE—In Open Stock

Light Weight American Semi-Porcelain, Standard Size. Artistic Border Decorations of the Latest Creations with Bright Gold Covered Handles. Sold in Open Stock. No Package Charge. For Composition of Sets See Page 121.

CAMEO ROSE DINNERWARE

Two-tone blue scroll panel, small pink rose medallions, gold-traced edge and verge line, bright gold covered handles.

A934—51-pc. Set. Set, **$11.65**

Cups and Saucers.
A913 — Cup 3½x2¼ in., saucer 5¾ in. Doz. (24 pcs.) $3.70

Plates
A914 — 4 in., actually 6¼ in. .... Doz. $1.60
A915 — 5 in., actually 7⅛ in. .... Doz. $1.85
A916 — 7 in., actually 9⅛ in. .... Doz. $2.88
A917 — 8 in., actually 9¾ in. .... Doz. $3.50

Coupe Soup Plate
A918 — 6 in., actually 8 in. .... Doz. $2.68

Baker or Open Vegtable Dish
A919—7 in., actually 9¼x7 in. .... Doz. $5.00

Dishes or Meat Platters
A920—8 in., actually 11¼x5⅝ in. .... Doz. $4.20
A921—10 in., actually 13x9¾ in. .... Doz. $7.50
A922—12 in., actually 15¼x11 in. .... Doz. $12.35

A935—100-pc. Set. Set, **$23.25**

Fruit or Individual Side Dish
A923— 4 in., actually 5⅝ in. .... Doz. $1.25

Pickle
A924—Actually 9½x4¾ in. Doz. $5.00

Salad Dish or Deep Round Vegetable Dish
A925—7 in., actually 8¼x2¾ in. .... Doz. $5.00

Covered Butter Dish and Drainer
A926—Diam. 7 in. Doz. $15.00

Covered Vegetable or Steak Dish
A927—7 in., actually 11x6¾ in. .... Doz. $17.40

Cream Pitcher
A928—42s, capacity 12 oz. Doz. $5.00

Sauce Boat
A929—Size 7½x3¾ in. Doz. $6.60

Covered Sugar
A930—30s, size 6½x4¼ in. Doz. $9.90

LUXOR BORDER DINNERWARE

Black and gold, pink rose scroll panels on black gold background, gold-traced edge and verge line, bright gold covered handles.

A736—51-pc. Set. Set, **$13.50**

Cup and Saucer
A716—Cup 3x2¼ in., Saucer 5¾ in. Doz. (24 pc.) $4.25

Plates
A717 — 4 in., actually 6¼ in. .... Doz. $1.90
A718 — 5 in., actually 7⅛ in. .... Doz. $2.15
A719 — 7 in., actually 9⅛ in. .... Doz. $3.30
A720 — 8 in., actually 9¾ in. .... Doz. $4.00

Coupe Soup Plate
A721 — 6 in., actually 8 in. .... Doz. $3.30

Baker or Open Vegetable Dish
A722—7 in., actually 9¼x7 in. .... Doz. $5.70

Dishes or Meat Platters
A723—8 in., actually 11¼x8⅝ in. .... Doz. $4.75
A724—10 in., actually 13x9¾ in. .... Doz. $8.50
A725—12 in., actually 15¼x11 in. .... Doz. $14.25

A737—100-pc. Set. Set, **$26.65**

Fruit or Individual Side Dish
A726 — 4 in., actually 5⅝ in. .... Doz. $1.40

Pickle Dish
A727—Size 9½x4¾ in. Doz. $5.70

Salad or Round Vegetable Dish
A728—7 in., diam. 8¼x2¾ in. .... Doz. $5.70

Covered Butter and Drainer
A729—Diam. 7 in. Doz. $17.10

Covered Vegetable or Steak Dish
A730—7 in., actually 11x6¾ in. .... Doz. $19.96

Cream Pitcher
A731—Capacity 12 oz. Doz. $5.70

Sauce or Gravy Boat
A732—Size 7½x3¾ in. Doz. $7.60

Covered Sugar
A733 — 30s, actually 6½x4¼ in. .... Doz. $11.40

TAN & ROSE BORDER DINNERWARE

Large pink rose cluster on black background, tan border with blue flowers and foliage, gold traced edge and shoulder, bright gold covered handles.

A1928— 42-pc. Set .... Set, $ 8.65
A1929— 51-pc. Set .... Set, 13.50
A1930—100-pc. Set .... Set, 26.65

Cup and Saucer.
A1905—Cup 3¼x2¼, saucer 5¾ in. Doz. (24 pcs.) $4.25

Plates.
A1906—4 in., act. 6¼. Doz. $1.90
A1907—5 in., act. 7 Doz 2.15
A1908—7 in., act. 9¼. Doz. $3.30
A1909—8 in., act. 9¾ Doz. $4.00

Coupe Soup Plates.
A1910—7 in., act. 8. Doz. $3.30

Baker or Open Vegetable Dish.
A1922—7 in., act. 9¼x7. Doz. $5.70

Dishes or Meat Platters.
A1911—8 in., act. 11¼x8⅝. Doz. $4.75
A1912—10 in., act. 13x9⅝. Doz. $8.50
A1913—12 in., act. 15¼x11. Doz. $14.25

Fruit or Side Dish.
A1914—4 in., act. 5⅝. Doz. $1.45

Pickle Dish.
A1915—9x4¾ in. Doz. $5.70

Round Vegetable Dish or Salad.
A1916—7 in., diam. 8¼x2¾. Doz. $5.70

Covered Butter and Drainer.
A1917—Diam. 7 in. Doz. $17.10

Covered Vegetable or Steak Dish.
A1918—7 in., act. 11x6¾. Doz. $19.95

Cream Pitcher.
A1919—Cap. 12 oz. Doz. $5.70

Sauce or Gravy Boat.
A1920—7½x3¾ in. Doz. $7.60

Covered Sugar.
A1921—30's, act. 6½x4¼ in. Doz. $11.40

HOMER LAUGHLIN Decorated American SEMI-PORCELAIN DINNERWARE

OPEN STOCK Pure white decorated semi-porcelain, lightweight, strong and durable, guaranteed against crazing. Has densely hard body, glazed so it will not readily break, chip or show criss-cross scratches as ordinary ware.

HOMER LAUGHLIN

WHITE HUDSON SEMI-PORCELAIN DINNERWARE

Pure White, Semi-vitrified body, will not craze. Light in weight, strong and durable. Neat, Attractive Shape, Very Serviceable.

DINNER SETS—See Composition of Sets Below

A135—31-pc. Set............Set, $2.30
A133—42-pc. Set............Set, 3.45
A134—51-pc. Set............Set, $5.45
A132—100-pc. Set............Set, 10.65

DINNERWARE IN OPEN STOCK

Teas and Saucers.
A100—Teas 3½x2½ in., saucers 6 in. Doz. (24 pcs.) $1.62

Coffee Cups and Saucers.
A102—Coffee Cups 3⅝x2⅝ in., saucers 6¼ in. Doz. (24 pcs.) $2.00

Plates.
A103—4 in., actual 6½-in..........Doz. 75c
A104—5 in., actual 7½-in..........Doz. 85c
A105—6 in., actual 8⅜-in..........Doz. $1.05
A106—7 in., actual 9⅜-in..........Doz. $1.25
A107—8 in., actual 9⅞-in..........Doz. $1.60

Fancy Bowls.
A112—5½x5⅜ in., capacity 23 oz....Doz. $1.90

Soup Plates.
A108 — 7 in., deep rim, actual 9 in....Doz. $1.50
A109—7 in., Coupe. Doz. $1.35

Bakers or Open Vegetable Dishes.
A111-7 in., actual 6¾x9-in..........Doz. $2.25

Individual Butters.
A113—3¼ in...Doz. 38c

Fruit or Individual Dishes, Round.
A117 — 4-in., actual 5½-in..........Doz. 57c

Dishes or Meat Platters.
A114—8-in., actual 8½x11¼ in........Doz. $2.00
A115-10 in., actual 10¼x13½ in........Doz. $3.60
A116-12 in., actual 11¾x15½ in........Doz. $6.00

Oatmeal Bowls.
A118—6 in....Doz. $1.18

Pickle Dishes, Oblong.
A119—3½x6¾ in. Doz. $2.28

Salad Dishes, Deep, Round.
A121-7 in., actual 8¼ in. Doz. $2.30

Covered Butter Dishes.
A122—8 in. Doz. $6.85

Covered Vegetable Dishes.
A123—6x8 in..Doz. $8.00

Cream Pitchers.
A124—Ht. 4½ in. Doz. $2.25

Jugs, Tall Shape.
A125—Ht. 7½ in., 24s. Doz. $3.80

Sauce or Gravy Boats.
A127—6½ in. Doz. $3.05

Sugar Bowls and Covers.
A128—Ht. 5 in. Doz. $4.60

"LOVE BIRD" DECORATED DINNERWARE

Pure white American semi-porcelain, neat new shape, decorated Forget-Me-Not, heart medallion, two love birds, ribbon bowknot and scrolls; small roses and twigs all in natural colors. Blue band edge, neat shoulder line, traced handles in blue. Sold in open stock or Sets.

DINNER SETS—See Composition of Sets Below

AO3837-42-pc. Dinner Set..........Set, $4.75
AO3838-51-pc. Dinner Set.......Set, $ 7.42
AO3839-100-Pc. Dinner Set..........Set, 14.74

DINNERWARE IN OPEN STOCK

Cups and Saucers.
A3813 — Cup 3½x2 in. Saucer 5½ in. Doz. (24 pcs.) $2.15

Coffee Cups and Saucers.
A3813½—Cup 3⅜x2⅜ in. saucer 6¼ in. Doz. (24 pcs.) $2.75

Plates.
A3814—4 in., actually 6-in..........Doz. $1.05
A3815—5 in., actually 7-in..........Doz. $1.15
A3816—6 in., actually 8-in..........Doz. $1.45
A3817-7 in., actually 8⅞-in..........Doz. $1.80
A3818-8 in., actually 9⅞-in..........Doz. $2.25

Soup Plates.
A3819—7 in., Coupe actually 8⅞ in. Doz. $1.85
A3834—7 in., deep rim, actual 9 in. Doz. $2.10

Fancy Bowls.
A3835—5½x5½ in., cap. 24 oz..........Doz. $2.65

Dishes or Meat Platters.
A3822 — 8 in., actually 7¼x11½ in. Doz. $2.65
A3823 — 10 in., actually 8¾x13⅛ in....Doz. $4.75
A3824 — 12 in., actually 10x15½ in. Doz. $7.80

Bakers or Open Vegetable Dishes.
A3820—7 in., actually 6x8⅝ in........Doz. $3.15

Individual Butters.
A3821—3¼ in. Doz. 55c

Fruit Saucers.
A3825—4 in., actually 5-in..........Doz. 80c

Oatmeals.
A3826 — 36s actually 6-in..........Doz. $1.65

Pickle Dish.
A3827—8½x5½ in. Doz $3.15

Salads, deep round.
A3828-7 in., actually 8½-in..........Doz. $3.15

Covered Butters.
A3829—7⅝ in. Doz. $9.45

Covered Steak Dishes.
A3830 — 7 in., actually 7¾x5½ in. Doz. $11.00

Cream Pitchers.
A3831—Capacity 9 oz. Doz. $3.15

Jugs.
A3836—Ht. 7¼ in., 24s. Doz. $6.25

Gravy Boats.
A3832—5¾ in. Doz. $4.20

Covered Sugars.
A3833—30s Ht. 3 in. Doz. $6.30

WIDE GOLD BAND DINNERWARE

Plain neat shape, decorated with 3/16-in. gold band. Body light in weight, strong and durable. Guaranteed against crazing.

DINNER SETS—See Composition of Sets Below

A656—31-Piece Set..........Set, $3.10
A653—42-Piece Set..........Set, 4.67
A654—51-Piece Set..........Set, $7.26
A655—100-Piece Set..........Set, 14.40

DINNERWARE IN OPEN STOCK

A600—Tea Cup, 3½x2 in. Saucer 5½ in. Doz. (24 pcs.) $2.25
A601—Coffee Cup, 3⅛x2½ in., Saucer 6 in. Doz. (24 pcs.) $2.70

Plates.
A602—4 in., act. 6 in. Doz. $1.03
A603—5 in., act. 7 in. Doz. $1.15
A604—6 in., act. 8 in. Doz. $1.41
A605—7 in., act. 8⅝ in. Doz. $1.80
A606—8 in., act. 9¾ in. Doz. $2.15

Soup Plates.
A607—7 in., deep rim, act. 8⅞ in.......Doz. $2.05
A608—Coupe, 7 in., act. 8 in..........Doz. $1.80

Baker or Open Vegetable Dish.
A609—7 in., act. 6½x8⅜-in..........Doz. $3.08

Fancy Bowl.
A610—3x5½ in., capacity 23 oz.....Doz. $2.56

Individual Butter.
A611—3½ in...Doz. 50c

Dishes or Meat Platters.
A612 — 8 in., act. 7¼x11½ in.......Doz. $2.56
A613—10 in., act. 8¾x13¼ in......Doz. $4.61
A614-12 in., act. 10x15½-in..........Doz. $7.69

Fruit Saucer.
A615—5 in., act. 5⅛ in. Doz. 77c

Oatmeal Bowl.
A616—6 in...Doz. $1.62

Pickle Dish.
A617—5½x8½ in. Doz. $3.08

Salad Dish, Deep Round.
A618—7 in., act. 8⅜ in. Doz. $3.08

Covered Butter Dish.
A619—7⅞ in..Doz. $9.25

Covered Vegetable Dish.
A620—7 in., act. 5½x7⅜-in..........Doz. $10.75

Cream Pitcher.
A621—Ht. 2½ in., capacity 9 oz......Doz. $3.08

Jug.
A622—Ht. 6¼ in., capacity 3 pts....Doz. $5.13

Sauce or Gravy Boat.
A624—5¾ in..Doz. $4.10

Sugar Bowl and Cover.
A625—Ht. 3 in. Doz. $6.15

"KWALKER" WHITE AND BLUE BAND DECORATED DINNERWARE

Plain, neat and refined. 1/16-in. blue band on edges with shoulder. Hairline, extra blue color narrow band on all hollow pieces. Blue colored traced handles.

DINNER SETS—See Composition of Sets Below

A8328-42-Piece Dinner Set..Set, $4.78
A8329-51-Piece Dinner Set...Set, $7.45
A8330-100-Piece Dinner Set......Set, $14.75

DINNERWARE IN OPEN STOCK

Cups and Saucers.
A8303-Tea cups 3⅝x2⅛ in., saucers 5¾ in. Doz. (24 pcs.) $2.25
A8304-Coffee Cups 3¾x2⅛ in., saucers 6 in. Doz. (24 pcs.) 2.70

Plates.
A8305-4-in., act. 6 in. Doz. 1.05
A8306-5-in., act. 7 in. Doz. 1.18
A8307-6 in., act. 8 in. Doz. 1.44
A8308-7-in.,act.8⅞ in. Doz. 1.80
A8309-8-in., act.9¾ in. Doz. 2.23

Soup Plates.
A8310-7-in., deep rim, act. 9 in..........Doz. 2.10
A8311-7-in., coupe, act. 8 in............Doz. 1.85

Bakers or Open Vegetables.
A8312-7-in., act. 6⅝-x9 in..........Doz. $3.15

Fancy Bowls.
A8313-3x5½ in.. Doz. 2.65

Individual Butters.
A8314-3⅛ in.... Doz. .53

Dishes or Meat Platters.
A8315-8-in., act. 7⅛x11½..........Doz. 2.65
A8316-10-in., act. 9-x13⅜..........Doz. 4.75
A8317-12-in., act. 10x15½..........Doz. 7.88

Fruit Saucers.
A8318-4-in., act. 5⅛ in. Doz. .79

Oatmeal Bowls.
A8319-6-in....Doz. 1.64

Pickle Dishes.
A8327-5⅜x9....Doz. $3.15

Salad Dishes, Deep, Round.
A8320-7-in.,act. 8⅛ in. Doz. $3.15

Covered Butter Dishes.
A8321-7⅛ in...Doz. $9.50

Covered Vegetable Dishes.
A8322-7-in., act. 6⅝-x11 in..........Doz. $11.00

Cream Pitchers.
A8323-Ht. 2½ in., cap. 9 ozs..........Doz. 3.15

Jugs.
A8324-Ht. 6⅛ in., cap. 3 pts..........Doz. 5.25

Sauce or Gravy Boats.
A8325-8 in.....Doz. $4.20

Sugar Bowls and Covers.
A8326-Ht. 3⅛ in. Doz. $6.30

DINNER SET COMPOSITIONS

"31-Piece" Dinner Set
6 only Cups
6 only Saucers
6 only Plates, 4-in.
6 only Plates, 7-in.
6 only Fruits
1 only Dish, 8-in.
TOTAL..............31 pieces

No Charge for Package on Any Goods

"42-Piece" Dinner Set
6 only Cups
6 only Saucers
6 only Plates, 5-in.
6 only Plates, 7-in.
6 only Fruits, 4-in., deep
1 only Baker, 7-in.
6 only Individual Butters
1 only Dish, 8-in.
2 pc. Covd. Sugar, 30's
1 only Bowl, 30's
1 only Cream
TOTAL..............42 pieces

"51-Piece" Dinner Set
6 only 4-in. Plates
6 only 5-in. Plates
6 only 7-in. Plates
6 only 7-in. Coupe Soups
6 only Cups
6 only Saucers
6 only Desserts
1 only Meat Platter
1 only Open Vegetable Dish
1 only Sauce Boat
2 pc. Covd. Dish
1 only Pickle
2 pc. Covd. Sugar
1 only Cream
TOTAL..............51 pieces

"100-Piece" Dinner Set
12 only 4-in. Plates
12 only 5-in. Plates
12 only 7-in. Plates
12 only 7-in. Coupe Soups
12 only Desserts
12 only Cups
12 only Saucers
1 only Meat Platter, 8-in.
1 only Meat Platter, 10-in.
1 only Meat Platter, 12-in.
1 only Open Veg. Dish
2 pc. Oval Cov. Dish
2 pc. Round Cov. Dish
3 pc. Cov. Butter & Drainer
1 only Sauce Boat
1 only Pickle Dish
2 pc. Covered Sugar
1 only Cream
TOTAL..............100 pieces

CHINA, CROCKERY, SEMI-PORCELAIN

NOVELTY FIGURES

Earthenware body, allover jet black gloss finish, realistic models, natural painted features ornamental and decorative.

A506 A507 A505

A506—Ht. 6½ in., ½ doz. in pkg. . . . . Doz. $6.00
A507—6½x6½ in. ½ doz. in pkg. . . . . Doz. $7.20

A504—5⅝x4 in. ¼ doz. in pkg. . . . . Doz. $6.00
A505—7x4½ in. 1/12 doz. in pkg. . . . . Doz. $8.25

JAPANESE CHINA CUPS AND SAUCERS

Pure white, light wt. China body.

PURE WHITE

A6136—Cup 3⅞x2 in., saucer 5½ in., 30 doz in case. Doz. (24 pcs.), $1.08
2 doz. in pkg. Doz. (24 pcs.), $1.15

GOLD BAND DECORATED.

A6137—Cup 3⅞x2 in., saucer 5½ in., 30 doz. in case. Doz (24 pcs.), $1.35
2 doz. in pkg. Doz. (24 pcs.), $1.50

NOVELTY EARTHENWARE ASH TRAY

A508—4½x4½ in., embossed design, matt finish, deep receptacle, 3 cigar rests, ½ doz. in pkg. . . . . Doz. $2.15

IMPORTED SEMI-PORCELAIN SALT BOX

A661—5½x4 in., ht. 6 in., white semi-porcelain body decorated with delft blue Holland water scenes, word SALT in black letters, tight fitting polished hardwood cover. . . . . Doz. $6.75

AMERICAN WHITE SEMI-PORCELAIN DINNER PLATES

H. K. Selection, Actual Size 9½ in. Diam.

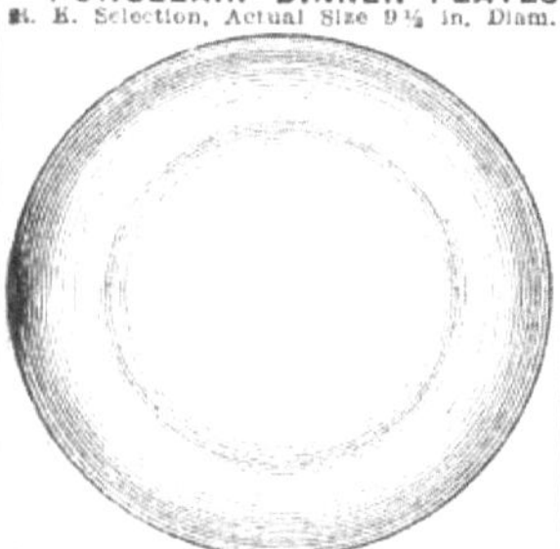

A01656—Actual size 9½ in. diam., pure white American semi-porcelain, pkd. 12 doz. in bbl., no less sold, wt. 170 lbs. (Total 12 doz. $10.50); Doz. 87½c

WHITE SEMI-PORCELAIN ST. DENIS CUP AND SAUCER

A01654 — White American semi-porcelain body, cup 3½x3¼ in., saucer 6 in., 12 doz. in bbl., no less sold. (Total $15.00); Doz. (24 pcs.), $1.25

JAPANESE CHINA DINNER SET

See Composition This Page.

Decorated—Underglaze in Blue Willow and Landscape scenes in border effect, blue decorated handles.
A016—Trade-marked "NORITAKE." 52-pc. set. Set. $13.50

YELLOW WARE APPLE BAKERS

Suitable for baking and serving for individual use.

A0784 — Diam. 4½x2 in., hard fired body, glazed inside and out. 12 doz. in crate. . . . . Doz. 42c
Less than crate. Doz. 45c

YELLOW UNDERGLAZED BROWN BAND CUSTARD CUPS

Hard baked body, highly glazed inside and outside.

A0780—Cap. 5 oz., 12 doz. in crate. . . . . Doz. 60c
Less than crate. Doz. 82c
A0781—Cap. 7 oz., 12 doz. in crate. . . . . Doz. 65c
Less than case. Doz. 92c

ROCKINGHAM TEAPOTS

Famous Rebecca at the Well design

Made from the best fireproof clay, glazed inside and outside.
A1646—42s, capacity 32 oz. 1 doz. in crate. Doz. $6.50
A1647—30s, capacity 58 oz. 1 doz. in crate. Doz. $8.50

Rockingham Teapot Starter Asst.

A01648—Asstd. as follows:
½ doz. Capacity 32 oz.
⅓ doz. Capacity 58 oz.
⅙ doz. Capacity 78 oz.
Total 1 doz. asstd. in bbl. . . . . Doz. $8.75

HALL'S FIREPROOF CHINA TEAPOTS

A01649 — Decorated with gold. Asstd. brown, blue and green. Snow white glazed inside, absolutely fireproof and sanitary. Capacity 5 cups. ½ doz. in box. Doz. $16.75

UTILITY YELLOW EARTHENWARE BOWL SETS

Extra hard yellow earthenware body, highly glazed inside and out, deep shape, pink and blue banded. Consists of one each, 6, 7, 8 and 9 in., sizes in set.

A4045—12 sets in box. (48 pcs.) Set, 42c Total, $5.04
A4045½—6 sets in box. (24 pcs.) Set, 45c Total, $2.70

YELLOW EARTHENWARE NAPPY SETS

Extra hard yellow earthenware body, highly glazed inside and out, panel shape plain edge, blue, banded. One each 4, 5, 6, 7, 8 and 9 in. sizes in set.

A4007—12 sets in box. (72 bowls.) Set, 62c Total, $7.44
A4007½—6 sets in box. (36 bowls.) Set, 65c Total, $3.90

COMPOSITION OF IMPORTED CHINA DINNER SETS

	52 Pc.		100 Pc.	
B & B Plates	6	6	12	12
Dinner Plates	6	6	12	12
Tea Plates	6	6	12	12
Coupe Soups	6	6	12	12
Desserts	6	6	12	12
Saucers	6	6	12	12
Cups	6	6	12	12
Med. Dish	1	1	1	1
Large Dish			1	1
Baker	1	1	1	1
Covered Dish	1	2	1	2
Casserole			1	2
Sauce Boat	1	2	1	2
Covered Butter			1	3
Sugar	1	1	1	1
Pickle	1	2	1	2
Cream	1	1	1	1
	52 Pc.		100 Pc.	

GLAZED AND TINTED EARTHENWARE CUSPIDOR

A4085 — Extra hard heavy earthenware body, green tinted, glazed inside and out. Diam. 7 in. ht. 4½ in. . . . . . Doz. $2.25

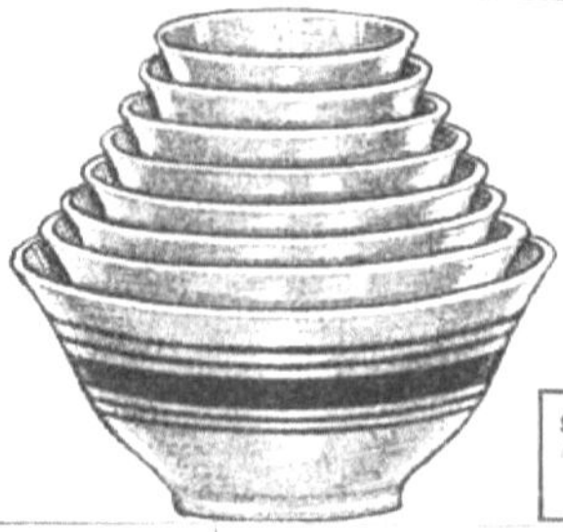

UNDERGLAZED YELLOW BOWLS, BROWN BANDED

Extra hard, heavy yellow earthenware body, highly glazed inside and out, deep shape, brown banded.

A4011—Diam. 5 in. . . . . Doz. $0.79
A4012—Diam. 6 in. . . . . Doz. .90
A4013—Diam. 7 in. . . . . Doz. 1.20
A4014—Diam. 8 in. . . . . Doz. 1.87
A4015—Diam. 9 in. . . . . Doz. 2.40
A4016—Diam. 10 in. . . . . Doz. 3.25
A4017—Diam. 11 in. . . . . Doz. 4.80
A4018—Diam. 12 in. . . . . Doz. 6.00

STARTER YELLOW BOWL ASST.

A4068—Asst. contains, ½ doz. each, 4, 5, 6, 7, 8 and 9 in. sizes. Total 6 sets in pkg. . . . . (Total, $3.90); Set. 65c

IMPORTED SEMI-PORCELAIN DECORATED BOWL SETS

6 Sizes in Set.

Good quality light weight semi-porcelain, pure white glossy finish, attractively decorated.

A658 — Deep shape, pink rose border decoration in wreath effect, joined with green foliage. One each of the following sizes, 5, 6, 6½, 7, 7¾ and 8 in. diam. Set (6 pcs.), $1.25

A657—Deep shape, brown, blue and green decorated; large tulips and blue daisies joined with green foliage. One each of the following sizes, 5, 6, 6½, 7, 7¼ and 8 in. diam. Set (6 pcs.), $1.45

BRISTOL SHALLOW STONEWARE BAKE PANS

A0775 — Hard baked fireproof body, glazed on inside, outside natural color. Asstd. as follows:
2 doz. 1 qt., diam. 7 in.
2 doz. 2 qt., diam. 9 in.
2 doz. 3 qt., diam. 10 in.
Total, 6 doz. asstd. in crate, no less sold. . . . . Doz. $1.35
A0775½—3 doz. asstd. in crate, no less sold. . . . . Doz. $1.50

IMPORTED SEMI-PORCELAIN DECORATED BOWL SETS

Light weight pure white highly glazed semi-porcelain, attractively decorated, 5 bowls in nest. 1 each of the following sizes, 8¼ in., 7¼ in., 6¼ in., 5¼ in. and 4¼ in.

5 Sizes in Set

A648—Panel shape, strawberries and foliage in natural red and green colors.
1 nest in pkg. (5 pcs.) Nest, $1.10
6 nests in pkg. . . . . Nest, 1.00

A646—Panel shape, bright blue decoration edged with black dotted line.
1 nest in pkg. (5 pcs). Nest, $1.10
6 nests in pkg. . . . . . . Nest, 1.00

This Guarantee Protects You

WE guarantee these prices against any advance until December 24, 1926, inclusive. Whenever for any reason we find it possible to make a lower price on any item we *immediately* reduce the price and all orders thereafter are billed at this reduced price. Thus our price guarantee protects you both ways. You are protected against any advance and given the benefit of any reduction from the day the reduction occurs.

WE GUARANTEE THAT ALL GOODS in our Catalog are the same quality as sold by all other first-class wholesale houses and exactly as described and represented by us.

All articles listed in our catalog are strictly FIRST QUALITY (with only two exceptions, which are: a few items in Enameled Ware sold as "Run-of-Kiln," and "Re-selected Thirds" in Chinaware which are fully described as such and are handled by all other first-class wholesalers).

We further guarantee *our prices* to be LOWER, on an average, than other wholesalers are charging NOW for the same goods, except on such few items as the manufacturer through his brands and trade marks establishes the wholesale selling price.

You are privileged to return to us, WITHIN 5 DAYS after arrival at your store, any goods ordered from our Catalog if not satisfactory to you; but on goods bought by customers here in the house and shipped as ordered, no returns will be allowed except for justifiable cause; and in any case no returns will be accepted unless made within 5 days.

AWC Signed *American Wholesale Corporation*

READ WHAT THREE of the LARGEST BANKS of BALTIMORE SAY:

The following Banks are our depositories. By permission we refer to them. Or see your local bank.

The National City Bank of New York.
The National Park Bank of New York City.
The Chase National Bank, New York City.
National Bank of Commerce of New York City.
Irving Bank and Trust Company, New York.

The Baltimore Trust Co., Baltimore, Md.
(Atlantic Exchange Bank and Trust Co.)
Citizens National Bank, Baltimore, Md.
Merchants National Bank, Baltimore, Md.
The Drovers & Mechanics National Bank,
Baltimore, Md.

SEE TESTIMONIALS ABOVE.

See also our rating of "AA A1" in "Dun" and "Bradstreet," which is the highest rating given to any concern.

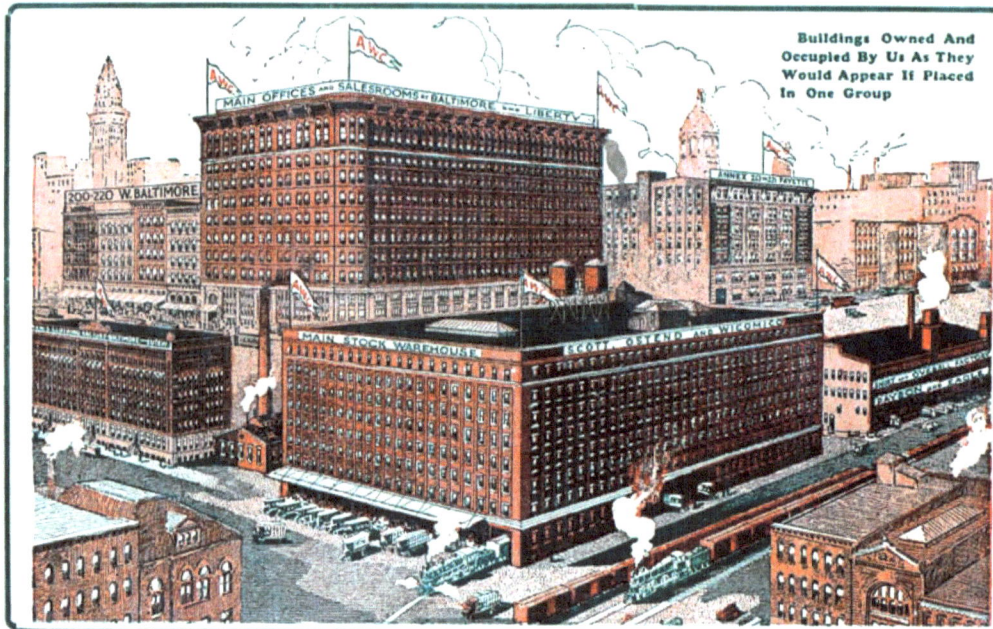

The Glass and Pottery Review

The Glass and Pottery Review contains 12 - 24 pages of informative articles and great pictures regarding your favorite antiques and collectibles. This publication is only sold online and is available only at our website - www.oldlinepublishingllc.com.

This quarterly newsletter is available either in a print version or an email version. Either version can be purchased securely right from our website. A shipping fee of $2.00 is included in the price of the printed version.

Each issue of **The Glass and Pottery Review** is sent on demand. That is, it is either mailed first class mail via USPS or emailed directly to you no later than the next business day. You do not need to subscribe as each issue requires that you purchase it individually. There's no doubt you will want to bookmark our site in order to return for future issues. Don't worry about forgetting, we'll send you a reminder when the next issue comes out so you can go right online and order. If you love glass and pottery you're going to love **The Glass and Pottery Review**!

If you would like to contribute material to this publication, we'd love to hear from you. Please contact us toll-free at 1-877-866-8820 or email us at oldlinepublishing@comcast.net. Let us know what your topic will be and when your material will be ready and we'll take care of the rest.

Catalogs On CD

Old Line Publishing is now offering an extensive line of eCatalogs. We have digitally reproduced every page of these trade catalogs in high resolution and in full color. We have then placed these images on compact disc for you to use. The quality of these images is so good that you can print them right on your home printer if you like, or you can simply view them on your computer.

There are nearly fifty catalogs available to choose from. Each compact disc catalog comes with a printed label and case for safe storage and easy identification.

All shipping and handling fees are included in the price of the catalog. All orders are shipped within 24-48 hours from when your order is received. These eCatalogs are designed to be used with Adobe Acrobat Reader 5.0 or greater. To order simply go to www.oldlinepublishingllc.com.

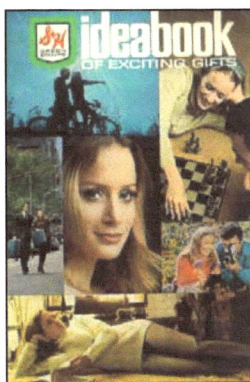

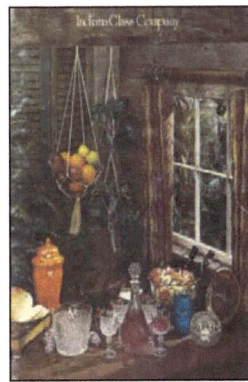

www.ingramcontent.com/pod-product-compliance
Lightning Source LLC
Chambersburg PA
CBHW061055090426
42742CB00002B/51